THE SUPERCOMPUTER ERA

Sidney Karin
and
Norris Parker Smith

HARCOURT BRACE JOVANOVICH, PUBLISHERS
Boston   San Diego   New York

Library of Congress Cataloging in Publication Data

Karin, Sidney, 1943–
  The supercomputer era.

  1. Supercomputers. I. Smith, Norris Parker,
1929–   II. Title.
QA76.5.K356 1987   004.1'1   86-32005
ISBN 0-15-186787-9

Printed in the United States of America

First Edition
A   B   C   D   E

For
NICKI HOBSON
and for
BERNHARDT HURWOOD

*in different places, and at different times,
they unfailingly urged friends to persevere*

Contents

Preface

The supercomputer era has arrived. Managers and researchers in a rapidly-growing number of scientific disciplines and industries are deciding that they need the most powerful computers available— the working definition of a supercomputer. Supercomputers are becoming less expensive and easier to use while they continue to grow in power. Supercomputing is now an important, distinctive segment of the computer market. It is no longer an obscure, specialized niche, no longer limited to government laboratories and a few industries with exceptional computational requirements. *The Supercomputer Era* was written in order to help make sure that basic information *about* supercomputers keeps pace with the rapid expansion in the *use* of supercomputers.

Comprehensive, up-to-date data about the machines, manufacturers, current uses of supercomputing, and sources of supercomputer services are intended to assist readers new to supercomputing in deciding what the supercomputer era may hold for them. This information can serve as a valuable reference for computer specialists as well as for people less familiar with supercomputing.

The Supercomputer Era is more than a reference work. It examines trends, it considers the future of supercomputing and the prospects for minisupercomputers which offer performance close to supercomputer levels at lower prices. The international dimensions of supercomputing are examined in detail, including the implications of Japan's entry into the supercomputer market. *The Supercomputer Era* is a broad-gauged introduction to supercomputing written in plain language. It emphasizes the jobs that supercomputers are doing—some familiar, some experimental—and the people who use supercomputers. It explores the varied human settings in which supercomputers work. The philosophies and objectives of these people and institutions are also shaping the supercomputer era.

Many readers will come to this book looking for specific information or will prefer to skip around in the text. A special effort has been made to write chapters so that each stands on its own, making it easier for the selective sampler as well as the front-to-back reader. Detailed information on the hardware available in the marketplace and sources of supercomputer services is concentrated in the two appendices.

In her excellent book, *The Computer Establishment*, Katharine Davis Fishman suggested that computer writers, even more than other journalists, must depend upon the kindness of others. This is especially true in the supercomputer era, because the new stays ahead of the printing press. The only way to keep up is by asking people who know.

In the notes which follow the appendices, tribute is paid to the many kind people who took time to talk about what they were doing, offering their confidence and trust as well as their knowledge. Credit is also given to those who may not have been quoted but who helped make it possible to draw this book together. The authors extend heartfelt thanks to the staff of the San Diego Supercomputer Center, especially Marilyn Shapiro and Erick Contag, and to the people of the Lawrence Livermore National Laboratory's News Bureau. We also offer deep appreciation for the cheerful enthusiasm and consistent professionalism of our colleagues at Harcourt Brace Jovanovich, Publishers. Much credit is also owed to Bill Gladstone of Waterside Productions, our agent, who had faith in the possibilities of this book from the start.

The authors acknowledge their debt to all these people who live in, and strive to understand, the supercomputer era. Without this foundation, it would have been impossible to assemble *The Supercomputer Era*.

CHAPTER 1 ─────────────

What Is a Supercomputer, What Is It Good for, and Is It Worth It?

> Start with the hard questions. What does "supercomputer era" mean? When did it start? Why now, rather than some other time? What is a supercomputer? How are supercomputers different from other computers? What do you get from that difference? What kind of people are using supercomputers, and what are they doing with them? What might this mean for people who are not computer specialists but whose livelihood might be affected by the supercomputer era? Eras in computing don't seem to last long; what comes next?

During the past few years—roughly the first half of the 1980s—a growing number of scientists, engineers, and businessmen discovered that conventional computers are too limited, or too slow, to meet their needs. Investigators in many fields found that in order to understand nature fully, the mathematics required is so complex that many millions or billions of calculations are needed to solve one small part of a problem. Unless they could obtain more computational power, their research would reach a dead end or a competitive opportunity could be lost.

This led to increasing demand for access to supercomputers, the most powerful computers in existence, capable of tens or hundreds of millions of calculations each second. Supercomputers now in advanced development, likely to be in operation well before 1990, aim at rates in the billions of calculations per second.

Requirements for computational performance at the supercomputer level involve more than idle curiosity. The fields in which investigators are most eager to obtain access to supercomputers are among the fastest moving, most exciting areas of modern science and technology. Their work could have direct, early impact upon the medicines which heal us, the aircraft we travel in, the cars we drive, the fuel which goes into those cars, the silicon chips which are the foundation of the modern information-based society, our capacity to foresee the weather, improved protection of buildings against earthquakes, and many other areas.

Scientific specialities which depend upon supercomputers include investigations of the innermost components of the atomic nucleus, studies of the origin of the universe and the development of galaxies, explorations of the molecular foundations of life, simulating in three dimensions the flow of blood through the heart, and probing the internal structure of the earth.

In the early 1980s, however, much of this growing demand was frustrated. Supercomputers were numbered in the dozens, with the worldwide total approaching 100. Most were operated by specialized government agencies, with a few installed at aerospace firms, oil companies, and universities. Access was limited to people working in a restricted number of specialties and those with thick wallets.

Then, in the middle years of the 1980s, a number of very important developments took place:

- Central governmments in the United States, Japan and Europe made funds available to stimulate the development of supercomputing and establish supercomputer centers available to academic researchers and to users in the private sector.
- A number of federal departments in the United States made new or expanded supercomputing facilities available to outside researchers.
- Local governments and universities in the United States and Canada funded the establishment of local and regional supercomputer centers.

- An increasing number of private firms, in a broadening range of industries, acquired their own supercomputers. This tendency has been most marked in Japan, with the United States close behind, Europe and Canada only slightly to the rear.
- The supercomputer marketplace, which had been a relatively obscure niche in the computer industry, became one of the industry's fastest-growing, most competitive sectors. This niche, which had been occupied by Cray Research, Inc., and Control Data Corporation, was invaded by three large Japanese manufacturers and IBM.
- In the United States, federal funding added greatly to the opportunities to learn about supercomputing and obtain hands-on experience. Throughout the supercomputer community, improved software, more powerful workstations with excellent graphics capabilities, better communications networks, and other developments are making supercomputers more accessible and easier to use.

Clustered within a short period, these developments are creating the conditions for a supercomputer era. Supercomputers are becoming a conventional, widespread, cost-effective tool for scientific research and engineering applications.

These developments underlying the supercomputer era are not only technological. The technology of supercomputing advanced steadily but not dramatically from 1976 to 1986. Economic, scientific, and political decisions are increasing the availability and accessibility of supercomputers. This in turn will stimulate an acceleration of progress across a broad range of key scientific and technological fields.

When did the supercomputer era start? Because it depends upon political, economic, and social as well as technological developments, taking place throughout the advanced industrial countries of the northern hemisphere, it is difficult—and artificial—to pick a specific date. The United States has been on the threshold of the supercomputer era longer than other countries, although Western Europe, Japan and Canada followed within a few years. A few industries, notably aerospace firms and oil companies, began to participate in the supercomputer era before others. In terms of making and using supercomputers, the supercomputer era has barely started in the Soviet Union and China and is far in the future for most of the rest of the world. Nevertheless, the technology which supercomputers help to create will have worldwide significance— not only in the 21st century, but for technologies now in active development.

The Beginning of the Supercomputer Era: Numbers and Projections

If a beginning must be picked for the supercomputer era, it might be the years 1985-1986. In those two years, the key developments which are giving momentum to the supercomputer era began to have a substantial impact upon the availability and use of super-computing. Why didn't the supercomputer era begin earlier? In 1976 or 1980 rather than 1985, for example? The answer is simple. The technology was there, the demand was building, but the other factors making for widespread, diversified use hadn't arrived.

In any event, at the beginning of the supercomputer era, su-percomputing is no longer a stepchild, but a dynamic sector in the computer industry and in science, engineering, and manufacturing. The growth of supercomputing has, indeed, accelerated so much that it is no longer easy to provide a precise worldwide census of supercomputers and related data. The following rough estimates sketch an outline:

- As of the spring of 1987, over 250 supercomputers were in use or on order throughout the world. Roughly one-third were outside the United States.
- The total value of supercomputer installations (including peripheral equipment and facilities) was on the order of $5 billion. Supercomputing sales were approaching $1 billion per year.
- Some forecasts anticipate an annual increase in supercomputer sales of 60% between 1985 and 1990. Conservative projections anticipate annual growth of 25%, compounding each year, for the foreseeable future.
- The number of people using supercomputers will soon be measured in the multiple tens of thousands. A conservative forecast

would put the total at 100,000 worldwide by 1990. This figure may well be exceeded sooner.

These are substantial figures, although not enormous in comparison with the entire computer industry or the world economy. It should be remembered, however, that supercomputing does not exist in isolation. Supercomputers are tools, used for a rapidly-growing range of scientific and manufacturing purposes. Moreover, supercomputers are general-purpose machines. One facility can serve dozens of different applications every day, hundreds each month. Furthermore, supercomputers are used primarily at the cutting edge of each technology, usually by the most talented, energetic investigators. Consequently, a few billion dollars or a hundred thousand people represent a great deal of leverage.

What Is a Supercomputer?

The most basic definition: "A supercomputer is the most powerful computer available at any given time." This is an unusual definition, because it is entirely comparative. Similarly, an Olympic champion in the marathon is the fastest runner in that event at that time. In terms of specific performance, this meant different things in 1972 and in 1984, and the winner's record in 1996 will be different again.

Performance of computers has advanced even more rapidly than improvements in Olympic records. What is super today becomes commonplace tomorrow, obsolete within a few years, and quaint soon after that. This chart demonstrates how performance of supercomputers has improved since the 1960s. It also serves as a tombstone, inscribed with the identities of machines that once were supercomputers but are no longer considered unusual or even very useful.

Supercomputer does not refer to a particular design or type of computer, although since 1976, when the CRAY-1 was introduced, the supercomputer market has been dominated by one basic design philosophy, emphasizing extremely rapid processing of vectors, a particular type of calculation. (For more information, see Chapters Two and Five.) Within a few years, this design philosophy may

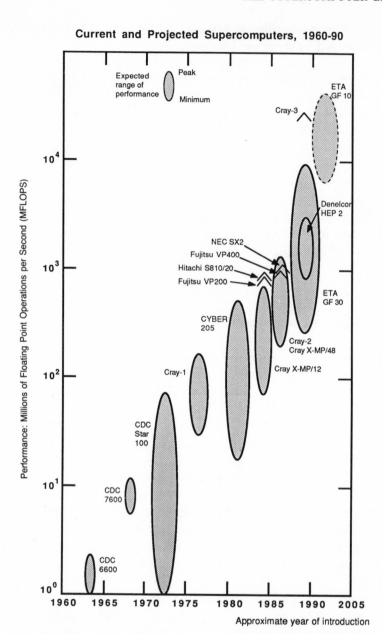

Current and Projected Supercomputers, 1960-90

Performance Ranges of Supercomputers.   (*Based upon a chart by Sidney Fern-bach in* "Supercomputers: Government Plans and Policies," *Office of Technology Assessment, 1986.*)

in turn be rendered unsuper as designs based upon new technologies such as multiple processors supplant it.

Supercomputers are compared to a spectrum of computational performance that has become crowded and confusing. During the early days of computing, in the 1950s and the first half of the 1960s, it was simple. There were mainframes (large general purpose machines), some smaller special-purpose computers (used, for example, in accounting) and that was that. In the mid-1960s, supercomputers achieved a distinctive separate identity with the development of the Control Data 6600. Then Digital Equipment Corporation, followed by other manufacturers, launched the minicomputer, offering substantial performance and relatively simple operation at a price far below that of a mainframe. In the late 1970s and early 1980s, the personal computer (fastidious specialists prefer to call it the microcomputer) came along, reducing price even further, improving compactness and simplicity, and providing remarkable, rapidly-growing performance.

The approximate relationship of supercomputer performance and the performance of these other categories can be shown proportionately. If the performance of contemporary supercomputers is assigned a value of 100, the values in proportion to supercomputers are:

- Mainframes: 1 to 10
- Minicomputers: 0.1 to 5
- Workstations: 0.1 to 1.0
- Personal computers: .001 to 0.1

In the past few years, the scene has become even more complicated. Manufacturers are promoting minicomputers with markedly higher performance, called superminis. Powerful stand-alone workstations, usually with special emphasis on graphics, are occupying a step on the performance ladder between PCs and minicomputers. A number of specialized machines have entered the marketplace, including array processors, which can be added to other computers to provide enhanced performance, especially for the repetitive mathematical operations at which supercomputers excel. Most recently, a number of firms are offering a new species called mini-supercomputers, claiming performance much superior to mainframes.

Manufacturers are advertising performance approaching that of a supercomputer at much lower prices.

What are the actual numbers? This would be easier if super-computer performance were tangible and could be measured on a speedway or dynamometer. Supercomputing involves more than raw speed. Supercomputers also possess exceptionally large, rapidly-accessible active memory. Because processing capability is so high, extremely efficient, high capacity input/output subsystems are needed. Performance is also affected by the specific problem or algorithm being run on the machine. There is an experience factor. Each generation of supercomputers, each new model, has a wide, unexplored terrain of unfamiliar characteristics. As this is mapped, understood, and put to use, the overall effectiveness of a system can be increased by a factor of 10 or more after a few years' experience.

One basic measure of computer performance is the rate at which it carries out floating point operations, essential for accurate, high-speed mathematical calculations. The counter for this is FLOPS, which stands for floating point operations per second. Any computer likely to be compared seriously with supercomputers is capable of at least a million such operations in one second, so performance is measured in megaflops.

Current supercomputers now in the marketplace operate at peak rates, using special test problems and algorithms developed to measure comparative performance, in the range of 160 to 400 megaflops. Some manufacturers claim higher figures, which are examined in Chapter 5 and Appendix I. It is possible to run actual, real-world programs consistently in the range of 30 to 80 megaflops, with some optimized programs running at more than 500 megaflops.

For comparison, the latest, most powerful conventional main-frame computers are approaching a peak of ideal performance around 10 megaflops. Day-to-day, real-world throughput would be perhaps a quarter of that figure.

What Good Does It Do?

A skeptic will ask: "Okay, ten times faster. So what? An Indy racing car looks impressive on TV and certainly goes like anything, but it doesn't do much good for someone in the trucking business.'' Supercomputers do not exist because they are neat machines, but because they add new, qualitative differences to science and business as well as quantitative improvements.

Scientists in fields as diverse as oceanography, astronomy, molecular biology, earthquake studies, statistics, and physics explain the advantages of supercomputers in a few words: ''new science, fresh approaches.'' Possibilities which had only been imagined or were entirely unanticipated are suddenly achieved or found to lie close at hand. Supercomputers become a tool of the imagination. The voluminous numerical results of extensive computations can be grasped and dealt with best if shown graphically, taking full advantage of the human capacity to respond to shape and color. Supercomputers become a tool of vision.

The unique computational power of supercomputers makes it possible to find solutions for many important scientific and engineering problems that could not be dealt with satisfactorily by theoretical, analytical, or experimental means. Numerical models and iterative simulation achieve a place of equality next to the established tools of scientific investigation. Supercomputers become a third way to do science, along with the blackboard and the laboratory. Supercomputing can become the laboratory, the only way to test hypotheses about problems too inaccessible, too distant in space or time, for experimentation or observation. Applications in which the exceptional capabilities of supercomputers have been critical include molecular dynamics, preliminary designs for a hyperspace plane, many aspects of astrophysics and cosmology, and a number of fields in high-energy physics. Advocates of supercomputing refer to a new renaissance, emphasizing the potential for application to the creative arts as well as science.

Engineers and scientists in many fields, including aerospace, petroleum exploration, automobile design and testing, chemistry, materials science, and electronics, emphasize the value of supercomputers as time-machines (see Chapters Three, Seven, and Eight). Computations requiring many hours or days on more conventional computers can be accomplished in a few minutes or seconds. A researcher or manager accustomed to checking out one or two variations on a problem in a week will gain a totally different perspective if she or he can obtain analyses of a half-dozen alternatives in a single day. In many areas (such as the design of extremely dense computer chips, improvements in the efficiency of jet engines, and the development of advanced materials) a su- percomputer is more than a time-machine. It is a necessity. No other computer could cope with the complexities of the problems that must be solved. The results are supremely practical. The use of supercomputers can mean the difference between profits and disaster for a firm competing in a market where early introduction of a product can mean a good market-share and rich returns.

The problems most frequently explored on supercomputers are not abstractions but actual processes observed in nature—extremely complex processes, requiring an exceptionally powerful computer in order to produce usefully accurate numerical simulations. Su- percomputers make it possible to move from two-dimensional maps or cross-sections to three-dimensional simulations that approximate the real world much more closely. Nonlinear problems involving the mathematics of abrupt, severe change become soluble. In the final analysis, everything is a detail, and supercomputers make it possible to analyze problems in much greater detail. Finer definition and more precise resolution make it possible to discover new forces or features that may be more important than had been realized.

It is important to remember that supercomputers are not uni- versally superior and not always the most cost-effective tool. For many purposes, computers with more limited capability are as good, or better, and are likely to be easier to use. It is usually wasteful to use supercomputer time for word processing or com- munications, and supercomputers may not be particularly apt at these functions. At supercomputer centers, smaller computers are used for these tasks. Chapter Two describes a complete super- computer system, including the smaller computers and other equip- ment which play supporting roles.

Throughout this book, flesh will be added to these abstractions through concrete descriptions of work now being done with su- percomputers, glimpses of people doing that work, reports of their reasons for turning to supercomputers, and their feelings about what they got out of it. These snapshots of supercomputer users at work may seem brief and technically inadequate to experts in each field. The intent, however, is to make them comprehensible to people in *other* fields.

In academic communities, members of specialized fields and academic disciplines are like separate groups passing through a maze in a classical garden. They all inhabit the same space, they encounter one another occasionally, but most of the time they pursue their separate courses without much intercommunication. A major objective of this book will be achieved if some readers leaf through pages about uses of supercomputers in another field of study and say, "Hey, what those guys are doing is a lot like this damned thing of mine. Perhaps . . . ."

This book is also aimed at managers whose business or research might benefit from supercomputers. They may not know a great deal about computers, but they are responsible for operations that already depend a great deal upon computers and might (or might not) gain from adding the most powerful machines to their inventory. Such managers may be under steady pressure from their research directors or production specialists, who produce hundreds of pages of reasons why they need supercomputer power. This book is intended to help computer specialists to explain their needs to their managers in language comprehensible to a nonspecialist.

What Comes Next? What Follows the Supercomputer Era?

Supercomputers in the 1990s will be very different from current models. Extensive changes are already in advanced development. The most direct avenue for improvements is more of the same: larger memories, more efficient chips, a shorter period between computations, more capacious input/output devices. This approach was taken with impressive results for the past ten years, continuing earlier trends. This chart shows the decreases in the cost of a given calculation which has resulted from these advances. Since the earliest days of computer technology, performance has improved more than one million times.

As of now, it looks like improving performance another million times will be more difficult. The potential of a more-of-the-same strategy is not exhausted. Researchers in Japan and the United States are working intensively to develop cost-effective gallium arsenide foundations for computer chips. Compared with the familiar

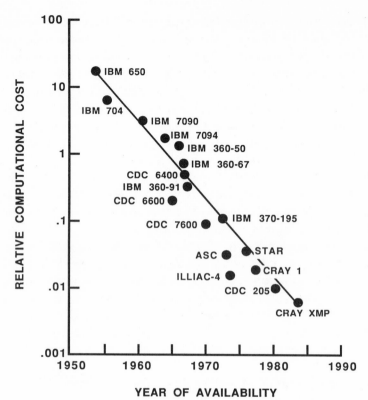

YEAR OF AVAILABILITY

Supercomputing Gets Cheaper, Faster. As performance of supercomputers has increased over the years, the cost of simulating a given problem has decreased steadily. This chart, based upon a diagram by Victor L. Peterson of NASA's Ames Research Center, compares the relative cost-effectiveness of successive supercomputers and mainframes.

silicon chips, these should have impressive advantages in speed, compactness, and low-temperature operation. Such research may slow but will not dispel the inescapable limit on any single computer processor. At time intervals of a few billionths of a second, electricity does not travel very far—just a few feet. The obvious solution is to pack circuits very tightly, but this results in a condition very much like the heating elements of an electric stove. A great deal of electric energy is confined in a small space and must be removed to prevent everything from burning up.

The next step is to use more processors: two, four, or a much larger number of vector processors or central processing units, able to work on a problem at the same time. Supercomputer makers have been moving in this direction since the early 1980s. The CRAY X-MP is available with one, two, or four processing units. The CRAY-2, introduced in 1985, has up to four processing units as well as an extremely compact design, very large memory, and an innovative immersion cooling system. The CRAY-3, expected within the next few years, is rumored to have 16 or more processors. IBM recently announced a six processor system.

ETA Systems, a supercomputer speciality company spun off from Control Data Corporation, is introducing initial test models of its ETA-10, which features up to eight processors, new chip designs, a very large memory, and faster operation due to immersion in liquid nitrogen. If all these innovations work at once, the ETA-10 could take supercomputing to a new level of performance, in the multi-gigaflop (billion flop) range. Japanese manufacturers, supported by a government-funded committee, are exploring similar technologies as they work toward a stated goal of 10-gigaflop performance by 1990. In universities and other laboratories all over the world, researchers are experimenting with machines which have dozens, hundreds, or thousands of processors. Some are already entering the marketplace. Adding to the confusion of nomenclature, some have been labeled "supercomputers."

Making a supercomputer with all these innovations is difficult enough. It is even more difficult to make it do useful work. Multiple or parallel processing is not a simple matter of addition. It was possible, but not easy, to control a team of 20 mules for hauling borax from Death Valley. A 40-mule team might be managed, although much harsh language would be exchanged between the mules and their drivers. A 100- or 1000-mule team would require far-reaching improvements in the technology of harnessing, communication between one end of the mule string and the other, and the personalities of mules and muleskinners. Large-scale parallel processing will similarly require advances in software that will take time—maybe a lot of time.

More uncertainty surrounds another potential transformation of supercomputer technology: the optical revolution. The use of optical fibers for communication over short as well as transcontontinental distances is now commonplace. Computers, including supercomputers, use optical fiber links along with metal wire, microwave, and satellite communications. Optical storage (using essentially the same technology as the high-fidelity compact disks which have invaded musical reproduction) has not yet been established firmly in the marketplace for supercomputer data storage devices, but the delay should not be long.

In principle, light would have many advantages over electricity, including greater speed and reduced heat, for transmission and processing of information within the computer itself. Many investigators are pursuing this problem vigorously. A solution would offer great prospects for the supercomputer technology of the future. How distant is that future? It is too early to tell, except that the future realization of optical computer processing is too distant for a book like this, which is limited to the immediate and predictable.

Meanwhile, there are plenty of other matters to attend to. Most supercomputer experts agree that the development of software has lagged behind the advances in hardware, even with contemporary technology. Exceptional improvements in software have taken place during the past few years, but the gap persists.

Supercomputers are so powerful and often so expensive that an extraordinary concentration of users may be needed at a single site in order to use a supercomputer fully and economically. Even then, users are likely to be dispersed among several buildings, a campus, or, more likely, a number of scattered locations which may be tens, hundreds, or thousands of miles apart. Increased attention to (and funding for) networking is one of the more important developments of the supercomputer era, but more effort will be required before all the pieces begin to fit together.

All in all, the supercomputer era is in its early stages, gathering strength and accumulating momentum, but far from maturity. The crucial point is that a large, rapidly-growing number of users are discovering the usefulness of top-of-the-spectrum computing. Most of them are not computer specialists. They do not care a great deal about the technology which provides them top-scale computer performance. Once they become accustomed to it, however, they are reluctant to accept anything less. At successive levels of increased performance, supercomputers will be a fundamental tool of science and business.

So far, the supercomputer era has been primarily an American era. Like most other major developments in computing, including the original design, then the mainframe, transistors, the minicomputer, integrated circuits, and the personal computer, supercomputing originated in the United States. Until the mid-1980s, supercomputer manufacturing was an American monopoly.

It could become a Japanese era. Japanese manufacturers are selling powerful and practical machines at attractive prices. The ETA-10, CRAY-3, and other American designs now in advanced development could leapfrog current Japanese models. Japanese manufacturers, working closely with universities and the Japanese government, are pursuing ambitious goals with characteristic persistence and ingenuity. Complacence or inattention in the United States could lead to quick erosion of the American lead.

The supercomputer era has begun. As long as people can find cost-effective ways to make some computers markedly more powerful than others, it is difficult to foresee an end.

CHAPTER 2 _____

Anatomy of a Supercomputer System

A supercomputer system, like other computer systems, requires more than the central computer itself. Using the San Diego Supercomputer Center as a concrete example, this chapter describes the machines and programs that make up a complete supercomputer system, including the people who make it work and who support the much larger number of people who use it. The chapter also serves as a general introduction to supercomputing by examining and explaining the features that give a supercomputer its exceptional computational power.

How does a supercomputer differ from other computers? Is it just bigger and faster? A cheetah can run much faster than a housecat, but a glance shows that it is fundamentally a specialized, somewhat larger member of the cat family. Put a elephant next to a cat, however, and the contrast is obvious.

Neither metaphor is entirely apt. If there were a cheetah with the size and power of an elephant, it might provide a better comparison. A concrete example is more to the point than any metaphor. This chapter will lay a foundation for the rest of the book by

17

describing one supercomputer system, the San Diego Supercomputer Center (SDSC) and introducing ideas and terms that need to be grasped in order to understand supercomputing. The discussion will emphasize basics. Readers familiar with large-scale computing installations may prefer to scan it quickly.

The SDSC is a reasonably representative example of a super-computer installation at this stage of the supercomputer era, but it is not a "typical" supercomputer installation and certainly not an "ideal" system. Those abstractions do not exist. The equipment and operations of different facilities for high-performance scientific computing vary over a broad spectrum depending upon the particular scientific requirements and the number of users, the objectives of each center, and a number of other considerations. Nevertheless, all supercomputer centers are composed of the same basic parts.

For supercomputer centers, like other complex institutions, purposes and philosophy shape operational and technological choices. The SDSC is one of five supercomputer centers in the United States that draw a substantial part of their funding from the National Science Foundation (NSF), which is making a total of $200 million available for this purpose over a five-year period (see Chapter Five for details on the NSF supercomputer initiative).

The SDSC is located on the campus of the University of California, San Diego, and derives part of its funding from the state of California and the university. It supports a consortium which now numbers 25 members, scattered from Hawaii to Maryland, including campuses of the University of California and other universities and research institutions in California. Investigators at other institutions who secure NSF grants obtain access on the same basis as researchers at consortium institutions.

This means that the SDSC has a very diverse national constituency. The central objective of the SDSC is to provide support for the acceleration of progress in scientific research by supplying high-quality services to its customers at institutions all over the United States. Through a process known as "time-sharing," the supercomputer can work on a large number of tasks simultaneously. Fifty, a hundred, or more users may be running problems on the computer system at the same time. These requirements have influenced the SDSC's selection of hardware and programs. Some components are more elaborate or powerful than at other facilities with different requirements or fewer customers. The principles remain the same.

GA Technologies, Inc., a private R&D firm in San Diego, focusing primarily upon energy research, which had had extensive experience with supercomputers as a participant in the Department of Energy's National Magnetic Fusion Energy Computer Center network, originated the SDSC concept. GA Technologies now manages and staffs the center. A number of other supercomputer centers in the United States have arranged for management and support from specialized firms, including the NSF-supported centers at Pittsburgh and Princeton, the National Cancer Institute's facility at Frederick, Maryland, and the NASA laboratory at Mountain View, California.

The Central Processing Unit (CPU)

When ordinary people (and for that matter many specialists) talk about "a computer," they mean the complex of electronic circuitry, including instructions and procedures built into the hardware, that does the calculations and makes everything go. For hand-held calculators and desk top PCs, it is a single semiconductor chip. For larger computers—and, in particular, supercomputers—this can be a mass of chips and wires as large as a three-drawer filing cabinet, or perhaps several rows of filing cabinets. Over the years, as circuits have been packed more closely upon semiconductor chips, CPUs (at all levels of power) have become more compact. The CRAY-2, a supercomputer introduced in 1985, is about as tall as a 10-year-old child, with a diameter about the same as the child's reach from fingertip to fingertip.

The main CPU at the SDSC is a CRAY X-MP/48, consisting of four CPUs linked to a single active memory with a capacity of 8 million 64-bit words. This does not mean actual words, but 64 binary expressions used to represent numbers and other symbols. Most mainframe computers operate with 32-bit words, which means that large numbers or numbers with many decimal places must be rounded off more brusquely, reducing the overall accuracy of calculations.

Older models of X-MPs run at a clock speed (a basic pace,

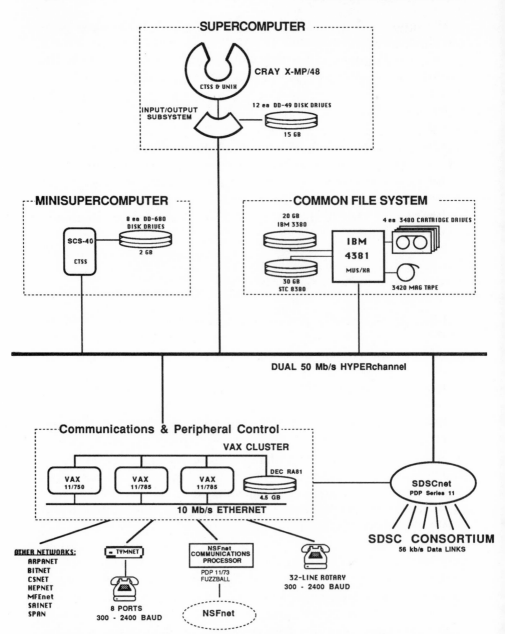

Schematic Layout of a Supercomputer System.   The basic components of the SDSC are found in other supercomputer systems, but there are many variations. For example, the SDSC operates an SCS-40 minisupercomputer. Some large centers operate more than one supercomputer system.   (*San Diego Super-computer Center.*)

like the beat of a symphonic conductor's baton) of 9.5 nanoseconds, or 9.5 billionths of a second. In late 1986, new models were offered at 8.5 nanoseconds. This high clock speed is one reason for the X-MP's great capacity. A large active memory is also essential for high effective speeds, because computers must store digits and then pick them up again during computations. The applications programs used on supercomputers are often very long and complex, requiring a great deal of memory. For many applications, a memory of adequate size is more critical than the raw speed of the CPU. Some X-MP installations (including the supercomputer centers supported by the National Science Foundation in Illinois and at Pittsburgh, and the new supercomputer at the National Center for Atmospheric Research) also have a Solid-state Storage Device (SSD). This consists of a massive collection of computer chips, connected to the CPU by a high-capacity communications channel, which provides additional rapid-access memory.

High-powered computers like the X-MP pack a great deal of circuitry into a small space. This is necessary because the clock speed is so high that electricity (which travels at a large fraction of the speed of light) can move only a few feet each time the clock ticks. A lot of energy is rushing around within that tightly packed space. The annual electricity bill of the SDSC is about one million dollars, and a large part of that is used by the CPU. (The new supercomputer building at the University of Minnesota uses heat thrown off by its supercomputers to heat its covered garage.) These physical facts set outer limits on the capacity of a single-processor computer. Achieving higher performance requires more than a faster clock speed.

The X-MP and other modern supercomputers sidestep this limitation through special multiple circuitry that can carry out one type of calculation, known as vector processing, through several pathways at the same time. The manipulation of vectors is a distinctive feature of the current generation of supercomputers, so much so that some manufacturers describe their supercomputers as "vector processors." (The principles of vector processing are outlined at the end of this chapter.)

Computer designers are also attempting to avoid the physical limitations on single processors by building machines that include more than one processor—from several, like the X-MP, to several

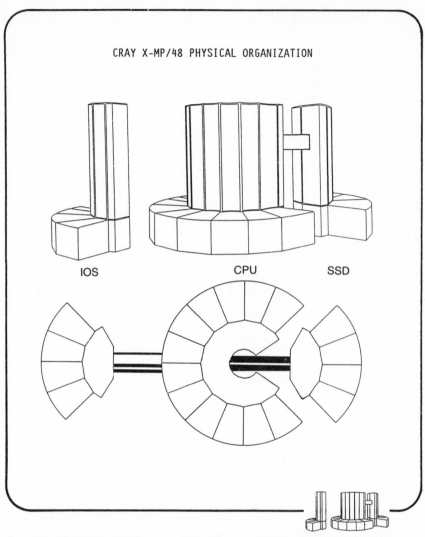

CRAY X-MP/48 PHYSICAL ORGANIZATION

IOS   CPU   SSD

Structure of a CRAY X-MP.   The IOS (Input/Output System) controls exchanges
of information between the CPU and the rest of the system. The SSD is a
Solid State Storage Device, a very powerful, fast active memory.

dozen or even thousands of processors. This approach involves
problems of programming as well as hardware that are discussed
in Chapter Eleven. The four processors of the X-MP/48 provide
the possibility of parallel processing. Currently, the SDSC operates
as if four computers were on the site. The machine routes a project

submitted (inputted) by a customer to one or another of the four processors. Soon, the system will be reconfigured so that customers can use all four together in a parallel mode.

How much does it cost? Supercomputer prices are subject to change and negotiation, but it is possible to give rough figures as of early 1987. The X-MP range includes models with one or two as well as four processors. List prices range from roughly $2.5 to $5 million for a single-processor version up to about $14 million for an X-MP/48. An SSD adds several more million dollars to the total price. The peak performance of a top-of-the-line machine approaches 1,000 megaflops.

The CPU of an X-MP is about as tall as the center of a professional basketball team and as wide as a medium-sized car. The processors are arranged in a *C* shape, or like a doughnut from which one large bite has been taken. The customer can choose the color of the plastic panels that run from top to bottom of each segment—at the SDSC, the panels are red and black. The seats that surround the segments seem to have been placed there for the convenience of visitors who wish to have their pictures taken, posed with the machine.

In fact, this high-tech seating is thoroughly functional. The X-MP disposes of the heat generated within its circuitry through a Freon cooling system that operates very much like a household air conditioner. The spaces under the seats are occupied by cooling equipment, serviced by large compressors in the basement underneath the machine. Other supercomputer designs take different approaches. IBM, for example, prefers chilled water; Fujitsu uses forced air; the CRAY-2 is immersed in a liquid fluorocarbon; and the new ETA-10 is designed to achieve optimal performance when cooled by immersion in liquid nitrogen, although it can run at room temperature.

The SDSC has another CPU, an SCS-40, manufactured by Scientific Computer Systems. This is a representative of a new breed of machines, the minisupercomputer, that provides performance approaching that of a full-scale supercomputer at much lower cost. The SCS-40 has peak performance capacity of 44 megaflops. The SCS-40 operates at a clock speed of 45 nanoseconds (roughly five times more slowly than an X-MP) but, like the X-MP, it is a 64-bit general-purpose computer. At SDSC it has been

A CRAY X-MP/48 uncovered. Technicians prepare to install the supercomputer at the San Diego Center. Note cooling equipment around base. (*San Diego Supercomputer Center/GA Technologies.*)

determined that the SCS-40 delivers more than the 25% of the performance of a single-processor CRAY X-MP claimed by the manufacturer—at about 10% of the cost. Of course, the cost of a supercomputer center involves much more than the cost of the CPU and memory. The company points out that this represents ten to 40 times the performance of conventional superminicomputers. In addition, compared to a full-bore supercomputer, it is a smaller, simpler, air-cooled machine, with less demanding requirements for installation. (See Chapter Eleven for more detail on minisuper-computers.)

Programs

By itself, a CPU is just a bunch of circuits—mute metal and fancy, expensive sand. Programs enable the system to do useful work.

They are sets of logically-consistent instructions that can be understood and executed by the CPU and guide the CPU and the other parts of the system.

The word *software* is interchangeable with *programs*. It started as a mildly witty mirror image of hardware. For non-specialists (and, unfortunately, for many computer people as well) the term has come to imply that software is somehow less important, perhaps less noble, than hardware. Get the hardware in good shape, it is thought, and the software can be taken care of somehow or another.

This is a naive, mischievous assumption. To be sure, software is written (or adapted) to fit the characteristics ("architecture") of a particular CPU, but this should not imply that software is of secondary importance. The history of computing is filled with examples of new systems and other projects that failed or were delayed because of trouble with programs. The time required to achieve fully functional software is often longer (and may be much longer) than the design and manufacturing cycle of the machinery, especially if the project is innovative. Many computer specialists as well as supercomputer customers stress that the development of software for supercomputers is lagging seriously behind the development of hardware, placing serious limitations on the overall performance of complete systems. This can be an especially significant difficulty because the potential performance range of supercomputers is much broader than that of ordinary computers. Supercomputers are typically applied to programs of exceptional complexity and size, and optimum program efficiency is crucial.

Operating Systems

There are two categories of software: the operating program and applications software. The operating program (usually called operating system) is the basic set of instructions that governs the functioning of the CPU and affects every other part of the computer system. An operating system is specific to a particular CPU or series of CPU's with similar design and characteristics. For example, most of this book is being written with the CP/M operating system, which was written for a class of eight-bit microprocessors now considered slow and somewhat odd, although they still work well enough for some purposes. The most widely used operating system for personal computers is Microsoft's MS-DOS, which is now being adapted to newer, more powerful, microchip CPUs. Most mainframes and minicomputers use distinctive operating systems that are not transferable from one line of machines to another. There is, however, an offsetting tendency toward standardization. Several manufacturers use IBM operating systems. Some are designing their systems so that they can be used with UNIX, a program developed by AT&T's Bell Laboratories and elaborated by many universities and software developers.

The SDSC uses the CTSS (Cray Timesharing System) operating system developed by the Lawrence Livermore National Laboratory. This program enables the SDSC to service its numerous, widely dispersed clientele. An individual user sitting at a workstation in Oahu or Maryland may have no idea whether the system is being used at that time by 2, 20, or 60 other people (although the curious user can easily find out how many others are at work). The system provides the same service, at essentially the same rate of response, as if the user were in some scientist's dream-castle, all alone with a supercomputer of his or her own. CTSS is also used at the University of Illinois supercomputer center that, like SDSC, is supported by the National Science Foundation's supercomputing intiative, described in Chapter Six.

Another program, COS (Cray Operating System), developed by Cray Research, is used by many other facilities operating Cray CPUs (for example, the NSF-supported center at Pittsburgh). This permits a certain degree of simultaneous use but is primarily for batch processing. The new CRAY-2 uses a system called UNICOS, based upon UNIX, although the first CRAY-2 to be delivered was operated on CTSS by the National Magnetic Fusion Energy Computer Center at Livermore. UNICOS is also in use at several X-MP installations. Other manufacturers are also moving toward wider operating system options, including some form of UNIX as well as IBM or proprietary systems. (See Chapters Ten and Eleven and Appendix I.)

Computer specialists are inclined to be conservative about operating systems, the primary link between the CPU and the real world. Change comes slowly, often in the face of stubborn resistance. Arguments about the merits and shortcomings of different systems sometimes seem to belong in the realm of theology rather than science. Miracles and damnation are both claimed loudly.

There is, however, reason for conservatism and strong feelings. Operating systems are typically very large and extremely complex programs—much more so than all but a few applications programs. A computer systems manager prefers to avoid dealing with more than one operating system at any site. This was a major reason for SDSC's choice of the SCS-40 rather than some other minisupercomputer—it emulates the CRAY X-MP instruction set and operates on CTSS.

Applications Software

Applications programs are the instructions that enable the computer system to deal with specific tasks. Hundreds of standardized (or relatively standardized) applications programs have been developed for use on supercomputers. Hundreds, perhaps thousands, of others have been written (or adapted from use on other computers) by institutions or individual researchers. An applications program provides instructions to the CPU and obtains output through the operating system. Thus, a program that runs on a particular operating system or hardware usually requires adaptation before it can be used with a different system.

Traditionally, the typical supercomputer user has been a scientist or engineer who is familiar with computers and can write or adapt applications programs. (This is not just scientific individualism; scientists who depend upon supercomputers are often working at the farthest edges of a particular area of inquiry; they must develop their applications programs, along with everything else, as they go along, like explorers travelling in an unknown region.) Compilers and other software tools for use on supercomputers are being improved rapidly, simplifying the tasks facing researchers and programmers. This is making it easier for beginners and people who cannot spare much time for program adaptation to make full use of supercomputer capabilities. The result: a broadened customer population for supercomputing.

Applications programs are also influenced by conservatism and convenience (and, from time to time, by theology). The FORTRAN programming language, introduced by IBM in 1957, remains the principal programming language for scientific applications. The great majority of programs for use on supercomputers are written in FORTRAN, and most special utilities programs for supercomputers aim at increasing the speed and efficiency of FORTRAN. The current investment in FORTRAN programs is so large that it defies estimation, but it must total many tens of thousands of man-years; perhaps a hundred thousand or more.

The SDSC and similar centers maintain an extensive library of applications software as a service to customers. These include programs for carrying out various kinds of mathematical operations and programs developed for computations used by a wide range of fields, including chemistry, engineering, and physics. Many were developed over the years by national laboratories in the United States and United Kingdom and are in the public domain. Others are licensed (at fees which range from nominal to substantial) by private software firms, universities, or others who own the copyright.

Memory and Storage

A visit to the typesetting room of a Chinese-language newspaper is a humbling experience. Newspapers in China use several thousand ideograms, each corresponding to a word or one part of a compound word. A typesetter stands in front of giant inclined trays, extending for several yards to the left and right. The individual pieces of type are contained in compartments on the trays arranged according to frequency of use, with the more obscure characters in the upper tiers and the extreme ends. Typesetters are usually sinewy and fast-moving, able to set a stick of type with amazing speed, reaching unerringly for the correct ideogram, in the appropriate type size. On a regular cycle, assistants restock the compartments with fresh pieces of type while the typesetters continue to work.

The typesetters are one part of an entire system. While they work, reporters are gathering information, researchers are digging out material for obituaries, looking up OPEC's total production of oil in 1984, and making sure that the latest statement by the Party Chairman is quoted accurately. Editors are cutting articles, making changes, sending them to the typesetting room to be set or reset, putting some on the spike, marking others for publication. In the library, called a morgue at old-fashioned Western newspapers, re-

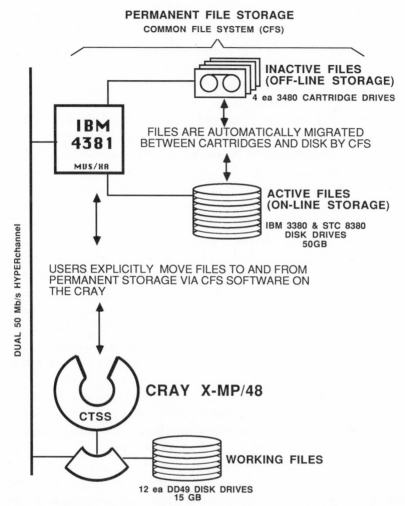

PERMANENT FILE STORAGE
COMMON FILE SYSTEM (CFS)

INACTIVE FILES
(OFF-LINE STORAGE)
4 ea 3480 CARTRIDGE DRIVES

IBM
4381
MUS/HA

FILES ARE AUTOMATICALLY MIGRATED
BETWEEN CARTRIDGES AND DISK BY CFS

ACTIVE FILES
(ON-LINE STORAGE)
IBM 3380 & STC 8380
DISK DRIVES
50GB

USERS EXPLICITLY MOVE FILES TO AND FROM
PERMANENT STORAGE VIA CFS SOFTWARE ON
THE CRAY

DUAL 50 Mb/s HYPERchannel

CRAY X-MP/48
CTSS

WORKING FILES
12 ea DD49 DISK DRIVES
15 GB

Storing Information: Active and Long-Term Files. This configuration at the SDSC is typical of large supercomputer centers, but specific equipment varies a good deal. (*San Diego Supercomputer Center.*)

searchers clip items from the paper and file them by category. The entire system requires hundreds of people and operates on a one-day cycle.

This is much like the role of memory in a computer, although a supercomputer requires many fewer people and operates on cycles measured in small fractions of a second. Like the typesetter, the

CPU must have a lot of compartments within close reach for temporary storage of pieces of data it is working on. The CPU draws on the stock of data to be manipulated in order to complete the task. It needs places to store short-term information, available for immediate access, as well as places to store data on a permament basis for later reference. Like a newspaper system, supercomputer systems rely upon a hierarchy of memory devices.

As noted earlier, the first level of storage of the Cray X-MP/ 48 consists of 8 million 64-bit words in active memory. X-MPs are available with smaller or larger active memories, including the extremely large, high-capacity, solid-state SSD option. Other supercomputer makers also offer alternative levels of active memory.

At the SDSC, the next level of memory device consists of 12 Cray DD-49s, very high-speed (and expensive) machines that store data magnetically on stacks of rigid disks—identical in basic design and function to the Winchester hard disks that are becoming an integral part of any serious desktop microcomputer system. The transfer rate between the CPU and this set of disks is, however, extremely high, 10 million bits per second. Moreover, unlike a PC, the disks in the DD-49's are not used for long-term storage, but only for short-term storage of data that may be required during a computation.

An IBM 4381 computer manages the other levels of storage. It oversees an array of IBM 3880s and StorageTek Company 8380s that are similar to the Cray disk machines but sturdier, slower, and less costly, with a total capacity of 50 gigabytes, or 50 billion 8-bit expressions. Despite this large capacity, such facilities become clogged with data very quickly. For example, an SDSC rule requires that unless a customer transfers a stock of data from temporary memory to more permanent storage (at the user's own facility or at the center) within 36 hours, it is erased automatically.

The final level of storage at the SDSC consists of an IBM 3480 tape system, also supervised by the IBM 4381 auxiliary computer. For years, the standard medium for this purpose was large reels of magnetic tape, about the diameter of a standard pizza, beloved by film directors looking for dramatic backgrounds. On the 3480, these have been supplanted by plastic cassettes (similar in size and design to videocassettes) that have much higher capacity than the old tape reels and can be accessed more quickly. For now, the cassettes are numbered, stored in racks, and must be picked out and fed to the reading machine by human hands. System operators and managers are awaiting eagerly the implementation of a reliable robot to carry out this task. At press time, Storagetek had just announced such a device.

Input/Output (I/O)

Information can be entered into a desktop computer in several ways: from a keyboard, over a wire from another computer, or from data stored on a floppy disk or hard disk. Once the data have been manipulated, the results can be displayed on a monitor, sent to a printer, transmitted to another computer, or stored on a disk— all forms of output. On a desktop system, even the most commonplace dot-matrix printer is controlled by a small microprocessor that maintains order in that subsystem and enables the printer to manage the flow of data from the CPU.

Supercomputers possess the same basic anatomy, but operation is complicated greatly by the enormous capacity of supercomputer CPUs, which require input/output (I/O) devices able to operate at appropriately high levels of speed and volume. This is not just a matter of hooking up enough wires of the right size. In supercomputer systems, I/O is managed by other computers. For an X-MP, I/O is directed by computer circuits in an obelisk a few paces away from the CPU; it looks roughly like the bite which was taken out of the original doughnut.

At the SDSC, and other supercomputer centers, the flow of data to and from users and among the components of the super-computing system is also managed by additional computers. The SDSC uses superminicomputers and minicomputers, the VAX and PDP-11 manufactured by Digital Equipment Corporation (DEC).

For most users of the SDSC, the results of a computation run (output) are routed back to their own locations, to be displayed on a local workstation, stored, or printed out. Output can also be printed at the SDSC—in ordinary text or graphics—on a high-speed Xerox 8700 printer which prints a full page at a time. A more unusual machine, the Dicomed D48CR, can transfer the graphic output of the supercomputer onto film. This makes it possible to show sequences of images, often color-coded, that are important for fields as diverse as astrophysics, molecular biology, aerodynamics, and structural engineering. Machines like the Dicomed are also essential tools for animators who use computers to produce sequences for film and television (see Chapter Nine).

Communications

The room housing all this machinery is not large—roughly the size of a basketball court—but adequate communications within it are a critical factor in the capacity of the entire system. Here again, it is a question of both hardware and software. The trunk carrier is a Network Systems Corporation dual fifty million bit per second HYPERchannel. Communications between the CPU and the DD49 high-speed disk drives take place over circuits with a capacity of 100 million bytes per second. Channels with substantial but smaller capacity link the CPU with the minicomputers that control the printer, other local output, and the exchange of messages with remote users. The operation of software that controls communications is based upon standards known as protocols. At the SDSC, communications to and from the CPU and the IBM 4381 which controls mass storage are managed using a standard called Simple Intermachine Protocol (SIMP). Other interchanges are governed by the Network Service Protocol (NSP) that is also used on the network linking the SDSC with remote users. Facilities utilizing TCP/IP (Transmission Control Protocol/Internet Protocol—developed by the Department of Defense's Defense Advanced Projects Agency), the standard protocol for the NSF's coast-to-coast backbone network, have recently been added to the SDSC communications complement.

  Computing does not stop at the I/O port. A facility like the San Diego Supercomputer Center depends upon a sophisticated, complex communications system to serve its customers. It is of course possible for a user to dial a number and send data to and from the SDSC over ordinary telephone circuits, linking the SDSC system with the user's own minicomputer or desktop. Some SDSC customers do this, although it is a slow process, especially in proportion to the extremely fast rate at which the supercomper does its work. (Remember that the CPU and its colleagues in the machine room are tossing data around at 50 or 100 million bits per second; a typical dial-up subsystem operates at 1200 bits per second; 2400 bits per second is becoming more common and some systems operate at somewhat higher speeds). Although the supercomputer is able to perform a task in a few minutes, it may require several hours to transmit the data from the user to the SDSC and a similar time to send the results back to the user. Line defects or interruptions, a minor irritant for voice communication, can leave a hole in the data or create gibberish.

For greater efficiency, the SDSC has set up a network of high-speed, high-quality dedicated communications channels (SDSCNET). Airlines reservation systems and other services that require constant, reliable, high-volume communication between remote terminals and computers rely upon similar networks of dedicated circuits. The SDSCNET consists of land-based circuits for relatively nearby customers and satellite links for communication with Hawaii and other more distant users. Most of the circuits operate at 56 thousand bits per second. The SDSC system includes minicomputers to manage this network and racks of equipment that monitor communication with remote sites. Members of the SDSC consortium are installing Remote User Access Centers (RUACs). These typically consist of a minicomputer, like the VAX 11/750, with a high-speed printer, disk and/or tape storage, and workstations. MFENET, a high-level protocol, is used to manage message traffic on the SDSCNET. It was developed at Lawrence Livermore National Laboratory.

The SDSCNET is large in terms of the number of operational nodes and the distances involved; not every supercomputer center will require similarly elaborate communications facilities. Communications are, nevertheless, an essential part of any supercomputer system. At the least, a center typically serves an entire laboratory or campus. The supercomputer will be tied into local networks and will probably be linked with remote sites. A supercomputer center with fewer customers may find it possible to install a communications management subsystem less powerful than SDSC's, but it is rarely practical to omit this function.

Numerous other supercomputer communications networks have been established or are being set up. The NSF-supported John von Neumann Center at Princeton, for example, has set up a network that emphasizes a very high-capacity channel known in the communications trade as a T1 circuit. The NSF has also established a national coast-to-coast trunk channel, and a number of local and regional networks are being developed. Additional discussion of networking developments in the United States and Europe can be found in Chapters Ten and Twelve respectively.

Scientists need to keep in frequent touch with one another. Scientists who use computers a lot find it natural to keep in touch through their computers. Thus, electronic mail and general communications become an important function of any network. The users of a supercomputer center like to be connected with their colleagues on as wide a basis as possible. The SDSC is linked with several networks used primarily or incidentally for electronic mail. It is also linked into a very extensive network operated by the Department of Energy, as well as NSF-sponsored networks, providing access to additional institutions for data transfer as well as electronic mail.

People

Diagrams of the anatomy of a computer system are often drawn by computer specialists; many fail to mention people, who seem to be considered incidental components at the ends of the input/output subsystem. The people who are served by a computer system—and who, incidentally, tell it what to do and judge the quality of its work—are conventionally known as "users." Katharine Davis Fishman, author of one of the most enduring books on computing, pointed out that the same term is used for computer customers and users of cocaine or heroin; after all, no one talks about users of tomato juice, cars, or for that matter old-fashioned iron typewriters. In any event, the term is now well established, concise, unambiguous, and difficult to avoid.

The most important people for any supercomputer installation are the people who use it. Who are they, where are they, and why are they using the system? The first year of the SDSC, from January through December 1986, provides preliminary answers to these questions.

Customers who actually used the center (as opposed to those who received allocations which were not yet used) during these 12 months represented 18 academic disciplines. Physics accounted for the largest amount of CPU time, about 27% of the total. Other major users included biochemistry (16%), chemistry (12%), atmospheric science (7%), materials science (5%). mathematics (3%), astronomy (3%), earth science (5%), mechanics (3%), and oceanographic science (2%). (The remainder was allocated in blocks to institutions, for use by a variety of disciplines.)

Users at a total of 99 institutions were allocated time on the SDSC during 1986. Major users (over 1000 hours of CPU time) included CalTech, the University of Hawaii, the University of California, Berkeley, UC San Francisco (the largest customer, with 2367 hours), UC Irvine, UCLA, UC San Diego, the Scripps Institution of Oceanography (UCSD and Scripps together totalled 2068 hours), and the University of Utah. Other major users (500–1000 hours of CPU time) were the Agouron Institute, Brown University, the University of Maryland, Stanford University, UC Santa Barbara, and the University of Washington.

Institutions whose researchers used 100–500 hours of CPU time were the University of Arizona, California State University Long Beach, the University of Houston, the University of Michigan, the National Center for Atmospheric Research, North Dakota State University, New York University, the University of Oregon, the Research Institute of the Scripps Clinic, UC Riverside, the University of Southern California, the University of Wisconsin, and Yale University.

A supercomputer center like the SDSC devotes a substantial part of its resources to assisting, educating, and encouraging the people who use it. In July 1986 the SDSC moved into a new 60,000-square-foot building that cost $7.5 million. (A facility of this size is not unique: the new supercomputer building at the University of Minnesota has more than 100,000 square feet of machine space and office/research/teaching space.) Much of this money was spent providing a suitable environment for the hardware and buying equipment needed to meet its appetites for electricity and cooling.

The rest of the building was designed to create an efficient environment for the people who support the machinery and learn how to use it. It includes an auditorium, several conference rooms, and smaller spaces that can be reconfigured quickly for training, seminars, and research. Each room is equipped with a number of jacks that permit access to two local networks within the building.

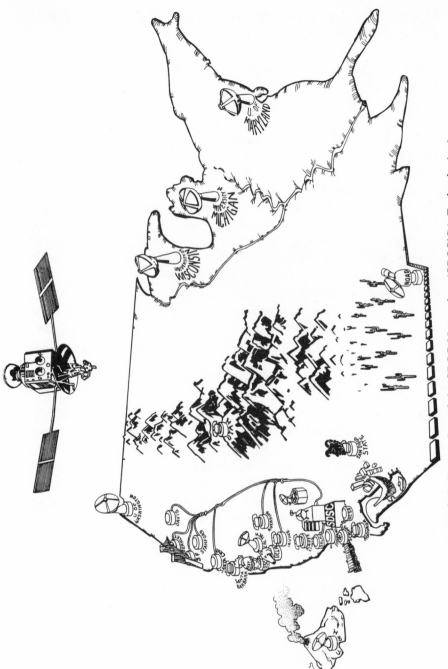

An Artist's Impression of the SDSC Network.   (*SDSC/GA Technologies.*)

Workstations and desktop computers—including more than 80 Macintosh Plus PCs donated by Apple—can be connected to these local networks for communicating with one another and working with the supercomputer system. Rows of PCs are set up in the auditorium for large-scale training sessions.

Like the other NSF-supported centers, the SDSC holds training sessions, summer institutes, and workshops. Training opportunities range in length from a single day to several weeks and are held at every level from introductory overviews to advanced sessions on programming. This is not an incidental fringe benefit for users but an absolutely central element in the operation of the center. Until now, few universities have possessed the facilities or motivation to teach about supercomputing. Typically, graduate students and post-doctoral researchers are the most active, creative users of supercomputers. If given enough basic knowledge about the hardware and programming tools, they will explore rapidly the applications within their field of study and go on to make significant advances in research. Researchers accustomed to other classes of computers or even new to computing also need training opportunities. Impressions of the 1986 summer institute at SDSC are reported in Chapter Thirteen.

Anyone accustomed to PCs appreciates the menus and "help" services provided by word processing programs, spreadsheets, and other applications programs for microcomputers. Frequently, the PC user is frustrated and annoyed by shortcomings in the manuals (known threateningly and often disappointingly as documentation) supplied with the hardware and software. The SDSC's services to customers include tens of thousands of pages of documentation about the hardware and other components of the system, including programs available in the SDSC program library. This is available to customers over SDSCNET (on-line documentation). A user puzzled by the documentation or unable to find an appropriate reference can call upon the SDSC staff via telephone, through the postal service, or by electronic mail for consultations and advice. A newsletter and other publications provide additional channels for informing users about the procedures, plans, and software of the SDSC. Other supercomputer centers, especially those serving a diverse clientele, provide similar services.

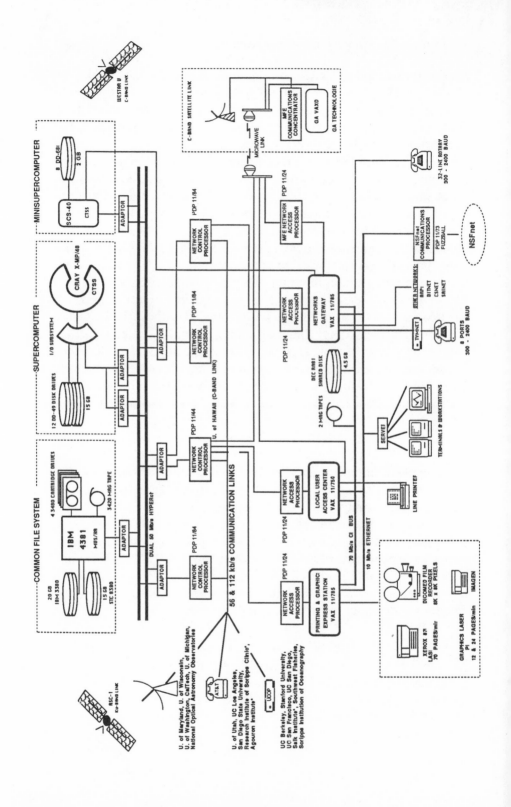

Objectives, Philosophy, and Management

The SDSC happens to be located only a few hundred yards from the central library of the University of California, San Diego, and it contains about as much information as a large university library. Although its operations are different, the philosophy of the SDSC is similar to that of a library. Like a library, it is an efficient mechanism for managing very large amounts of data, and it must remember that its final purpose is to serve customers. All this requires an expert staff. Essential functions, like selection, acquisition, cataloging, and restoration, are carried out in the rear rooms of a library; if done well, the customer who checks out a book need never think about all the work that goes on in the back. A library system typically supports branches and may service remote borrowers. A substantial library, like a supercomputer center, is a large investment. Both are also dynamic systems; like a library that must constantly be acquiring the latest books, a computer center must keep abreast of the newest hardware and programs. Both computer centers and libraries must continuously assess new technology and, from time to time, adopt it.

The SDSC also emphasizes sufficiency, reliability, predictability, and availability. The CPU and support equipment were chosen to provide sufficient capacity and power to deliver on-line service for its numerous and widespread users. The CRAY X-MP/48 was selected because it showed the best promise to meet these criteria. This powerful CPU has been in use since the early 1980s. It is

---

A Computer Specialist's View of the SDSC Network. SDSCnet lets remote users access the CRAY from their own desktops. The main systems at SDSC are (along the top of the diagram) the Common File System (for long term storage), the CRAY X-MP/48 supercomputer, and the new SCS-40 minisupercomputer. RUAC users (left, except Hawaii in center) connect to SDSC via dedicated high-speed data links (RUACs shown with asterisk have not yet come online). The lower right corner of the diagram shows additional ways remote users can connect to SDSC. Peripheral equipment at SDSC (bottom left) include document and graphics laser printers, and a color film recorder. A local area network provides connectivity to the SDSC staff through terminals and workstations (primarily Macintosh Plus microcomputers). (*SDSC/ GA Technologies.*)

The San Diego Supercomputer Center.   (*SDSC/GA Technologies.*)

known for problem-free start-ups, and the on-site support provided by Cray engineers is excellent.

CTSS was chosen as an operating system for similar reasons. It has been proven through years of use by the Department of Energy's National Magnetic Fusion Energy Computer Center (NMFECC), located at the Lawrence Livermore National Laboratory, as well as at several other installations. The SDSC chose another proven NMFECC product, the MFENET protocol, as its networking protocol—the traffic cop and management system for the communications network. The NMFECC is the grand-daddy of large-scale scientific computing networks. The SDSC drew on the NMFECC's years of experience in selecting support hardware and even in designing the building in which the system is housed. This was not done from a blind impulse to imitate, but in order to increase confidence in being able to develop a reliable system that could be put together quickly and achieve full-scale operations with minimum delay.

Other supercomputer centers, including centers supported by the NSF, have applied different philosophies and, as a result, have made different choices. Many have different objectives, focused upon specific applications or a relatively small number of fields of research. Some appear to consider that the library analogy is too passive. They do not stick to proven, low-risk components but aim explicitly at exploring the boundaries of developments in software and equipment. Scientists are bored easily by the predictable and the reliable. Computer scientists and operators of computational systems are no exception.

Some have opted for the CRAY-2, a newer design that operates at a faster clock speed than the X-MP and has an exceptionally massive active memory. Others are reaching farther into uncertainty and planning to install the ETA-10. The NSF-supported center at Cornell University has chosen the IBM 3090-400. Some supercomputer systems managers have chosen lower-cost options like the Cyber 205 or second-hand CRAY-1s and single-processor X-MPs which have come upon the market as users have upgraded to more powerful equipment. There is similar diversity in the choice of operating systems, support computers, and peripheral equipment. Appendix II describes a number of supercomputer systems in the United States in some detail, including descriptions of the institutions these systems support and the contrasting philosophies and objectives that these systems embody.

Vector Processing: Why Supercomputers Are Super

Numbers are numbers, and arithmetic is arithmetic, right? This is the instinctive attitude of the majority of the population (including many with advanced degrees) who escaped from serious attention to mathematics as soon as they could, somewhere around the ninth grade. Without getting into fine points, there are different ways to *do* arithmetic. In supercomputing, two ways are especially important: *scalar* processing and *vector* processing.

When we try to balance a checkbook in our head or use a pocket calculator to estimate how much wallpaper will be needed to decorate the den, we are doing *scalar* arithmetic. It is done one step at a time. Everything gets muddled if we attempt to do step three before step two has been done. Supercomputers are generally good at scalar processing, but only because they run fast and have a lot of sheer computational power.

Because everything must be done in sequence, scalar processing works very slowly for a task like calculating the paychecks for hundreds of workers, earning many different rates of pay, working different numbers of hours, plus variables like overtime, benefits, different rates of tax withholding, and so on. To give a simplified example:

Joan's hours worked × hourly rate − tax withheld = salary due
Charlie's hours worked × hourly rate − tax withheld = salary due
Hugh's hours worked × hourly rate − tax withheld = salary due
Ada's hours worked × hourly rate − tax withheld = salary due
Maria's hours worked × hourly rate − tax withheld = salary due

Scalar processing would require that each individual case be worked out horizontally, step by step. Even for this very limited example, many calculations must be done in sequence.

It is possible, however, to treat lists of numbers as *vectors,* performing repetitive similar calculations for hourly rates, tax withheld, etc., rather than a series of single calculations. A vector processor can work rapidly through these lists, performing all the multiplications at more or less the same time. This adds enormously to the actual operating speed, especially for applications programs which include a large proportion of repetitive operations, like the *Do Loop* in FORTRAN.

The high performance of the supercomputers now in general use is due in large degree to their special efficiency in doing vector processing. Scientific problems tend to involve many repetitive calculations. In addition, it is often possible to write a program (or rewrite it) so that the maximum proportion of operations can be carried out in this way. The process, which is somewhat like tinkering with a recipe so that it cooks quickly in a microwave oven, is known as *vectorization.*

Problems run on supercomputers tend to be much more complicated than getting the right checks out for ten million people. Through efficient vector processing and skillful vectorization, solutions can be obtained quickly—often in seconds or minutes, usually in a few hours for the most demanding problems.

Class X, Generation Y: What Does It Mean?

Computer terminology can be confusing, and it gets worse when confusing numbers are added.

Two terms often mentioned in connection with advanced computing are *Class VI* (occasionally Class VII as well) and the *Fifth Generation*. The origins and meanings of these two designations are very different.

Some years back, computer specialists tried to reduce confusion by defining performance goals for successive levels of high-performance computers. It was hoped that despite arguments about a megaflop one way or another, it could be agreed that a specific machine was Class IV, Class V, or whatever. It is generally agreed that the CRAY-1 was the first machine to meet the specifications for Class VI. Since then, it has become more complicated. The models introduced since then have generally been considered Class VI machines. Some specialists place the CRAY-2 in Class VII, however, and supporters of the ETA-10 say it will be the first true Class VII supercomputer. Others question whether a machine like the IBM 3090 with vector procesors qualifies fully as a Class VI machine.

In this book, we have bypassed references to Class VI and other classes in the hope of reducing confusion and avoiding technical disputes about models which may or may not qualify for Class VII. We have substituted descriptions like "contemporary supercomputers." The various models now available compete in the market with one another. It seems sensible to discuss all of them without worrying too much about categories. Appendix I includes manufacturers' claims of performance.

The *Fifth Generation* is the name of an initiative for new computer design, started in Japan in 1982, that has become the object of research and speculation around the world. It aims at a new kind of computer that will constitute a new generation, superseding the previous four generations, based respectively upon vacuum tubes, transistors, integrated circuits, and very large scale integrated circuits. The emphasis is on creating computers able to use human languages and perform like the human brain, or at the least act as an effortless link, even a collaborator, between a human operator and the problem being examined. (The Fifth Generation project is often confused with the Japanese high speed computer project, which was launched at about the same time and is described in Chapter Twelve.)

This is a different domain from the essentially straightforward requirements of high-performance supercomputing. Hence, the Fifth Generation lies outside the scope of this book.

CHAPTER 3 _____

Making Things That Sell: Supercomputing and Private Business

Use of supercomputers by private businesses is broadening after initial concentration in a few fields, especially aerospace and fossil fuels. Automotive, electronics, and chemical firms are now using supercomputers. Applications are increasing in industries exploring new materials and requiring solutions to complex engineering problems. The history and pyschology of supercomputing have influenced this pattern of adoption. AT&T, Apple Computer, Dupont, ALCOA, Exxon, Aerojet General, and General Motors are among the companies whose experience is examined.

A reader who earns a salary by worrying about profits and marketability may ask, "Supercomputer era sounds impressive, and a supercomputer may be all right for the scientists, but we have to think about the bottom line. Will it generate revenue, not in 1992 or 1997, but soon enough to help *me* get in line for consideration as a senior VP or even CEO? We already have plenty of computers. I couldn't live without the PC on my desk, and the smaller one I take on trips, but the ops committee just signed off on two new computers, big ones, and we all felt that was plenty for now. Ten or twenty million for some huge machine for the research people to tickle? Not now. The times are tough, and more likely to turn worse than better.''

These remarks could apply to any proposed acquisition of a new, unfamiliar device that has uncertain prospects, requires a large capital expenditure, and consumes lots of operational funds. Such statements are, perhaps, made more frequently about super-computers than about other big-ticket research tools whose value is established more firmly in the minds of business managers. Nevertheless, in these early years of the supercomputer era, busi-nesses in Japan, the United States, and Europe are now increasing use of supercomputers at an accelerating rate. The history of su-percomputing, the psychology of adapting to supercomputers, and the economics of supercomputer management make it easier to understand the initially slow acceptance of supercomputing.

How Supercomputing Started

Weapons and Codes

Governments are usually torpid, timid creatures, slow to change, especially unimaginative about new technology. Through most of history, this been especially true of military establishments. During World War II, however, the belief that science equals power was added to the articles of military faith. It has been engraved even deeper during the decades of competitive peace that followed.

The first computers or near-computers were used for military purposes, to calculate trajectories of conventional artillery shells and to assist the designers of less conventional weapons working for the Manhattan Project at Los Alamos. After the war, the Los Alamos National Laboratory, its offshoot, the Sandia National Laboratory, and then the Lawrence Livermore National Laboratory, established in 1952, were consistently among the first buyers of each successive new model that offered higher computational capacity.

The events which take place during nuclear fission and fusion are very complex, occur within a extremely brief span of time, and are exquisitely difficult to measure. Computers can simulate what takes place during those tiny fragments of time, making it possible to improve the safety and reliability as well as the yield of nuclear weapons. The more computer power, the better. This was not an exclusively American preoccupation. The nuclear weapons establishments of the United Kingdom and France were equally anxious to obtain powerful computers and were among the earlier users of supercomputers in Europe.

Supercomputer facilities available to the Atomic Energy Commission (predecessor of the Department of Energy) at the weapons laboratories were also used to explore peaceful applications of the same basic physics. Nuclear fusion could apply the physical principles which make stars shine to produce power from an inexhaustible source, the hydrogen found in seawater. Achieving this appealing goal requires some extraordinarily difficult engineering as well as sophisticated physics. It is necessary to confine fuel plasmas within extremely powerful magnetic fields or compress fuel with concentrated energy, delivered by massive lasers, in a very small space. The equipment needed to carry out fusion experiments is massive and very expensive. Computer simulations can help in designing this equipment, avoid multi-million dollar mistakes, and also help to define productive experiments.

During World War II, calculating machines—crude computers in a way—were used for cryptography, coding and decoding secret messages. The tales of the German Enigma and Japanese Purple systems, and the success of the Allies in deciphering them, have been told many times. High-speed computers, with their aptitude for manipulating sophisticated algorithms and dealing repetitively with enormous sets of data, are extremely useful in carrying out the dual task of protecting one's own communications and gaining access to the secret messages of an adversary. Once again, the more power the better, and more power is never enough. Government agencies responsible for communications security and code breaking have also been among the earliest, most consistent, and most demanding customers for supercomputers.

This early history of high-performance computing generated a paradox. The national atomic energy laboratories in England as well as the United States—known for secrecy and isolation—have been fertile sources of operating systems, applications programs (in many fields of engineering as well as nuclear matters), storage systems, and other innovations that have made important contributions to the growth of supercomputing in the private sector. As early buyers of most supercomputer models, programmers and hardware experts at the national laboratories have helped manufacturers find solutions for initial problems in new designs.

Some sectors of industry and research were also quick to appreciate the virtues of supercomputers and took steps to put them to use. These included the aerospace industry, the oil and gas industry, and atmospheric research (see Chapters Seven and Eight). For aircraft makers and oil searchers, the contribution of supercomputers to their profits was immediate and important. Weather forecasting is one of those unpleasant responsibilities which are not likely to produce predictable profits, so it is left largely to governments. Supercomputers were acquired for these purposes in Europe, Japan and Canada as well as the United States.

A Moral Tale: Researchers Betrayed by Central Computers, Rescued by the VAX

Supercomputing is not a separate phenomenon; it is involved inextricably in the general course of computational history. The burdens of history are heavy. Many industrial researchers and academic scientists or engineers who are still active (some of them now managers of large research or production operations) were introduced to computers 20 or 25 years ago. The early high-performance mainframes were expensive. It was assumed that their capacity, which seemed so vast at the time, could be used fully and efficiently only if central facilities provided administrative, research, and other services for an entire firm, division of a large company, or campus.

Networking was primitive or nonexistent. Input/output devices were also primitive, depending upon stacks, sometimes enormous stacks, of punched cards. Customers lined up at the computer center, submitted their boxes of cards, and then went back to await the call that their job was done, their data ready at last. If something had gone wrong, the defect had to be found, and then the whole arduous process was repeated. Not surprisingly, many researchers concluded, "If this is the computer revolution, then the hell with it," and went on to other things.

Powerful, relatively inexpensive minicomputers appeared in the late 1960s and early 1970s. They became a universal tool of industrial and academic research. Researchers were delighted. Money could be squeezed from a research budget to buy one of these machines without going through tedious layers of review boards. It was possible to bypass data processing managers anxious to preserve central control. Operating systems like AT&T Bell Laboratories' UNIX and the Digital Equipment Corporation's TOPS-10 and VMS permitted a number of researchers to use one machine simultaneously. For most ordinary problems, a user could put in data, run a program, get the results, and try again, all in one afternoon or perhaps within a few minutes, without leaving his or her office. Improved input/output devices, especially disk drives, added to the ease and speed of computing. Minicomputers were also easily adapted to experimental production-line use for computer-controlled manufacturing and inventory control.

Hewlett-Packard and other computer makers did well in this market, but its symbol became the DEC VAX. The VAX performed the same service for science as Chevy and Ford pickup trucks did for American agriculture: VAX minicomputers were easy to buy, surprisingly powerful, gratifyingly versatile, and above all could be kept right outside the rear stoop.

In the late 1970s and early 1980s, when some universities and industries began to think seriously about taking advantage of the power of supercomputers, many people accustomed to the accessibility and immediacy of minicomputers were wary of the prospect of a reimposition of central control. A facility on the other side of town was bad enough. Now they might be required to relate to centers hundreds or thousands of miles away. Persistent shortcomings of communications and networking, even at the best-run centers, made this concern even more valid.

As the 1980s began and supercomputing was beginning to diffuse more widely, a familiar scene in the history of technology was recreated. "A tractor? This ox may be contrary, but he's *my* ox, he pulls the plow when I tell him to, and he's paid for." "A good yew bow doesn't blow up in your face, I can reload it faster than any musket handler, and I can count on it even when it rains." The people who were skeptical about supercomputers were not, for the most part, hostile to computing. They were familiar with the computers they had, and they liked it that way.

Demand and Saturation

Science is, however, both the daughter and mother of contention. A great many people in universities and a considerable number in the private sector wanted to get at a supercomputer very badly. They agitated within their own institutions and within their professional specialties, saying that supercomputing was essential for further progress in their work. Study panels were formed, and petitions were presented to the federal government and Congress (see Chapter Six).

Some of these people knew that they needed more computational power, but had not yet had a chance to use a supercomputer. Others had had a taste of supercomputing and wanted more. In any event, once they had access to a supercomputer, another distinctive phenomenon of computing, especially supercomputing, appeared: saturation.

"Computing capacity is like love," according to Glenn Ingram of the National Bureau of Standards. "When you don't have it, or don't have enough, life looks grim. When it comes your way, everything is wonderful. Then, after a while, you begin to think that it might be nice to have a little more—or a whole lot more. Before long, everything looks grim again until you find a way to get what you just *know* you need." Managers of supercomputing systems also make a comparison with another eternal issue, almost as emotional as love: on-campus parking. No matter how much is built, it fills up right away and remains so. Whatever is done in an attempt to allocate parking spaces fairly, a lot of people always end up mad. Regardless of the comparison, supercomputing facilities that are accessible to a fairly broad clientele, have adequate communications, and are not perceived by customers as over-priced usually come close to full utilization within a few months after they begin full-scale operations.

This has been true time and again for the National Magnetic Fusion Energy Computer Center at Livermore, one of the earliest supercomputer systems to serve a national clientele. Each time it added more powerful equipment, it was expected that the new capacity would take care of things for quite a while. With each increase, the most optimistic projections for use were exceeded much earlier than anticipated. Ingram, with decades of experience as a manager of computer systems, was surprised by the speed at which demand for the Cyber 205 installed at the National Bureau of Standards in the spring of 1985 came close to its capacity.

Money makes a difference. Typically, institutions that consider acquiring supercomputers are large, many of them very large, with decentralized budgeting and management. Will the supercomputer be a centralized corporate or campus resource, or will it belong to one unit or a single fast-track project? Does it go into an existing computer service center, or elsewhere? Is time on the supercomputer available to anyone within the whole organization who wants it for a serious purpose? Are subunits within the organization charged for time, required to transfer funds ("funny money") from their budget to a central account? Or are blocks of time parcelled out ("resource allocations")? If time is allocated, by what criteria, and who decides the allocation? Do the prices for computer time reflect corporate overheads, or are they limited to direct costs? Decisions on these points can make the difference between underutilization, early total saturation, and some happy balance in between.

Supercomputers at Work

I: Designing Computers and Chips

"People do not design computers any more; computers do." This statement remains an exaggeration, but it can be rephrased like this: "People cannot design computers efficiently without the aid of computers." For the most part, conventional computers are used to design computers and the chips that are their fundamental components. More and more, however, electronics companies are deciding that they need the added computational power that supercomputers provide.

Bell Labs: in the Home of the Transistor and UNIX. Since 1980, AT&T Bell Laboratories has been using supercomputers to help its engineers design chip circuits and to explore the physics and chemistry of the chips themselves. Japanese manufacturers have been doing this for some time, and Fairchild Semiconductor recently acquired a supercomputer for the same purpose. Control Data/ ETA and Cray use supercomputers in order to design new super- computers and produce simulations that enable software engineers to create and check out programs to be used on new machines. Now, Apple Computer is operating a powerful CRAY X-MP, used primarily to design and simulate new products. All these companies are using supercomputers in order to obtain direct, immediate returns in the marketplace.

The AT&T Bell Laboratories facility at Murray Hill, New Jersey, is the prototypical high-tech research campus—the real thing. In June, the trees are assertively green; there is enough open space to accommodate a golf tournament, several Little League cham- pionships, and a few soccer pitches simultaneously without crowding. The buildings are geometrical modern but done in good taste; they appear to have been designed by a live architect, not a concrete salesman. Inside, the commonplace reasserts itself; the main halls and cafeteria have a degree of style, but the workspaces are a maze of partitions, just like everywhere else. Managers seem to assume that computer people, like mushrooms, thrive best when deprived of sunlight.

A lot of things very prominent in the history of computing were developed at Bell Labs, including the transistor and the UNIX operating system. Nils-Peter Nelson, supervisor of the Systems Support Group at Murray Hill, is not an ordinary computer center bureaucrat. His favorite slogan is a quotation from computer pioneer Dick Hamming: "The purpose of computing is insight, not numbers."

The computer center in which Nelson works is the home of a two-processor CRAY X-MP, installed in November 1985. The ver- tical panels of the CPU are not the customary brightly-colored vinyl: they are enlargements of the circuitry of a chip designed on a supercomputer at Bell Labs. The X-MP replaced a CRAY-1 that started up at Murray Hill in January 1980. AT&T uses lots of computers of every possible size. It added the Cray to its inventory in order to permit its scientists and engineers to gain sharper insight into the inner life of computer chips. It also sought to speed up the process of designing and producing integrated circuits. (The two objectives are, of course, complementary.)

The chip makers have been riding a fast horse for decades, but now it is turning into a nightmare. Great increases have been accomplished continuously; each successive generation of chip has had more capacity, more power—not just somewhat more, but many times more. The cost of active memory, once a major factor in the total price of a computer system, has shrunk steadily, in absolute as well as relative terms. The size of processor chips for microcomputers and other applications has decreased enormously, while capability has increased equally fast. As chips become more crowded, however, it is becoming increasingly difficult to design and manufacture each generation of improved chip.

An integrated circuit looks like a piece of lawn that is heavily overpopulated by very orderly gophers. As seen by the lawn-owner it looks two-dimensional, but to the gophers it is three-dimensional. There are several layers on a chip (the surface and substrates) of different chemical composition, somewhat like the grass blades, the root level, and the dirt below. Gophers possess a good deal of cunning and can make adjustments when they bump noses while tunneling. Electrons are not clever, and so the entire, complex, desperately crowded system must be without flaws.

Design of a new chip begins with the substrate material, usually silicon. A series of other substances, called dopants, is added carefully. Their type and concentration determines the electrical properties of the substrate and hence the performance of the chip itself. Phenomena like electromagnetic scattering, heat transfer, and the distribution of energy within the substrate can be studied. Once the designer has used the computer to simulate the cross-section of dopants, the devices (the transistors and other electronic components) are simulated. Devices are now so small that electrical effects can no longer be explored as if they were strung out on a wire in one dimension. Two-dimensional models are now usual, but three-dimensional simulations are required to achieve satisfactory accuracy. Increasing density of smaller and smaller devices will also require consideration of quantum mechanics in addition to the classical mechanics that have sufficed so far. Finally, the designer examines the model on the circuit level. It is also necessary to remember that customers will on occasion bump, overheat, and otherwise mistreat the equipment in which the chips will be installed. These effects must also be simulated, along with the electrical characteristics and performance of the circuit.

While chips have become more difficult to design, the market lifetime of each class of chip has become shorter, almost like fad products. The manufacturer who gets in first with a product and stays in front has a great advantage over competitors who lag behind. The front-runner establishes market-share. As experience is gained with the new item, unit costs go down and profits rise. Late arrivals must cut prices to compete; this may hurt them more than a market leader who has had time to establish a more comfortable cushion between costs and price and keep increasing efficiency of production. The intersection of these two considerations means that a manager of chip R&D must walk around with a clock ticking in his head. A time machine is immensely appealing.

Especially at first, the CRAY-1 at Murray Hill was not an efficiency machine, as such things are usually measured. They used SPICE, the standard software for circuit design. Because it permitted only 10% vectorizing, the vector processing capability that is the distinctive advantage of the CRAY-1 and similar machines could only be exploited partially. Nevertheless, according to Nelson, the supercomputer was cost-effective in the scalar mode—in effect, doing ordinary primary school arithmetic. It may not have been operating in its most efficient mode, but it was still much faster than any alternative.

The cycles of iterations for AT&T's development of the 256K chip were cut by a number of months. AT&T was the first into the marketplace with the megabit chip, which was designed much more rapidly than would have been possible without supercomputing. The high-quality simulations possible on supercomputers paid off in another way: the 256K and megabit chips came in error-free.

Replacing the CRAY-1 with an X-MP has increased efficiency. Along with improvements in software, SPICE can be vectorized more readily, leading to corresponding improvements in productivity. A process known as gather-scatter makes it possible to move fragments of information to and from active memory rapidly while a calculation proceeds. As a result, the machine can spend more time in the vector-processing mode, making fullest use of its capabilities. It is easier to do three-dimensional modeling. This was difficult on the CRAY-1, due to memory constraints more than lack of processing speed.

The supercomputer installation at Murray Hill services thousands of AT&T Bell Labs scientists and engineers at facilities spread around New Jersey, the outer fringes of the New York metropolitan area, and other locations. About 300 are active users of the Cray. This may not seem a large number, and the rate of utilization falls somewhat short of theoretical total capacity. Yet, as Nelson points out, the total salaries of these users exceed the annual cost of operating the supercomputer by a very wide margin. The ultimate benefit is product—above all, product ready at the right time.

The Murray Hill center is also a test-bed for new software. Originally, the CRAY X-MP was operating under COS (the established Cray standard, primarily for batch processing) with UNICOS (the Cray adapation of UNIX) operating within COS as a "guest system." A changeover to UNICOS took place at the end of 1986. This is being done, Nelson says, due to UNICOS' advantages for time-sharing and interactivity. He believes that CTSS, an alternative operating system for time-sharing on Crays that is used at some other installations, requires too large a support staff. (At the San Diego Supercomputer Center, six full-time staff members are devoted to supporting CTSS and its languages and utility programs.) Nelson also foresees a millenium in which UNICOS will fit into a comprehensive work environment, based upon UNIX, that would, ideally, permit a user to input a problem into a system and obtain results without having to be concerned with the sordid details of the machinery and software that make it possible.

Apple, Cray, Apple, Cray, Apple . . . Apple Computer is a large company, a long way from the garage where it all began. It passed through a period of uncertainty but then achieved substantial profits and accumulated a comfortable stock of cash while other companies competing at the smaller end of the computer market were struggling or collapsing. Even IBM wheezed a little, made uncharacteristic excuses, and accelerated its early-retirement program in order to reduce staff. Success has, however, elevated Apple into a tough league. Compared with IBM, DEC, and the major Japanese companies, Apple's product-line is narrow, its resources slender.

In order to keep up the pace, Apple has done what the other big boys do: select the capital equipment it needs to maximize its competitiveness and use that equipment aggressively. One of the most striking features of this policy is a CRAY X-MP/48. It was installed in the heart of Silicon Valley in March 1986, in a building where all the support requirements had been built from bare concrete in six weeks of three-shift maximum effort.

R. Kent Koeninger of Apple says that the Apple investment in a supercomputer has one overriding purpose: "To gain time. It buys Apple time to get its product to market faster. It is possible to try many more designs, many more different ideas. Without a supercomputer, the process would have to be skimped or would take too long."

It is not easy to evaluate this decision without knowing about the product (or products) that Apple hopes to harvest. Apple has learned another lesson from IBM and its other major competitors. If the opposition doesn't know what you're trying to do, it is harder for them to hurt you. The X-MP cannot be accessed by telephone lines, only over a 10 million bits per second Ethernet servicing several Apple buildings within a few miles of the supercomputer. In an interview, Koeninger declined to characterize the simulation software being used at Apple, lest this suggest the type of project that Apple researchers are exploring.

Apple is forthcoming about the operating system. The X-MP has been running exclusively on UNICOS—the first such X-MP installation. Koeninger, who came to Apple from NASA's nearby Ames research facility, was also involved in the first use of a two-processor X-MP running on COS. They encountered the initial difficulties common in a new machine, and Koeninger would not have been surprised if the start-up of Apple's four-processor machine using UNICOS would have similar problems. In fact, everything went remarkably smoothly, and the X-MP is used interactively without difficulties. Initially, Apple preferred the well-established COS, but during the factory trials of the machine it was decided to try UNICOS right away. "We thought we would take our lumps up front, before there was a heavy load," Koeniger remarked, "but then there weren't a lot of lumps."

For now, Apple is using the X-MP as if it were four separate processors sharing the same memory. In the future, Koeninger says, they expect to move to multi-tasking, or using all four processors simultaneously. He explains that some of the simulations that Apple is emphasizing adapt well to multi-tasking. Engineers throughout Apple have access to the Cray for their own projects, unless the machine is busy with a long run of a high-priority project.

How does all this fit into the garage-to-riches-in-sandals mythology of Apple? Koeninger emphasizes that Apple did not just leap in one bound from the Apple II/Lisa/Macintosh to the Cray. Apple had done simulations earlier on minicomputers, including DEC PDP-11s and VAXs. Well before the decison was made to acquire the X-MP, Apple had plenty of people with solid experience using supercomputers. Other machines were considered, but they lacked the horsepower or had other drawbacks.

The supercomputing community is growing rapidly, but it is still small enough to spread good stories far, fast, and wide. One of the better ones is repeated widely. When asked about the apparent anomaly of Apple buying a Cray to design new products, Seymour Cray reportedly replied, "Why not? I use a Macintosh to design Crays."

II: Chemistry

Fresh Insights at Dupont. The ambiguity—or diversity—of reactions to supercomputers is illustrated by the experience of Dupont, the first chemical company to install its own supercomputer. Prior to this acquisition, computing resources in the Scientific Computing Division of Dupont's Central Research and Development Department consisted of a cluster of ten VAXs and an IBM 3081 with a Floating Point Systems 164 array processor attached. A CRAY-1/A went on line in early 1986 and was available to customers within the company a few months later.

Molecular dynamics and molecular orbital theory have become well-established fields for the use of supercomputers (see Chapter Four). Chemists and biologists argue from time to time over rights of possession of molecular dynamics, but there seems to be plenty of work to do for everyone. (University managers of high-speed computers say that computational chemists are like locusts—if turned loose, they eat up all the computational capacity in sight.) Frederic A. Van-Catledge of Dupont's Scientific Computing Division says that Dupont researchers in these areas followed the form. These workers had already secured access to supercomputers operated by Boeing Computer Services or Cray Research. When a supercomputer was operating right there in the home neighborhood, they moved in. Soon, they accounted for 60 to 70% of total utilization.

The problem has been to spread the use of supercomputing across the company. Van-Catledge points out that it was necessary to convince researchers in other specialties that the new supercomputer was both a quality machine and a time-saving machine. The analysis of fluorocarbons, for example, has always been tiresome and demanding. A relatively straightforward problem required four months on a VAX 11/780, running eight hours every night. Dupont researchers dealing with this and other problems are discovering that the performance possible on the Cray can change their entire pattern of work. Conservative projections indicate that calculations requiring 25 hours on a VAX or 2 1/2 hours on the IBM 3081 can be completed in 30 minutes on the Cray. Van-Catledge cites another problem which can be done in 231 seconds on the CRAY-1/A, compared with 7320 seconds, or just over 2 hours, on a VAX 8650.

Researchers do not react to such savings of time by saying, "Hooray, it's done," putting up their feet, and reading the funnies or the stock market reports. They use the new-found time to do more. This does not only result in more efficient use of time. It also results in fresh insights. Quick turnarounds, making it possible to run through a number of cycles of analysis in a single day, enable researchers to perceive unexpected patterns and break new ground.

Van-Catledge reports that a wide range of problems are being explored on the new supercomputer. Fibers are a very important part of Dupont's total business. Monte Carlo statistical sampling methods are used to simulate breakage thresholds and breakage patterns in fibers. Fractals (a mathematical model used to simulate complex surfaces) are employed to examine the propagation of cracks in composite materials. Other fields being investigated include chemical kinetics and the electronic structure of solids.

Developing New Catalysts: "Pushing a Supercomputer as far as it Can Go." Tony Rappe, an assistant professor of chemistry at Colorado State University, has been using computers since his days as a graduate student at Cal Tech. Most of his research time is now devoted to the application of quantum chemistry to catalysis. He says, "This is at the forefront of what can be done on a supercomputer—pushing a supercomputer as far as it can go." More than 160 hours on the Cyber 205 at Colorado State are needed to generate the field for reactions he has been studying.

Rappe's attention is currently concentrated upon a class of substances known as zeolites. Around 250 atoms, predominately silicon, oxygen, aluminum, and sodium, are arranged in a structure called a supercage. Zeolites can be used for catalysis; possible applications include upgrading crude oil and reducing pollution from combustion by breaking up nitrogen monoxide into familar carbon dioxide and nitrogen. The problem is to determine the best form of zeolite.

Rappe says that researchers in Japan are "substantially ahead" in this work. Professor Keiji Morokuma of the Institute for Molecular Studies in Japan is using Hitachi supercomputers to support his research. Rappe has been working with Dr. T.H. Upton at Exxon and has adapted for use on the Cyber 205 programs which have been run on a Floating Point Systems 164 array processor.

Work in this field requires quantum chemistry. There is very little symmetry, and ordinary shortcuts do not work. Rappe is using an algorithm that he had applied to studies of the numerous reactive states (35 in all) of the element scandium. "We are not looking toward dynamics in the foreseeable future," he says. "Time steps are not used, just static thermodynamics. The algorithms for the quantum approach are a lot more expensive than those for molecular dynamics, perhaps 10,000 times more expensive, in terms of computational time." His work with zeolites is not based on sampling: the model includes the entire structure of the supercage, all the atoms and all the electrons. He is very much at home with the Cyber 205; indeed, he arrived at Colorado State six years ago, when the supercomputer was just being installed. In addition, he has obtained supercomputer time at Purdue. He points out that the Cyber 205's capacity for very long vectors is very well adapted to his kind of problem.

Tony Rappe is at the intersection of industrial development and basic research, a situation considered natural in Japan but not as common in the United States. When asked when his work with

Exxon might produce direct, practical results, he smiled and said: "Moderately soon." In order to protect proprietary interests, he declined to define either word precisely.

III: New Materials, New Problems

Plain steel and solid concrete—even straightforward aluminum and familiar plastics—simply aren't enough any more. Increasingly, advanced materials that combine the unique properties of ceramics, polymers, and metals in highly engineered laminate and composite systems are specified by product designers. Aerospace and defense industries are leading the way, and automobiles are not far behind. Other applications, ranging from communications satellites to food packaging, are developing rapidly. Engineered materials are lighter, stronger, more resistant to corrosion and fatigue than conventional materials. In the past, an entire component might be machined from a single monolithic piece of material. In the future, it is more likely to be an assemblage of several parts, each engineered to meet specific design criteria.

The round-the-world flight of the *Voyager* was possible only because the aircraft was made almost entirely of composite materials, saving weight needed for fuel. Barry Fell, a chemist for Hexcel Corporation, which fabricated many of the parts for the aircraft, points out that conventional steel firewalls to protect the crew from fire in the two engines would have weighed 70 pounds each. Instead, the *Voyager* used composite ceramic firewalls which weighed two pounds each. The lightweight material provides equal fire resistance.

Peter Bridenbaugh, Alcoa's Vice President for Research and Development, points out that the successful integration of materials into laminate or composite systems requires massive computational capacity. Some materials, like ceramics, lack the comforting pre- dictability of metals, especially in structural applications. It is difficult to make sure when a particular part may crack—like the single cup, out of a dozen, which emerges in two pieces from the dish- washer. Conventional engineering tests are difficult to apply to materials systems that may consist of a metal mesh embedded in a ceramic matrix. Models of interfacial or adhesion behavior, for example, require calculations so complex that they are feasible only on a supercomputer.

In Bridenbaugh's opinion, too few researchers within Alcoa, and in American industry as a whole, have had experience using supercomputers. "There is a general lack of supercomputer expertise among the Fortune 500," he says. There is also a need for more people trained to manage supercomputing systems and provide program development support for researchers. The horizons and thoughts of engineers have increasingly become defined by the capabilities of their VAXs, erecting artificial boundaries which impede creativity. Bridenbaugh also urges more effective, rapid transfer of new technology from academic and federal laboratories to industry.

Understanding and controlling a material's microstructure has a direct impact upon product design, performance, and manufacturing, Bridenbaugh says. Alcoa's desire to control tightly each of these areas demands high-speed computational capabilities as well as integrated manufacturing systems capable of dealing with very large, complex problems. Bridenbaugh points out that the most cost-effective tools for these purposes appear to be supercomputers or high-performance parallel-processor machines.

IV: Engineering

Moving Toward Supercomputers—At Last. Mechanical, electrical, and architectural engineers have been using computers for a long, long time. Much of their day is spent finding out what happens when something is subjected to weight, pushed, hammered, bent, heated, or cooled. Will it break or shatter, and when? What additional engineering, what added material, what bracing or other safety factor is needed to keep this gadget from flying apart or prevent this building from falling down? This takes a lot of figuring. In the old days, engineers relied mostly on an analog device, the slide rule. They welcomed digital machines, which are quicker, more accurate, and provide much more precise results.

Hundreds of specialized programs have been developed to assist engineers in carrying out specific computational tasks. Usually, engineering programs are run on minicomputers or mainframes. High-performance workstations have developed so rapidly that they are relied upon increasingly for very substantial engineering computations. Programs are also adapted or developed for use on supercomputers. Many of these applications programs have been developed at national laboratories and are in the public domain. Others were developed privately and are under copyright. A license for commercial use by a manufacturer can be downright expensive, but such programs can be highly cost-effective, so users grit their teeth and pay.

Engineering applications typically apply a grid to the object under study or divide its surface into a number of polygons. (Similar approaches are taken in programs for aerodynamics, weather prediction, and computer animation—see Chapters Seven, Eight, and Nine.) A simulation can then determine what will happen when the object is subjected to load, deformed in various directions, or crushed. The grid points (in effect, a method of sampling) bend, twist, and crumple in an approximation of the behavior of the actual material.

Engineers did not stampede in pursuit of supercomputing power, except for specialized problems like circuit design. Now, however, a growing number of engineers are entering the supercomputer era. They feel increasingly confined within the capabilities of smaller machines and are eager to deal with more complex, exacting problems. Because of the very large number of users and the broad range of potential applications, this could become a major source of demand for supercomputing. At some supercomputer centers, such as the University of Minnesota, engineering applications consitute a third or more of total utilization.

Aerojet General: Making Sure that Rockets Work. How does an engineer design fuel pumps and other rotating components which may run at speeds of 20,000 to 100,000 revolutions per minute, are subjected to extremes of temperature ranging close to absolute zero, undergo severe acceleration forces, must be reusable, and must provide total reliability? How about rocket combustion chambers which must meet the same requirements at temperatures up to 2000 degrees centigrade? Walt Langhy and his colleagues at Aerojet General's applied mechanics department engineer components for civil and military rockets and the propulsion system for the proposed National Aerospace Plane. They are now using supercomputing to help them meet these demanding objectives.

Rocket design has never been an easy trade, but the requirement for reusability makes it even more difficult. Anyone who has ever looked at the metal erosion and general wear of a well-used sparkplug knows that a combustion chamber is a very tough environment, even in an ordinary commuter car. Aerojet General engineers must make life-cycle projections for rocket engine thrust chambers. They must simulate and predict accurately the "creep"—redistribution of material within the chamber—that is caused by repeated firings. Designers of turbo pumps must deal with problems of rotor dynamics, centrifugal stress, and blade vibration as well as questions of fluid dynamics. Operation under cryogenic conditions, involving the extreme cold of liquid hydrogen, complicates matters further.

Langhy and his coworkers are using a ground station near the Aerojet General facility at Sacramento to reach the X-MP at the San Diego Supercomputer Center over a 56 kilobit per second channel. The work he does on structural analysis involves thousands of elements; solutions on a minicomputer encounter serious problems of saturation. He also needs interactive graphics. A CPU with the capacity (including memory) of an X-MP/48 and an operating system like CTSS, which permits operating in an interactive mode, are essential. A powerful supercomputer is especially important for analyses that involve entire engine systems, not just single components within the system. The problems encountered are nonlinear as well as linear.

Software requirements vary. For structural analysis, Langhy uses well-established programs like NASTRAN and ANSYS. Adapting his codes for use on the X-MP required only a few months of work in late 1986. Ken Kirk, who works on computational fluid dynamics, is in an earlier stage. He and his associates are developing new fluid dynamics codes that will be able to deal adequately with the movement of propellants through an engine system. Existing codes do not have enough coordinate flexibility, and full three-dimensionality is needed. They require the power of the X-MP to develop these codes, a process which, Kirk estimates, will require several years.

Automobiles: Rethinking the Purpose of Research. General Motors, Ford, Nissan, Chrysler, Adam Opel (GM's West German subsidiary), and SAAB-Scania of Sweden are among the world's largest engineering firms. A large part of their total costs is devoted to R&D: developing new models, engineering new materials and individual parts, making manufacturing processes more efficient, and improving fuel efficiency and passenger safety. All these companies operate supercomputers, and Daimler-Benz is reported to be kicking tires, deciding upon a supercomputer of its own. Other car manufacturers in Japan and Europe make extensive use of supercomputers at universities, research institutes, and service bureaus.

GM has installed a CRAY-1/S, and George Dodd, Head of the Computer Science Department of GM Research Laboratories, reports that it has proven a very tractable resource; it is providing the results that GM sought. GM is using the CRAY-1/S for many purposes, including the analysis of combustion inside engines, structural analysis, the design of stamping dies, speeding up the transition from the clay model of a new product to actual component design, and aerodynamics. They are moving into crash simulation, which can reduce costs in the highly expensive process of testing actual cars to see what happens. The supercomputer validates and extends laboratory experimentation, such as testing airflow over a new design in a wind tunnel. It makes it possible to explore three-dimensional solutions for problems like the analysis of both the chemistry and fluid flow of combustion.

Above all, Dodd says, the supercomputer makes it possible to rethink how research is done. Computers can be used for something more than arithmetic. Results from an experiment that used to be available after two or three weeks can now be available two or three times a day. Problems that had seemed overwhelmingly large can now be solved easily, stretching the imaginations of researchers. For aerodynamic simulations, for example, computation is now the shortest element in the cycle. It requires about 40% of total time to develop the model, 20% to compute, and 40% to evaluate results. In many areas of GM's research, the size of models is so large that memory rather than computational speed is the limiting factor.

The supercomputer configuration which GM acquired is aimed at meeting user needs for the next several years. Future requirements include increased memory and an improved capability to manipulate very large data bases. All in all, Dodd says, the supercomputer "has had a significant and positive impact on research at GM. It means that computational capability drives experimentation, rather than limiting it."

V: Other Customers—Financial Firms
and Smaller Businesses

Can supercomputers help economists and investment specialists to understand what the economy is doing—and what might happen? Supercomputer makers believe so. Banks, insurance companies, and other financial institutions that must analyze the investment market and project future economic conditions already use very complex econometric models. Supercomputers could make it possible to analyze a larger number of variables in greater depth and provide results quicker. For Cray or ETA, it would be a whole new market, potentially a large one. IBM could build upon its extensive base of conventional, non-vectorized 3090s and other machines installed in financial institutions.

Periodic reports indicate that financial institutions and supercomputer makers are talking about possible sales. So far, no firm deals have been confirmed. It seems likely, however, that this will be one of the next frontiers to be crossed by supercomputing.

Smaller businesses? Skeptics are hard to quell: "Yeah, GM, other big car companies, Dupont, even Apple, they can afford these machines. If most of the Fortune 500 isn't too swift about using supercomputers, so much the better for smart but smaller folks like us. I know exactly how I can use one. But if I go to my backers for another big jolt of investment capital, they'll run me out of town. When you don't have the cash to buy one, how do you get a piece of one?"

The replies to this question are among the most important developments of the supercomputer era. For the first time in the history of supercomputers, there are now several satisfactory answers. The unprecedented expansion in supercomputer availability now taking place offers a variety of options short of outright purchase. These include private-sector participation in the new centers supported by the National Science Foundation, such as the San Diego Supercomputer Center. Other state and regional supercomputing programs welcome business customers, often at reasonable rates. Some, like the University of Minnesota's supercomputing center, have a stated charter to support local firms. Commercial service bureaus do not come cheap, but they are efficient and can offer a

no-nonsense opportunity to evaluate the usefulness of supercomputing for a particular requirement. (Options for smaller businesses
are noted in Appendix II, summarizing sources of supercomputing
capabilities.)

CHAPTER 4

Quarks, Molecules, and Galaxies: Supercomputers as Scientific Instruments

Many fields of science were early recruits to the supercomputer era. Supercomputers have become accepted tools of research in molecular biology (the impact upon drug development has begun already), quantum chromodynamics (exploring what appear to be the ultimate components of matter), the study of the universe, and many other disciplines. The differences in scale of size and time spanned by these fields are enormous, but the problems being solved by supercomputers and the needs of researchers are often similar.

It would be easy to assume that Paul Bash, David De Young, and Julius Kuti have little in common.

Paul Bash has just completed the requirements for a Ph.D. in biophysics at the University of California, Berkeley. He did research for his dissertation in the Computer Graphics Laboratory of the University of California, San Francisco, an institution devoted to the healing arts and biological studies. During most of 1986, he was scrambling to find time to complete his doctoral work without interrupting his continuing research.

David De Young is an established astronomer who divides his

time between the offices of the National Optical Astronomy Observatories in Tucson and activities at the Kitt Peak National Observatory, where he is associate director. Julius Kuti is a professor of physics at the University of California, San Diego. His field is theoretical physics, especially the particles within the nucleus of the atom.

De Young works with time spans measured in the multiple billions of years and distances so great that it is difficult, even for astronomers, to estimate them with much confidence. Bash works on a scale so small that individual atoms stand out clearly. A nanosecond (one billionth of a second) is a typical interval between one event and the next. Kuti's interests take him within the atom and into the deepest recesses of the atomic nucleus, where particles with improbable names are bound together by forces which remain very imperfectly understood.

Physics, biology and astronomy are sciences with long, rich, and very different histories. In the popular imagination, biologists spend their days at workbenches in white coats, working with cultures, centrifuges, and microscopes. Astronomers use telescopes, send satellites to eavesdrop on Neptune, and talk about black holes on TV. Specialists in high-energy physics have come in two species. Theorists avoid barbers, spend a lot of time looking at blackboards, and go on long, tree-shaded walks. Experimental physicists put more pens and pencils in their shirt pockets than ordinary folks. They use giant apparatus to pelt one kind of particle with another at immense speeds. None of these sterotypes is totally wrong, but all are out of date. One salient similarity links these otherwise disparate scientists. All rely upon computations, and in particular upon supercomputers, to conduct their research. Not all their colleagues share this preoccupation, but more and more are joining Bash, De Young, and Kuti in turning to supercomputers.

In large part, supercomputers become necessary instruments for these disciplines because the march of science often leads into swamps where an investigator can become lost in too much data, too much uncertainty, or both. New techniques and new ideas create greatly increased amounts of information which cannot be comprehended readily through conventional methods or do not respond to traditional methods of analysis.

This is particularly marked in astronomy. Through much of

this century, astronomers have been learning new ways to look at the universe, adding to the varieties of signals they collect from the firmament. In addition to signals in the frequencies of visible light, astronomers also observe radio waves, X-rays, and other portions of the electromagnetic spectrum that lie outside the narrow capacities of human sight. Telescopes for observing signals in all parts of the spectrum are increasingly becoming multiple. Signals from a selected object are noted simultaneously from a number of different observation points that may be very distant from one another. These distinct, separated streams of information can be combined into a single image with much higher resolution (more detail and precision) than a single instrument of great size.

One example is the National Radio Astronomy Observatory at Socorro, New Mexico. It uses 27 dish-shaped antennas, each 82 feet in diameter, that can be moved around on a Y-shaped set of railroad tracks, each arm of which is 13 miles long. Networks of continental size are in development. These multiple-point observatories gather an enormous amount of data, so much that the observations literally do not make sense until they have been assembled together by a computer. It can be compared to the scattered pieces of a jigsaw puzzle, just a jumble until fitted together. The process is most efficient if the pieces can be joined together promptly and accurately, a job which supercomputers do best.

Astronomers, particularly cosmologists who study the origins and development of the universe and its parts, were also dissatisfied because even the most revealing observations were snapshots. They lacked the dimension of time and so did not illuminate the dynamics of the universe. Biologists shared this frustration. Several decades of rapidly-advancing research have taken biologists deep into the living molecule. Not quite living, however, because the living cell and the molecules which make it up are in constant motion. X-ray crystallography and other established means reveal protein structure, but the dynamics are frozen. In both these disciplines, contrasting in so many ways, simulations made possible by supercomputers are able to show the dynamics of the universe on the galactic as well as on the molecular scale. The dimension of time, combined with the capability of supercomputers to generate very detailed graphic representations, can result in moving images.

Julius Kuti encounters a different problem. In exploring the

Theoretical physicist Julius Kuti.   (*University of California, San Diego.*)

inner workings of the atomic nucleus, traditional methods of analysis
that have served theoretical physicists for decades produce vague,
unsatisfactory results. Experimental physicists find it difficult to
contribute adequately to understanding of these phenomena. Analysis
has not gone far enough to guide the experimentalists in defining
their objectives and configuring their apparatus. In order to understand these problems and the role of supercomputers it seems
best to start on the smallest scale, the realm of Professor Kuti and
his colleagues in quantum chromodynamics.

Quantum Chromodynamics:
When and How Do the Gluons Come Unglued?

Quantum chromodynamics is not the latest fad in computer-matched
cosmetics; it is the study of particles called nucleons that reside
inside the nucleus of the atom. This is a domain rich in metaphor.
The word "chromodynamics" is used because the constituents of
nucleons have distinguishing characteristics called "colors," and

"flavors," tagged with names like "up," "down," and "strange." It is possible to gain some understanding of what Professor Kuti is doing without dipping too deeply unto the poetry of nucleons. The two creatures which make up the nucleon of greatest interest are the quark (a kind of particle) and the gluon, the term for the attraction which binds quarks together in a nucleon known as "strong interactions."

According to Professor Kuti, throughout the history of physics, each successive level of penetration into the mysteries of matter turned out to be fairly straightforward. The atom and the nucleus each had constituents that could be broken apart when enough energy was applied in the right way—"If you kicked them hard enough," as Kuti puts it.

Quarks resist kicking. At temperatures now prevailing in the universe, they cling together—a phenomenon called quark confinement. Analytical methods alone could not explain this, nor set a limit on the temperature at which the quarks might be separated. It was hypothesized that there might be a transition point—an extremely high temperature at which the quarks would come apart and buzz about in what is called a quark-gluon plasma. Cosmology threw some light. A few microseconds after the universe originated in what is known as the Big Bang, everything consisted for a while of a quark-gluon plasma, which shortly cooled into more conventional matter.

Neither analysis nor cosmology could give more than a vague indication of the temperature and conditions at which the huddled quarks transform into wandering quarks. Professor Kuti explains that it was necessary to combine analysis with numerical computations. A mathematical tool was at hand: the Feynman Path Integral. This was created by Richard P. Feynman, the Nobel prize winning physicist from Cal Tech who has left the footprints of his inquiring, original personality all over physics and in many other endeavors, including lock-picking, drumming, and the official presidential inquiry into the causes of the *Challenger* disaster. Using this mathematical tool is a formidable task. There are several million variables. The full powers of a supercomputer are required to achieve useful results.

The first paper describing the application of computations to this problem appeared in 1980. The work was done on VAXs and a small IBM machine and was, as Kuti describes it, "very limited." Since 1983, computations have been carried out on supercomputers. Kuti and his associates at the University of California, San Diego and University of California, Santa Barbara currently use about 600 hours per year on a Cyber 205 located at Florida State University and supported by the Department of Energy. His group also uses an ST-100 array processor, made by Star Technologies, which is installed at Santa Barbara.

What have the computers wrought? Professor Kuti says that they have "demonstrated rather convincingly" that the transition state at which quarks become deconfined is found at about 200 million electron volts, equivalent to a temperature of many trillions of degrees. They also discovered certain properties of the transition into a quark-gluon plasma that had previously been unknown. Currently, Professor Kuti and his colleagues are explaining how colored quarks are bound together into the observed varieties of particle—"colorless," of course. The ways in which the colors fit together are roughly analogous to the attractions between positive and negative particles in the atom. This is very relevant to the Standard Model, a hypothetical matrix of particles now widely accepted among theoretical physicists. The methods being used also make it possible to demonstrate another feature of quarks, called asymptotic freedom. When quarks are extremely close to one another, they move freely within the nucleus, but at longer (but still small) distances, they are bound tightly.

What lies beyond the Standard Model? Kuti notes that there is a great deal of interest among physicists in a theory which hypothesizes that objects called super-strings may manifest themselves as the ultimate replacement for point-like particles. Supercomputers might be employed to study super-strings, but there is as yet no counterpart to the Feynman Path Integral. "And," Kuti adds, "if doing quantum chromodynamics on a supercomputer is hard, that looks a lot harder." It seems likely to require supercomputers considerably more powerful than those now available.

The study of quantum chromodynamics has become what Kuti describes as a "substantial cottage industry." The quantum chromodynamics community includes a few hundred people, of whom perhaps 100 or less have used supercomputers.

Points, Meshes, and Grids: Seeing Nature Whole

Dave De Young describes himself as a theoretical astrophysicist. He sifts through data about phenomena like quasars, the active galactic nuclei that are the most violent known objects in the universe. He compares this to an observer in space who trains his instruments upon an automobile factory on earth. The distant observer notes a large, oblong object that produces a steady stream of energetic, apparently self-guiding smaller objects that follow no fixed rules. There seem to be inputs of some kind, but the instruments are too crude and the observer's imagination too extra-terrestrial to define them clearly. There is no way to penetrate inside the large flat object where all this takes place. Astronomers can come to similar conclusions about galactic nuclei, producing various models of the central engine which produces so much energy. It is, however, difficult to devise observational tests that will prove or invalidate those models.

Paul Bash confronted a similar conundrum in his investigations of the transfer of ions through the outer barrier of a cell. In principle, the lipids (fatty substances) on the cell exterior would repel the ions. It was known that specialized gates through the cell wall function like drain pipes in a retaining wall. If ion transfer took place according to static models obtained through conventional means, the poor little things would never make it, but they do. As in the problems of Dave De Young and Julius Kuti, conventional analysis was not much help, and alternative models cast little light.

Dave De Young and Paul Bash are participants in a transition that is becoming more and more common among scientists and engineers around the world. They are approaching problems like these as dynamic processes, including the crucial dimension of time and many other forces such as heat and gravity.

When dealing with complex natural processes like these, science has typically attempted to obtain a manageable path toward a solution by selecting pieces that can be pulled out of the problem and ignored or set aside. It is hoped that this would not degrade excessively the value of the findings. Three-dimensional processes may be reduced to two dimensions. In astronomical issues like the formation of galaxies, interstellar gas clouds may be ignored. Al-

Apoorva Patel, research physicist at the University of California, San Diego (front) and Paul Bash, now a post-doctoral researcher in the Department of Chemistry at Harvard University, during the initial computations on the CRAY X-MP at the San Diego Supercomputer Center, December 1985–January 1986. (*SDSC/GA Technologies.*)

though every biologist knows that life swims in water, it may be necessary to deal with dried specimens or otherwise leave water out of consideration. It is hoped that the pieces that have been removed can be put back later, but then the problem may once again become too complex for analysis.

Bash, De Young, and thousands of colleagues in a wide range of disciplines are now taking a different route toward simplification. They do not remove processes ("leaving all the physics in there," as some investigators put it). Instead, they set up approximations of the entire process. A contour map shows the three-dimensional shape of a mountain on a two-dimensional map. If the contour interval is fine (a few hundred feet) the map may provide a reasonably accurate representation of the mountain; a hiker can recognize each individual peak without confusion. If the contour interval is coarse (a few thousand feet) the map no longer identifies individual features very well, and some important features may not be represented at all. The mountain climber needs even more precision; a detail the size of a desk which is missed by most contour maps may block an ascent.

The approach followed by De Young, Bash, and other researchers in many disciplines is similar to a contour map. They represent complex natural phenomena through a sampling procedure—establishing a grid, mesh or network of points, each of which symbolizes one portion of a three-dimensional (or, at times, two-dimensional) object or process. This procedure is fundamental to a number of other disciplines, including fluid dynamics and atmospheric research (see Chapters Seven and Eight). In engineering and other fields, surfaces are treated in a different but analogous way. A bridge or wing under stress may be divided into a large number of polygons, each of which represents a portion of the surface. This technique is also used for digital animation (see Chapter Nine).

In some cases, the mesh is uniform. A typical galactic system may include many hundred billion stars. In a coarse mesh, each point may represent about a billion stars; in a finer one, only several hundred million. In any event, like the coarse-interval contour map, detail will be lost, but it is not practical to concentrate on certain parts of the system to obtain more detail. When dealing with smaller problems, the mesh can be varied. In structural analysis of a bridge, for example, large uniform surfaces that do not receive severe stress can be represented with large polygons; finer detail is used for joints and major stress-bearing components. A grid used for studying aerodynamic flow around an aircraft will be finer-grained at the wingroots and around the engine nacelles, focusing less sharply on the flat sides of the fuselage. Capable grid-designers are much sought after. Even among thoroughly-experienced computer users, it is considered a black art, which does not imply magic but inscrutability. People who know how to do it find it difficult to tell others how it is done, and other people find it even more difficult to do it right.

Paul Bash and Dave De Young also inhabit a world of imagination which does not demand the straight-line progressions of conventional linearity. Nonlinear situations, in which the path from A to B to

K is not easily predictable and may involve startling changes and sudden reversals, offend our common sense and wish for order. Nonlinearity is, however, much more usual in the world than might be expected.

Nonlinear situations abound in the familiar day-to-day world. Automobile fuel consumption is nonlinear with regard to speed. A car that gets 30 miles per gallon at 40 miles per hour may only get 25 mpg at 55 mph. This is familiar. At 70 mph, however, consumption may drop—nonlinearly—to 15 mpg. If your appetite were to increase as you ate, making you hungrier and hungrier the more you consumed, you would rapidly (and nonlinearly) empty the refrigerator and the pantry shelves and then clean out the neighborhood market.

Bash and De Young take full advantage of the most powerful machines in reach. They yearn for more computational power. De Young talks about a "threshold of coarseness"—if greater computer power makes it possible to tighten the mesh, to reduce the interval between the contour lines, features that were obscured previously may stand out and take on real significance.

More detail can make a profound difference. Imagine that our only impression of the *Mona Lisa* was obtained from a great distance and very generalized—a representation of a woman, but otherwise not exceptional. Then we get closer and are able to observe the painting through an instrument which provides increasingly fine resolution. Slowly, the *Mona Lisa* as we know it appears: a fine painting of an appealing, enigmatic woman. In this case, the threshold of coarseness, the point at which information begins to take on real meaning, is very close to a complete, detailed representation. In other cases, it may be found at a rougher approximation of reality.

Discovering Supercomputers

Paul Bash has been at home with computers for a long time. In the summer of 1985, he attended an NSF-sponsored supercomputer institute at Boeing. "I knew nothing about supercomputers," he explains, "but I found it very easy. Only there wasn't enough time to accomplish much."

In late 1985, Bash learned that time might be available while the new CRAY X-MP at the San Diego Supercomputer Center was going through its initial check-out. During the Christmas season, Bash descended upon San Diego with his ion-transfer problem. He used a computer code that added temperature and velocity to static representations of the process. The dynamics were established by a series of images. Each glimpse was separated by very brief time steps of ten or 15 femtoseconds (trillionths of a second). The changes from one step to the next were derived through calculations based upon Newtonian mechanics. As Bash puts it, "We added a box of waters." The plural is not poetic, like the waters of Babylon, but descriptive: a conceptual container, not filled with abstract "water," but with individual atoms of water.

Bash did most of his work in the computer graphics laboratory at UCSF. Using minicomputers and sophisticated software, much of it developed in the UCSF laboratory, researchers there produce dynamic graphic representation of natural processes. The people in the business have avoided fancy acronyms and compound terms: they refer to their output as "movies." Bash's year-end work in San Diego resulted in a brief movie that shows the ions (brightly colored according to an arbitrary code) finding their way among the waters, bouncing cheerfully as they pass through the gap in the surrounding protein molecules. A process that had seemed paradoxical becomes thoroughly comprehensible. For Bash, this is computational molecular biology. He talks about it with boundless enthusiasm and much optimism. He looks impatiently toward a near future in which analysis that now requires 60 hours on a CRAY X-MP can be completed in a few hours or less.

To an observer encountering all this for the first time, it seems dramatic and revolutionary. Yet it is based solidly upon work in biology, chemistry, mathematics, physics, and computations that has been going on for more than 30 years. Peter Kollman, a professor of chemistry at UCSF, sketches the history. He traces the origins to 1954, when Dr. Robert Zwanzig, now a professor of physical science at the University of Maryland, published an article about free-energy perturbations. Zwanzig showed what might be done in investigations like those carried out by Bash, but at that time there was no way to find out whether his insight was correct or not— computational power was simply inadequate. When we contacted Professor Zwanzig in 1986, he recalled the article immediately.

Zwanzig is a versatile scholar who has had many interests over the years. He indicated politely that that he was now more interested in other matters. "I have put all that out of my head," he said.

Others at institutions all around the United States and in Europe did pursue the matter, building up an intellectual framework and computer programs which are available to researchers like Paul Bash. Early computer solutions were demonstrated in 1982; use of supercomputers began in 1984 and 1985. Bash points out that this accelerated the research greatly. Work that might have required years to accomplish—or could not be done at all—could be completed within three or four months. Most researchers in the field are now finding their way to supercomputers, although lack of adequate time remains a frequent complaint.

Practical Results: Molecules and Medicines

A better understanding of the energetics involved when molecules bind to proteins has important implications for drug design. It will soon be possible to substitute simulations for experiments. What are the consequences if you change the enzyme, or this or that molecule in the enzyme? This can be accomplished through laboratory procedures, but these are slow and expensive.

Peter Kollman emphasizes that computer modeling is still dependent upon data about the crystalline structure. It is also necessary to identify the target structure: for example, the pathogen (virus or other dangerous substance) which a desired drug must eliminate or neutralize. So far, there are relatively few cases for which the crystalline structure is known and the target structure has been identified. Where both exist, Kollman looks toward practical results (the development of new drugs with the help of computer simulations) within a few years.

Arthur Olson, senior staff scientist and director, Molecular Graphics Laboratory, of the Research Institute of Scripps Clinic in La Jolla, California, points out that studies of molecular dynamics are already being reflected in new drugs now under development. He says that all major pharmaceutical companies have computer groups and are working with computer graphics. These techniques do not yet permit a pharmacologist or computer driver to sit down at a workstation and design a drug to order. It is possible, however, to simplify and shorten the process of developing and testing alternative versions of a potential drug to find which have the greatest therapeutic power and fewest side effects.

Olson has some stupendous movies of his own. One shows an enzyme whose duty is to attract and neuter free radicals of oxygen that can be very damaging to living tissue. It is a dimer, two protein molecules linked together. The movie shows the enzyme from various points of view and examines its structure, showing, among other things, how this enzyme in humans differs from its counterpart in cows. (It doesn't differ much—this enzyme has been doing its thing for many millions of years and is essentially the same in bacteria as well as in mammals.)

Then Olson's movie shows the enzyme using an electrostatic field to lure a free radical into a pocket that possesses exactly the right chemical components and electrical charge. There, through electrons in the proteins, the radical is converted into ordinary oxygen, which is benign, and hydrogen peroxide, which is less toxic and will in any event be scavenged by another specialized enzyme. This movie was made at Scripps based upon the results of X-ray crystallography and calculations by Paul Weiner and Peter Kollman of UCSF and John Tainer, Elizabeth Getzoff, and Jane Richardson of Duke University.

Another movie shows the structure of the polio virus—selected because it has been studied so exhaustively. The virus is a sphere, or more precisely a near-sphere built up of polygons exactly like Buckminster Fuller's geodesic dome. This outer structure protects the RNA inside until it penetrates a host cell and can begin to dictate the genetic future of that cell. Studies of structure make it easier to understand function and develop an understanding of the dynamics of the virus.

So far, the group at Scripps has used minicomputers for work of this kind; it has also acquired a Convex C-1 minisupercomputer. A simulation of the rhinovirus, a virus found in the nose and a common cause of the common cold, was carried out on the Cyber 205 at Purdue University. Scripps is now connected to the San Diego supercomputer, and Olson says that they plan to make regular use of it.

Galactic Dynamics and Viewing Time

Many astrophysicists, especially those who deal with phenomena beyond the Milky Way galaxy in which the earth resides, embraced computers long ago. The subjects of study are out of reach of experiment. Information obtained through observation is inclined to be dim and ambiguous. Computer simulations make it possible to examine change over time. Scientists in this field deal with objects so huge and complex that the full power of current supercomputers is needed—at a minimum.

Bruce Smith, an astrophysicist at NASA's Ames Research Center, uses supercomputers to study the evolution of galaxies. What determines the shape of a galaxy? Why are some spiral, others disc-shaped or elliptical? Classical astronomical theory held that rotational flattening, interacting with the formation of stars, shapes the form of a galaxy. Smith remarks, "It is not that simple. It is not just rotation."

Smith studies the effects of gravity and other forces as well as rotation over time in terms of a cubical mesh with one hundred thousand particles. This provides a coarse approximation of the astronomical reality. Smith is now experimenting with Ames' new CRAY-2. It enables an improvement in resolution which permits Smith to obtain much fuller representations of the workings of mass, time, and motion as galaxies grow and decline.

Joan Centrella, associate professor of physics at Drexel University in Philadelphia, is an articulate advocate of the application of supercomputers to astronomy. She concentrates upon cosmology and galaxy formation. Like Paul Bash, Bruce Smith, and Arthur Olson, she prefers to explain what she is doing by showing movies, but it is not possible to include within a book a showing of a cosmological movie. At a 1985 seminar on supercomputers at the University of Maryland, however, Dr. Centrella provided a running commentary for her images, which is the next best thing. In collaboration with Adrian Melott of the University of Kansas, Dr. Centrella did these simulations at Digital Productions in Los Angeles, whose main business was producing animation sequences for films and TV (see Chapter Nine).

To let Dr. Centrella speak for herself, or for her movie:

What we are doing is modeling the gravitational clustering of the universe. We are going to take a portion of the universe, a physical cube. The time clock will start running at one million years after the Big Bang [which astronomers presume was the origin of the universe]. You will see, initially, a distribution of matter which is what we think the universe looked like very shortly after the Big Bang. You will then fade to a particle description of that matter, and watch those particles cluster under the force of gravity as the model continues to evolve.

There is our typical cube in the universe. And that is the distribution of matter: very low amplitude, long wave length, density perturbations. This is what they look like with a quarter of a million computer points moving in a box. As the box is rotating around, gravity is acting, the universe is expanding, and these particles are clustering to form superclusters and clusters of galaxies. As the model continues, you see, once gravity gets strong enough, the clusters begin to form and become very, very dense and we are left with a laminate structure computer image in density contours—nested levels of density contours. That is our final model.

As in molecular biology and other fields, simulations of such phenomena on supercomputers make it possible to test alternative models with minimum delay. Dr. Centrella adds, "We also have experimented with repeating the model, where the matter was distributed differently, and it had very, very different properties. We ran out of money and we couldn't do this image in much the same way."

Programs of this size eat up computational time, even on powerful computers like Digital Productions' CRAY X-MP. A single slide, a simulation in three dimensions showing density contours of the universe after gravitational collapse, required 10 minutes of calculations. The entire two-minute film needed 30 to 40 hours of CPU time.

Dave De Young is interested in the problems of nonlinear hydrodynamics raised by the jets of extremely energetic gas that have been observed to propagate away from galaxies, collimated like a beam of laser light. What are they? Something had to push them out. How old are these jets? How do they start? Analysis is not of much help, and the theories that can be worked up are essentially speculations. The best exploratory tool is numerical simulations of the jet propagation and evolution. The problems are of such magnitude that they require a supercomputer.

The Kitt Peak Observatory has been using the San Diego Supercomputer Center on a dial-up basis since November 1985. It has been linked by satellite since July, 1986, and De Young says it is too early to evaluate the impact. He emphasizes, however, that the power possible through a supercomputer is needed in order to include enough physics in models of large astrophysical systems. Without a supercomputer, it is necessary to leave out phenomena like interstellar gas, stellar death, and super-novas, leading to incomplete solutions of an incomplete problem. His objective is to obtain models that are sufficiently detailed and specific to be proven wrong. Otherwise you have as many models as you have astronomers, he says, and the various astronomers are inclined to hang onto their preferred models throughout their careers.

As one of the managers of a national observatory, De Young also hopes that the computational capability available through the connection with San Diego will be used for image analysis. The largest telescope at Kitt Peak, a 4-meter reflector, is oversubscribed four times over (an excess of demand over supply that exceeds even many supercomputer facilities). This means that many applications involving excellent science must be set aside or delayed for a long time.

An investigator patient or lucky enough to obtain viewing time can typically make two or three exposures each night on photographic film. If the images gathered through the telescope are registered on CCD (charged coupled devices) instead of photographic plates, it is possible to obtain 20 or as many as 100 frames in one night. The investigator also has the option to secure fewer images but penetrate much more deeply or obtain a more detailed resolution.

Images on photographic plates are familiar, obtainable almost immediately without additional fuss. The initial output of a CCD, on the other hand, is a great pile of numbers. A computer is required to transform the numbers into images; a supercomputer is needed to do it with reasonable speed. There is a potential trade-off between additional or larger telescopes, which are expensive and take a long time to build, and supercomputers, which are less expensive, are available with shorter lead-times, and can be used for other purposes.

De Young believes that a supercomputer equivalent to current machines, or even more powerful, is essential in order to integrate data from multiple sectors of the electromagnetic spectrum (X-ray, radio, and other sources in addition to the visible portions of the spectrum).

Radio Astronomy: the Computer as a Viewing Device

This view would be endorsed at the National Radio Astronomy Observatory's (NRAO) Very Large Array (VLA) near Socorro, New Mexico. Indeed, computers are a necessity, not just an option, at the VLA. It depends wholly upon computers in order to obtain comprehensible images from its huge antennas that ride on tracks extending for kilometer after kilometer across the desert floor. Since the VLA went into operation in 1980, new techniques have brought about dramatic increases in its ability to improve resolution.

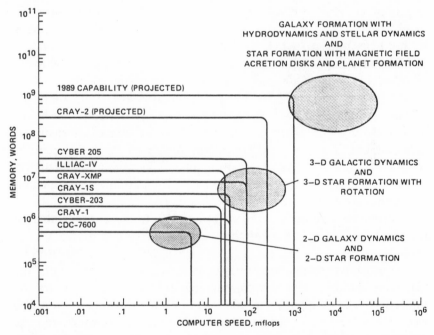

Unfinished Business. This chart, by Victor L. Peterson and James G. Arnold of NASA's Ames Research Center, depicts present computational capacity (lines) and present and projected requirements (shaded ovals) for astronomy and astrophysics.

These techniques require a great increase in computational capacity. The computers now used at the VLA cannot process images within reasonable lengths of time, and the NRAO is seeking funds for a supercomputer.

The resolution (accuracy and precision) of a telescope depends upon the size of the aperture, the wavelength of the electromagnetic spectra being studied, and the interference of the atmosphere. The wavelength of visible light is relatively short; consequently optical telescopes of relatively small diameter provide good resolution. (Nevertheless, multiple arrays of optical telescopes, also coordinated by computer, are employed in France and are gaining acceptance elsewhere.)

When radio astronomy began in the 1940s, it used single antennas. These revealed a great deal of fascinating, previously unanticipated things going on in the universe, but their resolution was limited because radio waves are relatively long. A single-antenna radio telescope capable of resolution equal to that of an optical telescope would be miles in diameter and extremely costly. No one is sure it could be made to work.

Digital computers make it possible to use a widespread array of relatively small antennas as if they were a single antenna with a very large aperture: a technique known as aperture synthesis. Signals received by each separate antenna are collected and then analyzed by a computer, which produces the image for study by astronomers. The potential collection quality of the entire array is reduced by unevenness in the atmosphere (very much like optical telescopes) and errors resulting from the limited number of antennas and finite observing time.

Researchers at the VLA have found ways to create much sharper images by compensating for these causes of error. As an NRAO proposal states, "When the VLA was originally proposed in 1971, it was expected to produce images in which the ratio between the brightest features and the faintest believable features would be limited by various errors to 100:1 (the dynamic range). . . . [The use of new error-correction techniques] has greatly increased the quality of the best VLA images from the 100:1 dynamic range specified in the original proposal to over 10,000:1, but at the cost of greatly increased computation time."

A "raw" image of the powerful radio galaxy Cygnus A shows two dark irregular blobs surrounded by a lot of clutter and a few small spots that seem to be emitters of much energy. After use of a deconvolution algorithm that corrects for inherent incompleteness of the measurements, most of the clutter is removed, and the detail of the blobs becomes much clearer. There is a hint of a line connecting the two most visible blobs with one of the energy-emitting dots, but it is too vague to convey much information. A vastly sharper, more nuanced image emerges after the effects of the atmosphere are removed. It shows a thread of energy linking the two blobs with the central dot, which is a galaxy visible through optical telescopes.

R.D. Ekers and P.A. Vanden Bout of the NRAO note in an article that "Scientifically, such an image is priceless, since it unequivocally demonstrates the role that the central galaxy plays in continuously fueling the radio lobes [the two blobs]. The extraordinary energy flowing from the galactic center leads to the critical inference that a black hole exists in the center of this particular radio galaxy."

These particular enhancements were carried out through many hours of processing on the VLA's existing equipment, a VAX 11/780 with an added Floating Point Systems 120B array processor. NRAO has used the National Science Foundation's Phase I program to obtain time at Digital Productions' CRAY X-MP (also used by Joan Centralla under the same program) and develop software for processing synthesis telescope images on the Cray. According to Ekers and Vanden Bout, preliminary timing tests indicate that the gain in speed over existing resources is a factor of 20 to 30. The VLA has also experimented with supercomputer facilities at its New Mexico neighbor, the Los Alamos National Laboratory.

The NRAO is seeking funds to acquire a supercomputing capability of its own, to be located at the VLA site. This will make it possible to carry out projects that are completed too slowly or are simply not feasible with current computing resources. It will also enable the VLA to serve more efficiently the scientists who come from all over the world to use its facilities—in 1984, a total of 600 astronomers came, from 140 institutions.

CHAPTER 5 _____

Today's Supercomputer Marketplace: Choice and Competition

Within the past several years, the number of major competitors in the supercomputer market has increased from two to six. Many other companies are offering machines with high performance—approaching supercomputer levels—at much lower prices. Cray continues to dominate, but there are many alternatives in a market that offers a broad range of cost-effective choices for buyers and many uncertainties for investors.

In the early 1980s, two companies in the upper Midwest of the United States produced the world's entire stock of supercomputers. Cray Research, which concentrates entirely on supercomputers and related equipment, carries out research, development, and manufacturing in Chippewa Falls, Wisconsin and has its corporate offices in the Minneapolis-St. Paul area of Minnesota. Control Data Corporation (CDC), which manufactures a broad range of computer-related products, is also in Minneapolis. The CRAY-1 series, initiated in 1976, and Control Data's Cyber 205, introduced a few years later, were the first of the contemporary generation of supercomputers, differing in design but roughly comparable in performance.

Cray broadened its range of models in the early 1980s and

consolidated a lead in sales which gave Cray about two-thirds of the market in the mid-1980s. A tidy market, easy to shop, much like the 1970s market for airliners: Cray was Boeing, Control Data trailed behind, like McDonnell Douglas, and there were no real competitors.

The supercomputer marketplace was transformed within a few years. Many more suppliers, competing intensely, and an even wider range of model choices replaced the Midwest duopoly. The Cray-Control Data duet has become a sextet; two choruses have begun to crowd the stage. Three Japanese manufacturers, Fujitsu, NEC, and Hitachi, announced new lines of supercomputers. By 1985 and 1986, they were making deliveries in Japan and laying a foundation for marketing in the United States and Europe. After an absence of two decades, IBM re-entered the market for high-performance scientific computing.

The first chorus is composed of companies making high-powered computers that approach supercomputer performance at much lower cost. (These machines are called "minisupercomputers" because "supermini" is becoming established as a term for minicomputers with more than usual power.) The other chorus consists of an even larger number of firms offering multiprocessor machines—many of them massively parallel, with scores or even thousands of processors. Some manufacturers are claiming very high performance for their new parallel designs, surpassing by far the products offered by more conventional manufacturers. Through repeated and at times doubtful repetition, the assertion "world's fastest computer" is becoming devalued.

Options and nameplates are also numerous. Fujitsu markets in collaboration with Amdahl in the United States and Siemens in Europe, and many components are manufactured in the United States. NEC is negotiating a close arrangement with Honeywell of the United States and the French computer company Groupe Bull which could apply to supercomputers as well as other products. Control Data has created an associated company, ETA Systems, for supercomputer development, manufacture, and marketing. The international balance of manufacturing is evened somewhat by IBM, which assembles many of its high-performance 3090s in France. Cray and other U.S. companies use memory chips from Japan as well as the United States. Most of these competitors offer several

Outline of Supercomputing History

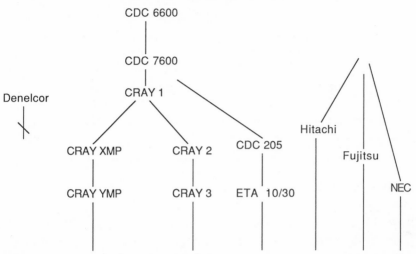

Outline of Supercomputing History. (*Richard Freund, San Diego Supercomputer Center.*)

models whose performance and price cover a wide range. The principal variables are the number of processors, the size of active memory, the option of a high-speed solid-state memory device, and, in some cases, different clock speeds.

This chapter is an introduction to today's supercomputer marketplace. More detailed descriptions of models and options offered by supercomputer makers can be found in Appendix I, and Chapter Eleven speculates on the future, with special attention to the prospects—and problems—of parallel designs.

How Many Makers Can Crowd into the Same Niche?

Supercomputers are one of the most rapidly-growing sectors of the overall market for computers, but remain a specialty niche. How can all these contenders hope to make money, and who will win out? How did the tidy situation of a few years ago turn into the crowded, turbulent market of the late 1980s? The first question is difficult to answer, although it appears that money-losers will outnumber the winners. (Other sectors of the computer business have enjoyed briefly the extraordinary mathematical phenomenon of a 200% market, which consists of 20 or more firms, each seeking a 10 or 20% market share).

A few paragraphs of history are needed in order to approach an answer to the second question. Control Data was the only supplier of supercomputers on a commercial scale during the 1960's and early 1970's. The 6600 (introduced in 1963) and the 7600 dominated a small market that was limited to specialized government agencies, a few aerospace and petroleum firms, and a scattering of universities. A CDC engineer named Seymour Cray was the principal designer of the 6600 and 7600.

IBM had made two tries. The first was STRETCH, a pioneering, creative project begun in 1955. It was too ambitious, did not meet performance goals, and was withdrawn from the market after building several machines. In the 1960s, IBM worked on a series of powerful machines, known collectively as the "Models 90" that were intended to be superior to the CDC 6600. Difficulties were encountered once again, more money was lost, and the effort was abandoned after only a small number of machines had been delivered. IBM thereafter grazed in other pastures.

Seymour Cray left Control Data and started his own company, which began to ship its first product, the CRAY-1, in 1976. In the early 1980s, Control Data countered with the Cyber 205. Soon thereafter, Cray began to produce the X-MP—a combination of up to four processors, each a descendant of the CRAY-1, but more powerful. This was followed in 1985 by the introduction of the compact, memory-rich CRAY-2.

Meanwhile, the Japanese, who had wrested a majority of their domestic mainframe market from IBM, moved into supercomputers. Characteristically, three of Japan's large electronics companies— Fujitsu, Hitachi, and NEC—entered the market at about the same time. Although none of them shipped large numbers of machines, they began to account for most supercomputer deliveries in Japan (although Cray sales were very respectable) and laid the foundations for export efforts (see Chapter Twelve).

All three Japanese firms decided to add supercomputers to their existing lines of computers. Japanese manufacturers have tended to base their mainframe offerings upon compatibility with IBM,

Seymour Cray, founder of Cray Research, Inc., and now a consultant to the company, with a CRAY-2. The object immediately behind him is a clear plastic cooling tower that dissipates heat carried away by the CRAY-2's fluorocarbon coolant. (*Cray Research, Inc.*)

emphasizing lower price, better performance, and collaboration in sales with U.S. computer companies. The Fujitsu and Hitachi machines, in particular, are basically upgraded mainframes with vector processors attached. This is not necessarily an inferior product; it can have advantages in simplicity of design and the ability to adapt software running on IBM machines for use on supercomputers.

Like the Caliph of Bagdad in the *Arabian Nights* stories, IBM prefers to permit others to sample the food before joining the banquet. It would be undignified to suspect the possibility of poison, but it makes it much easier to relax and enjoy the meal. IBM had tried a taste of supercomputers some time ago, as noted earlier,

Lloyd Thorndyke, President of ETA Systems, Inc., holding a complete CPU board for an ETA-10. ETA-10's can be ordered with as many as eight of these CPU's. A Cyber 205 is in the background. (*EPA Systems, Inc.*)

and, after an embarrassing touch of indigestion, decided it would stick to good old plain cooking.

In 1986, however, IBM came back to the supercomputer buffet with the 3090-200 and 3090-400, two versions of its current top-of-the-line mainframe. As expected, IBM enhanced the performance of these machines by offering embedded vector boards, providing modest levels of supercomputer performance. IBM also provided a large, strengthened memory system. IBM is moving aggressively into parallel processing, announcing the 3090-600 (six processors) as well as internal research projects addressing higher forms of parallelism. The 3090s with vector boards are serviceable machines, able to operate an enormous library of familiar, capable applications software. In 1986 IBM was beginning to ship these machines to academic as well as industrial buyers in the United States and abroad. IBM has recently announced faster versions of these machines with up to six processors.

Performance: The Slippery Slope

Supercomputers are bought for only one reason: to obtain markedly quicker, better solutions for exceptional computational requirements—needs that cannot be met (or cannot be met except at the cost of severe penalties in lost time) by the thousands of perfectly competent mainframes and hopped-up minicomputers that are already on hand or can be bought for much less. But how can performance be measured, how much performance is really needed, and which models deliver the best performance? These questions cannot be answered with final precision for any computers, and supercomputers pose especially difficult problems.

If a manager were ordering heavy-duty dump trucks, it would be simple. There are few manufacturers, specifications for carrying capacity and horsepower are easy to draw up, and maintenance experience can be obtained. A company can define its requirements and go ahead reasonably confident that its needs for performance and cost-effectiveness will be met.

Supercomputers are different. As noted in Chapter Two, a supercomputer CPU is the heart of a complex system. On the one hand, its level of performance defines the capability of the whole system, but, on the other, actual total performance is affected by the capacity of everything else. It is analogous to selecting the engine for a dump-truck system. More horsepower doesn't mean much if the tires won't carry the load and the brakes go out every week. Rated horsepower and EPA miles per gallon may be arbitrary figures, difficult to attain on the road, but everyone knows how to discount them when buying a vehicle. Supercomputers are not as simple.

In early English, the word bank—and, by association, its close cousin bench—meant "a sloping mound." (We still go down an em*bank*ment to board a riverboat.) This fragment of etymology relates to supercomputers because the performance of these machines (and other computers) is traditionally measured through "benchmarks." The implication, of course, is that these are solid points of reference, like the brass markers, anchored in rock, which guide surveyors and cartographers. Computation is, however, nowhere near as straightforward a discipline as surveying. The process known as benchmarking (computer people, like other technologists, love to turn healthy nouns into lame verbs) involves measuring the speed at which a given computer completes certain standardized tasks. A standard set often used for this purpose is called the Livermore Loops, which refers to a series of calculations of different lengths and characteristics rather than rides at an amusement park. Other standards developed at the Argonne National Laboratory and elsewhere are also used. Some computer specialists have become acknowledged experts on benchmarking, roaming the earth to subject new models to their tests.

Nevertheless, the process is uncertain and subjective; benchmarking can become a slippery slope. This is not because computer manufacturers are especially wicked or greedy, or because benchmarking specialists are naive. It is simply difficult to come up with a perfect, objective measurement of computer performance. If different applications are used, the answers are different. The complications grow when the model being tested has unfamiliar architecture and is operating at or beyond the familiar limits of computational performance.

As things stand, competing claims about peak speed do not necessarily determine the usefulness of a computer. The central fact is that a researcher who can lay hands upon any contemporary system has access to enormous computational capability. Differences in working memory, network capacity, or other matters can be more important, in terms of delivering results, than CPU speed as such. Other factors, such as software performance, system reliability, start-up time, training, manufacturer support, and potential future upgrading must also be considered in making a choice.

In an effort to protect the reader from a barrage of numbers, the best estimates of performance capabilities of supercomputer models now in the market are shown in the chart on page 6. The performance ranges shown for each model are not just a cautious fudge. Actual speed on a particular application depends upon many factors. The most important is the nature of the application and the software used to deal with it, especially the percentage of total computing that can be vectorized. Time, experience, and peripherals make a great deal of difference. Skilled operators working with a particular system for six months or a year can improve overall output by factors of 100 or even higher.

Manufacturers and Customers

Even for a Fortune 500 company, a supercomputer system is a major purchase. At prices that begin at $2.5 to $5 million and go up quickly from there, customers feel they have a right to a great deal of help and attention from manufacturers—after installation as well as before. Manufacturers respond eagerly. They recognize that they are going to lose a lot of sales unless they develop each prospect carefully. The profitable additional sales of upgrades and follow-ons are at least as important.

The quality of service to customers and relationships between manufacturers and users are among the most important areas of competition among companies that make large-scale computers, especially supercomputers. Other types of computers may be becoming commodities, like mousetraps or microwave ovens, bought primarily on criteria of price and features and sold in plain cardboard boxes. Supercomputers remain an exception. Customers preserve intense loyalty toward certain manufacturers and models. This involves more than sentiment and gratitude. A great deal of effort may be required to adapt applications programs that have been optimized for a particular architecture and operating system.

For a customer entering the supercomputer market for the first time, the initial choice of a CPU supplier is crucial for several reasons. It will commit the customer to a particular operating system, which in turn shapes software development and the customer's applications. A universal system (based perhaps on UNIX) is sought by many computer managers but is a difficult and perhaps distant goal (see Chapter Ten).

Earlier models, like the CRAY-1 and Cyber 205, were "this-is-it, folks" machines. Prospects for upgrading were limited. Now, however, upgradeability has become a fundamental tool in supercomputer marketing strategy. A CRAY X-MP buyer can start with a single processor and a relatively low level of memory. Later on, it is possible to move on to two and then four processors and larger memories. Similarly, the Amdahl/Fujitsu line offers several models, all the same basic design but offering marked upgrades in capacity. Nothing is ever consistent. For some problems, the Amdahl 1400 is much more powerful than the 1200; for others, there is very little improvement. IBM and other makers follow similar strategies.

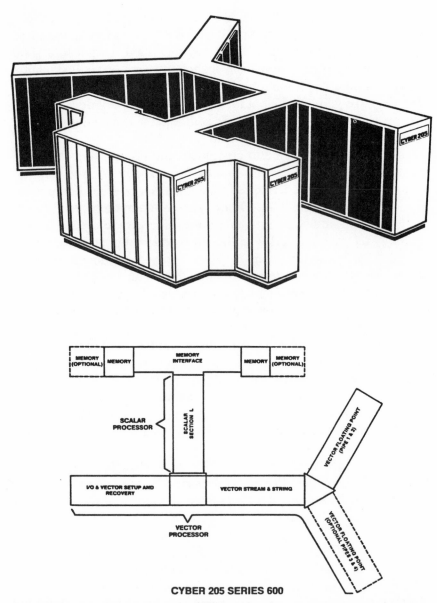

Layout of a Control Data Corporation Cyber 205.   The Cyber 205 is capable
of handling unusually long vector operations. The drawing shows the additional
vector pipeline and memory that may be added as options.

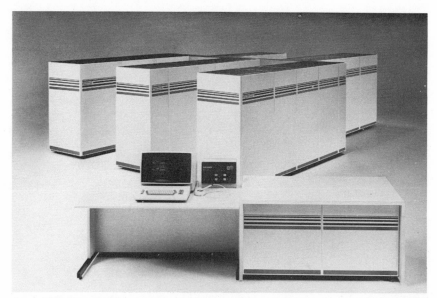

Amdahl/Fujitsu 1200 Supercomputer. Its appearance is typical of designs derived from mainframes. The floor space requirement is larger than that of a CRAY machine, but its forced-air cooling reduces installation costs. (*Amdahl Corporation.*)

Upgrading can often be accomplished with minimum disruption and without discarding an existing operating system. Some enhancements are field upgrades, done more or less overnight at the customer's own site. Others are accomplished through a quick replacement. Manufacturers are becoming very broad-minded about taking an earlier model off the hands of a customer—like a GM dealer facilitating a series of trade-ins from Chevrolet to Olds to Cadillac. (This is establishing an active market in second-hand CRAY-1s and lower-end X-MPs, benefitting universities and other less affluent buyers.)

Supercomputer companies do not only sell to companies or other institutions. They look for individuals—the VP for research, prestigious scientists, others in that institution who want additional computational power very badly and will spend a lot of time and energy getting it, and computer specialists eager for a try at a bigger machine. (The business card of such a person in one customer

IBM 3090 Model 400 four-processor mainframe computer with vector-processing attachments. (*IBM.*)

company, Apple Computer, identifies his title appropriately as "Cray Evangelist.")

The marketing staff of a supercomputer supplier has two tasks. They must convince their key contacts in the institution that their product is the best buy. After they have recruited evangelists, they must help them to convince their managers, often right up to the board of directors, that the purchase would be cost-effective. A camel's nose option made available at an attractive price makes it easier for the evangelists to overcome any objections from their superiors and introduce the manufacturer into the tent. If this strategy works, the capacity made available by the initial, conservative purchase fills up quickly. Before long, the whole camel is inside the tent. Everyone is content, especially the supercomputer company whose sales staff are now helping the evangelists to work up figures that demonstrate the need for a bigger camel.

The relationship can in fact be very cooperative. Especially for early-adopters who have the greatest appetite for large increases in performance and large, highly skilled staffs of software specialists, collaboration between manufacturer and customers can be extremely close. Uncertainty surrounds every new design, even one representing an incremental change from an earlier one. When changes are more radical, the association is even more intimate. The first CRAY-2 was delivered to the National Magnetic Fusion Energy Computer Center at Livermore in the spring of 1985. Specialists from NASA's Ames Laboratory and Cray worked closely with Livermore experts during the transition from one-processor operation to full-scale use. Six months passed before it was integrated fully into the center's services. Ames spent additional months in bringing its own CRAY-2, delivered in late 1985, from the developmental stage to full operation.

In the United States, this developmental role has usually been played by major federal laboratories and universities. NEC is placing its most powerful model with a U.S. university consortium, the Houston Area Research Center. NEC and other Japanese manufacturers have made similar placements with Japanese universities. The University of Minnesota has acquired an extraordinary array of low serial number models from Cray and Control Data and is now in line for an ETA-10. The ETA-10's first baptism, however, is taking place at Florida State, funded primarily by the Department of Energy. For arrangements of this kind, which can provide a manufacturer with valuable advice and experience as well as exposure to the market, suppliers typically make their equipment available at advantageous discounts or as outright gifts.

Amdahl/Fujitsu emphasizes in its marketing brochures that its supercomputers (which it describes straightforwardly as "Vector Processor Systems") are based on IBM architectures and compatible with IBM's System/370 architecture, the principal IBM design philosophy up through the 3090. The intent is to appeal to potential buyers who are already using IBM equipment and who wish to gain much higher performance without the pain and delay of large-scale software conversion. IBM is following the same basic strategy. Hitachi also emphasizes IBM compatibility. NEC offers models of differing performance, using a distinctive non-compatible operating system but offering compilers which make it easier to adapt existing applications programs.

Minisupercomputers: "Why Buy Buick? Get a Ford!"

The power of an earthquake, able to topple the most ambitious buildings and take the unwary by surprise, rumbles up from below. This has happened repeatedly in the computer business. Minicomputers and, later, capable word processing systems seized market sectors from mainframes or established new niches. In the 1980s, manufacturers of minicomputers were forced to run hard by steady pressure from rapid improvements in personal computers and high-performance workstations.

For supercomputers, the ground is beginning to shake. Minisupercomputers offer a potential threat to supercomputers roughly similar to the role played by minicomputers when they took a lot of business away from mainframes 10 or 15 years ago. The slogan is simple and can be effective: "Not the same power, perhaps, but a lot of power—perhaps all you need—at a good price and with less fuss."

Alliant Computer Systems Corporation, for example, offers the FX/Series of machines, selling at $100,000 to $1,000,000, which are compared to supercomputers in its advertising but described more cautiously as scientific and engineering computers in its brochures. More than 12 times the performance of a VAX-8600 is claimed for the top-of-the-line FX/8, whose processors operate in parallel.

Culler Scientific Systems Corporation asserts that its PSC (Personal Super Computer) performs at a rate of 3 to 4 megaflops at a price under $100,000. Other Culler models range in price from $250,000 to $1,000,000, with claimed performance up to 16 megaflops.

Floating Point Systems, Inc., which also produces large-scale parallel processors that claim performance at supercomputer levels, is a leading producer of array processors. These are usually used in conjunction with other high-performance computers to enhance performance of certain types of repetitive mathematical problems. For many applications, array processors are used widely as a way to approach supercomputer performance.

The SCS-40, produced by Scientific Computer Systems, was described in Chapter Two. As noted there, one of the points in its favor was the decision by SCS to use an architecture compatible with the CRAY X-MP and all its software. Other manufacturers of minisupercomputers emphasize the efficiency of their FORTRAN compilers or ease of use with UNIX. They are also reaching into the burgeoning arena of workstations: Alliant has forged an alliance with Apollo, and the Culler PSC is in effect an add-on to a Sun workstation.

This sampling of the minisupercomputer market is brief and limited. Other companies offer similar products. None has as yet established a leading position in a new, evolving market. For supercomputer customers—or, more precisely, customers in need of substantial, but not necessarily massive, computational power—minisupercomputers could provide an alternative worth close examination. The performance levels now possible are certain to improve sharply before long. The term "high-performance scientific and engineering computing" could become even more imprecise than it is now, referring to a broad spectrum extending from substantial but lower levels of performance up through intermediate models to the most powerful machines, full-scale supercomputers.

The Market: Buyers and Investors

After a number of years of steady growth in relative obscurity, the market for supercomputers is now entering the big time. IBM is back in town, breathing smoke and stomping its feet. Expansion of the market is accelerating as potential buyers increase among industries as well as universities and government laboratories. Estimates of the growth of the market differ, but even the most conservative projections expect double-digit annual growth indefinitely.

The growth in engineering applications is especially notable. Often these programs are less computationally intensive than classical supercomputer problems like fluid dynamics or seismic studies. Supercomputers offer advantages in quicker turnaround time and higher overall performance but may not always be essential. IBM could aim primarily at applications of this kind, especially for customers already using IBM equipment and software. IBM pioneered the marketing strategy of getting customers—and keeping them—by round-the-clock intensive care. Especially for large, profitable systems, it adheres firmly to that tradition. If IBM concentrates on this lower-middle sector of the market, minisupers could become its main competitors, especially on the lower fringes where entry cost may be as important as raw performance.

Competition could be most intense in the upper-middle range. The Japanese manufacturers can continue to sell supercomputer power to their established customers, but each company has a relatively slender base. The Japanese companies seem determined to pursue worldwide market share. They have in the past had the money and patience to invest in intensive, attentive, persistent marketing and attractive prices. Recognizing that the intimate manufacturer-customer relationship characteristic of supercomputer marketing does not travel well across cultural boundaries, the Japanese makers are emphasizing foreign associates in their main overseas markets. The Japanese firms may be willing to combine intensive (and expensive) product development with aggressive price concessions—a tactic that has served them well in other markets in the past. A stronger yen and weak domestic demand have, however, affected the profitability of even these powerful firms since early 1986. There is no immediate sign of any decisions to cut back on supercomputer marketing and development. If discouraging bottom lines continue in Japan, however, some of the Japanese makers may decide to concentrate on other products with a firmer existing marketing base and surer profits.

At the upper end of the supercomputer market, Cray possesses many strengths: a large, solid, loyal customer base; plenty of funds and little debt; a broad range of products and prices; an active, diversified development effort; a solid service organization; and a well-established name. Another new product, the Y-MP, is expected soon. The CRAY-3 also lurks. In February, 1987, Cray introduced a new, markedly less expensive model and cut prices on other low-end machines—a direct challenge to IBM, the Japanese, and the minisupercomputers. In the supercomputer marketplace, the wreath of "safe choice" that permits corporate purchasing agents to sleep more easily belongs to Cray, not IBM.

The next challenge to Cray may come from the ETA-10. Its objectives are ambitious, and the design is aggressively innovative. If actual performance measures up, if ETA delivery schedules are met, and if the software meets the complex demands of the ETA-

10's architecture, it could gain a place among the more demanding scientific users.

Prediction is deception, especially when one is predicting what seems a dead certainty. Not too long ago, there were some people in California who did not believe in God, but everyone was sure they could count upon the Bank of America, the Southern Pacific, PG&E, and Chevron. Now God is gaining a little, but all the others are in trouble of one kind or another.

The supercomputer market is no exception; indeed, it is more uncertain than most, certainly more uncertain than the market for banking or ground transport. Supercomputers are, by definition, at the extreme edge of technological unpredictability in the computer market, which in turn is among the most volatile in the world economy. Until recently, the computer business also seemed to offer sure-fire profits for anyone who was reasonably well equipped to compete. In the mid-1980s, even the strongest, best established competitors, in Japan as well as the United States, are struggling, slipping back, or failing outright.

At first glance, supercomputers, which right now are doing better than the rest of the industry, would seem a good prospect for investors looking for sound high-tech stocks. Cray and other leading contenders are worth a close look, but the entire super-computer segment, like the rest of the computer industry, could become a rich mulch for migraine.

For the prospective buyer of a supercomputer or other high-performance system, however, the rest of the 1980s offer a gratifying choice among good deals. Even more than usual, it is essential that a potential buyer define objectives clearly and make a thorough assessment of actual computing needs, staff capabilities, financial resources, and future requirements. The customer who does all this thoroughly and diligently should find the present supercomputer market very rewarding.

CHAPTER 6 ⎯⎯⎯⎯⎯⎯⎯⎯⎯⎯

Today's Revolution: The Expansion of Supercomputer Availability

The dramatic expansion in the availability of supercomputer services during the mid-1980s is one of the most important developments of the supercomputer era's initial years. In the United States, major centers supported by the National Science Foundation and other new university facilities serve academic and industrial users. Scientists and engineers may also arrange to make use of new or upgraded systems operated by specialized federal agencies.

Before 1984, a university or industrial scientist or engineer in the United States whose research required supercomputer capabilities faced discouraging alternatives. Only a few institutions (Colorado State University, the University of Minnesota, and Purdue University) operated their own supercomputers. A would-be user of supercomputers could move to one of those places, redesign the project to satisfy the specialized criteria of one of the national laboratories, wheedle the cash to buy time from a supercomputer service bureau, or collaborate with a more fortunate colleague.

Many found a way. In the early 1980s, the number of supercomputers (all made in the U.S.) devoted to academic research in

Western Europe was larger than the number in the United States, especially in proportion to the relatively small number of European research universities. Larry Smarr, now head of the National Center for Supercomputer Applications at the University of Illinois at Champaign/Urbana, became an often-cited item in the history of computing. He could not obtain supercomputing time in the United States to carry out his astrophysical simulations, so he went to Germany, where he was able to do his work at the Max Planck Institute—on a Cray made in the USA.

Successive panels, composed of scientists from many fields as well as computer specialists, examined this situation and issued reports deploring it. One theme was stressed repeatedly: the United States could lose its leadership in technology because its scientists lacked adequate access to this fundamental tool of advanced research. Admonitory fingers were pointed toward Japan and Europe, where supercomputers were being installed and used at a growing rate. The prediction: imminent and perhaps irreversible loss of America's international competitiveness.

Petitioners from universities looked primarily to Congress and the National Science Foundation, the principal source of federal funds for academic research in most scientific disciplines. Support for research in certain fields is provided by the National Institutes of Health, NASA, the Department of Energy, the Defense Advanced Research Projects Agency (DARPA), other parts of the Department of Defense, and smaller federal agencies. Similar arguments for additional supercomputer capacity were directed to these departments, and to the Congressional committees which oversee their funds.

More or less simultaneously, a surprising number of these projects found favor in Congress and among the budget makers of federal agencies. Ears that did not heed earlier appeals emphasizing scientific need became responsive to arguments about preserving America's prestige, American jobs, and American technological leadership. Legislators and administrators frustrated by the difficulty of finding solutions to problems of industrial policy, protectionism, exchange rates and the cultural differences between Japanese and American factories discovered a talisman. It wasn't easy to fix all those other things, but it was possible to do something about the supercomputer shortage.

The prevailing attitude of the American scientific community toward federal patronage is one of cooperative paranoia. All science is good, but science that might consume exceptionally large sums of federal support can be dangerous, threatening a reduction of all the other shares. High-energy physics (especially its current proposal, the superconducting supercollider) and astronomy have provided focal points for these anxieties, and now genetics is having a turn. The congressional response was rapid, very generous, and remarkably free of contention. The usual anxieties of the scientific community were for the most part bypassed, perhaps because many institutions and a wide range of scientific disciplines would benefit.

The NSF plans to devote $200 million for the support of the supercomputing intiative over a five-year period, beginning in fiscal 1985. It started by buying time at existing facilities and moved swiftly to select and fund five new projects—at Cornell University; the University of Illinois at Champaign/Urbana; a joint project of the University of Pittsburgh, Carnegie-Mellon University, and Westinghouse; at the University of California at San Diego (operated by GA Technologies, Inc.); and the John von Neumann center at Princeton, N.J., managed by a consortium of universities located mainly in the Northeast. These projects began operations in 1985 and 1986. (Detailed information about these centers, their equipment, and their objectives can be found in Appendix II, Section 1). The Department of Energy, NASA, the National Cancer Institute, the National Center for Atmospheric Research, and the National Bureau of Standards set up new facilities or expanded supercomputer installations available to nonfederal researchers (see Appendix II, Section 3). The overall result has been a very large amount of new capacity.

All over North America, states and universities that did not secure formal federal support—or preferred to go their own way—also launched supercomputer programs. Supercomputer facilities were established or expanded at the University of California at Berkeley, Calgary University, Florida State University, the University of Georgia, the Houston Area Research Center, UCLA, the University of Minnesota, the University of Texas system (facility located at Austin), and Toronto University. The total capacity of these other installations already exceeds the resources available under the NSF initative and is continuing to grow (see Chapter

Twelve and Appendix II, Section 2; a list of universities participating directly in the NSF initiative and other supercomputer programs follows this chapter).

As described in Chapter Three, these increases in availability of resources for academic research based upon supercomputers were paralleled by a substantial, if less dramatic, increase of supercomputing in American industry. These simultaneous and mutually reinforcing tendencies have resulted in an explosive expansion of opportunities in the United States for access to supercomputer capability—forming the foundation of the supercomputer era.

The objectives and priorities of these facilities and the terms and criteria for access vary widely. Generally speaking, the university centers (whether NSF-funded or otherwise) are open to the full range of academic disciplines. Most of the capacity at the NSF centers is allocated without charge to academic applicants who satisfy basic criteria, including the scientific merit of the project (established by peer review) and the investigators' need for supercomputer capabilities to accomplish their research objectives. Researchers may apply on an equal basis even though their institution may not be a member of any supercomputer consortium.

At other university facilities, priority may be given to users from a particular campus, affiliated institutions, state, or region. Federal facilities specialize in certain disciplines or fields of investigation. Most reserve the majority of their time for government use, but the proportion available for outside use is, nevertheless, a substantial resource.

Terms for access to these centers by private corporations are even more diverse. All five NSF centers have programs for industrial sponsorship, affiliation, or other participation. In addition to computer time—each center may reserve 10% of its capacity for these purposes—the centers offer private firms the opportunity to keep up with supercomputer technology and explore the suitability of supercomputers for their own requirements. Affiliation makes it possible to do this at a small fraction of the cost of setting up a supercomputer in the company.

The prices and terms of such participation differ from center to center. Similar programs of corporate affiliation are being developed at university centers which are not receiving NSF support. Some of the them (the Houston consortium, for instance) are actively courting private participation. Private corporations are generally asked to pay (either through annual participation fees or by the hour) for access to university-based supercomputers.

Criteria for access to supercomputers at federal facilities are also diverse. The National Cancer Institute's new facility welcomes outside researchers in biomedicine. NASA's Numerical Aerodynamic Simulation program reserves a total of one-quarter of its capacity for scientists and engineers from the aerospace industry and universities. The Department of Energy has been enlarging its capacity at the National Magnetic Fusion Energy Computer Center, available to researchers in a broad spectrum of energy-related fields. The National Center for Atmospheric Research, National Bureau of Standards, and the Environmental Research Laboratories of the National Oceanic and Atmospheric Administration (NOAA) (served by the National Bureau of Standards) have long emphasized cooperative and collaborative research (see Appendix II, Section 3.)

Finally, a number of supercomputer facilities sell time. Even before the advent of the new university centers, this provided a "taste-before-buying" alternative for corporate users. Many major users have consumed increasing quantities of supercomputer time before deciding to buy their own machines. Others believe that the capital cost and administrative burden of operating a supercomputer center are not justified or are too much trouble; they purchase the time they need and leave it at that. (Facilities and procedures at Boeing Computer Services, one of the largest service bureaus, are described in Appendix II, Section 3.)

Especially at universities, the rates and conditions for acquiring supercomputer time are far from uniform. Discounts are sometimes offered for evening and weekend use. Reduced rates may also apply to users who accept a secondary priority, which means that their work may be accomplished later than a job given full priority. At many institutions, other special arrangements can be made.

Training in supercomputing is also expanding very rapidly. The NSF-supported centers and many other facilities offer one-day introductory workshops for potential users, more thorough seminars, summer institutes for graduate students and other researchers, and additional opportunities. Summer institutes and other courses are supported by NSF grants. The Department of Energy offers summer institutes in supercomputing for promising high school students;

other courses and summer internships are available at supercomputing centers in the national laboratories. Supercomputing facilities
at universities offer similar opportunities.

Within a short time, the bleak but tidy scene of supercomputing
availability has been transformed into a fertile, even competitive
one. Researchers who, not long ago, were looking for *any* supercomputing opportunities are now following up rumors of time that
might be found at a good rate (or, perhaps, for free) at a facility
that is not fully utilized. Despite the recent explosion in the availability of supercomputer capacity, however, it seems likely that
any pockets of underused capacity will vanish quickly. Improvements
in networking (described in Chapter Ten) should improve access
to supercomputing facilities all over the country.

As the computer era gathers momentum and demand from
science and industry continues to accelerate, the current increases
in the availability of supercomputers will soon prove insufficient.
It is still difficult for many meritorious projects that require hundreds
or even thousands of hours of supercomputer time to find a center
able to accomodate them (see Chapter Thirteen). In order to respond
to this demand, the revolution in the availability of supercomputer
capacity must be a continuing revolution, not just a brief flurry of
activity.

**North American Institutions Participating in Supercomputing:
Members of Consortia and Academic Affiliates
of NSF-Supported Centers, Other Consortia,
and Campuses with Supercomputers**

Key:

CTC: *Cornell Theory Center—Cornell National Supercomputer Facility*
         (consortium members)
HARC: *Houston Area Research Center* (consortium members)
JVNC: *John Von Neumann Center* (consortium members)
NCSA: *National Center for Supercomputing Applications* (Illinois;
         affiliates)
PSC: *Pittsburgh Center* (academic affiliates)
SCC: *Single-campus computer center* (may be networked)

SDSC: *San Diego Supercomputer Center* (consortium members)
NSF: *Site of NSF-supported center*
NCAR: *Member of National Center for Atmospheric Research consortium*

Note: Applicants not affiliated with consortium members have equal access to NSF-allocated supercomputer time at NSF-supported centers

Northeast and Middle Atlantic States:

Brown University (JVNC)
Carnegie-Mellon University (PSC, NSF)
Case Western University (PSC)
Columbia University (JVNC)
Cornell University (NSF, NCAR)
Cornell Medical Center (CTC)
University of Delaware (CTC)
Drexel University (NCAR)
George Washington University (NCSA)
Harvard University (NCSA, JVNC, NCAR)
Johns Hopkins University (CTC, PSC, NCAR)
Institute for Advanced Study (JVNC)
Lehigh University (PSC)
University of Maryland (SDSC, PSC, NCAR)
Massachusetts Institute of Technology (JVNC, NCAR)
City University of New York (CTC)
New York University (NCSA, JVNC, NCAR)
State University of New York at Albany (NCAR)
State University of New York at Binghamton (CTC)
State University of New York at Stony Brook (CTC)
University of Pennsylvania (JVNC, PSC)
Pennsylvania State University (CTC, NCSA, JVNC, PSC, NCAR)
University of Pittsburgh (PSC, NSF)
Princeton University (JVNC, NCAR)
Rensselaer Polytechnic Institute (CTC)
University of Rhode Island (NCAR)
University of Rochester (CTC, JVNC)
Rockefeller University (CTC)
Rutgers University (JVNC)
Syracuse University (CTC)
Temple University (PSC)

Woods Hole Oceanographic Institution (NCAR)
Yale University (PSC, NCAR)

Southeastern States

University of Arkansas (NCSA)
University of Florida (PSC)
Florida State University (SCC, NCAR)
University of Georgia (SCC)
Georgia Institute of Technology (PSC, NCAR)
University of Houston (HARC)
Louisiana State University (CTC)
University of Miami (NCAR)
University of North Carolina, Chapel Hill (CTC)
North Carolina State University (NCAR)
Oklahoma State University (NCSA)
University of Oklahoma (NCAR)
Rice University (HARC, NCAR)
University of Tennessee (CTC, PSC)
Texas A&M University (CTC, HARC, NCAR)
University of Texas, Austin (HARC, NCAR)
University of Texas System (SCC, at Austin, serving all U.T. institutions)
Triangle Universities Computation Center (Duke University,
    University of North Carolina, North Carolina State) (PSC)
University of Tulsa (NCSA)
Vanderbilt University (NCSA)
Virginia Polytechnic Institute (CTC)
University of Virginia (PSC, NCAR)
Washington University (PSC)
University of West Virginia (PSC)

Midwestern States

University of Chicago (NCAR)
University of Illinois, Champaign/Urbana (NSF, NCAR)
University of Illinois, Chicago (CTC, NCSA)
University of Indiana (NCSA)
Iowa State University (NCAR)
University of Iowa (NCSA)
University of Michigan (SDSC, PSC, NCAR)
Michigan State University (PSC)
University of Minnesota (SCC, NCAR)

University of Missouri (NCAR)
University of Missouri, Rolla (NCSA)
University of Nebraska at Lincoln (NCAR)
North Dakota State University (NCSA)
Northwestern University (NCSA, PSC)
Notre Dame University (NCSA)
Ohio State University (PSC, NCAR)
Purdue University (SCC, NCAR)
Saint Louis University (NCAR)
University of Wisconsin (SDSC, PSC, NCAR)

Mountain States

University of Colorado (JVNC, NCAR)
Colorado State University (SCC, NCSA, NCAR)
University of Denver (NCAR)
University of Idaho (NCSA)
New Mexico Institute of Mining and Technology (NCAR)
New Mexico State University (NCSA)
University of New Mexico (NCSA)
University of Utah (SDSC, NCAR)
Utah State University (NCAR)
University of Wyoming (NCAR)

Far Western States

University of Alaska (NCAR)
Agouron Institute (SDSC)
University of Arizona (JVNC, NCAR)
University of California, Berkeley (SDSC, SCC)
University of California, Davis (SDSC, NCAR)
University of California, Irvine (SDSC)
University of California, Los Angeles (CTC, SDSC, NCAR, SCC)
University of California, Riverside (NCSA, SDSC)
University of California, San Diego (NSF, SDSC)
University of California, San Francisco (SDSC)
University of California, Santa Barbara (SDSC)
University of California, Santa Cruz (SDSC)
California Institute of Technology (SDSC, NCAR)
University of Hawaii (SDSC, NCAR)
Naval Postgraduate School (NCAR)
National Optical Astronomy Observatories (SDSC)

University of Nevada (NCAR)
Oregon State University (NCSA, NCAR)
Salk Institute (SDSC)
San Diego State University (SDSC)
Research Institute of Scripps Clinic (SDSC)
Scripps Institution of Oceanography (U.C. San Diego) (SDSC, NCAR)
University of Southern California (SDSC)
Southwest Fisheries Center (SDSC)
Stanford University (NCSA, SDSC, NCAR)
University of Washington (NCSA, SDSC, NCAR)

Canada

University of Calgary (SCC)
McGill University (NCAR)
Ontario University (shares with Toronto)
University of Toronto (SCC, NCAR)

CHAPTER 7 ─────────────

Flying Machines

Supercomputers now play an essential role in the design of
aircraft and jet engines. Before supercomputers, it was impossible to obtain reasonably complete solutions of the basic
equations describing the flow of air, water, and other fluids.
Supercomputing has joined wind tunnel research and flight
testing as basic tools of aircraft development. Computational
fluid dynamics, dependent upon supercomputing, is becoming
more crucial as the design process becomes more expensive,
the stakes increase in the international market for civil and
military aircraft, and competition grows more intense.

Supercomputers are flying machines. To be sure, the wing loading
and other characteristics of an average supercomputer are not con-
ducive to flight. Extensive design changes would be necessary
before a typical supercomputer could become airborne. Under the
best of circumstances, its flight behavior would be sluggish and
the glide path abrupt. Nevertheless, supercomputers are indeed
flying machines. Without them, it would be difficult to design the
fuel-efficient, high-performance aircraft of today and impossible to
develop the hypersonic space planes of the future.

High Stakes in High Technology

The stakes are high. Producing modern aircraft, especially airliners and high-performance military aircraft, is an extremely expensive, demanding business. This is true for jet engines as well as airframes. In the United States, only a few very large companies have survived. The aircraft industries of Europe and Japan are able to undertake major projects only by forming consortia like Airbus Industries. American companies are doing the same: for example, Boeing's cooperation with Japanese firms on the 7J7 project and the collaboration between General Electric, one of two major U.S. makers of jet engines, and the French firm SNECMA.

The service life of modern airliners is measured in tens of years, and cumulative lifetime costs are critical. An efficient aircraft with a performance edge over competitors can be a better buy for customers and so remain in profitable production for a long time. Aircraft are already remarkably efficient; improvements in performance and cost-effectiveness are difficult and costly. Developmental costs for a wholly new type of aircraft or engine design are measured in the multiple billions of dollars. Most current models under development are evolutionary, retaining basic fuselage design, major turbine components of a jet engine, or other existing features. Narrow advantages, measured in a few percentage points, in areas like engine thrust, fuel consumption, or airfoil efficiency may mean large savings over the life of an aircraft—the difference between a profitable model and a disastrous flop. In military aircraft, where service lifetimes are also very long, an edge in fighting ability, ease of maintenance, and lower cost can have real, lasting implications for national security.

For decades, American manufacturers dominated the global market. Occasional European models, especially from French and British firms, would do reasonably well in some segments of the market, but only Boeing (and to a lesser extent McDonnell Douglas) were able to meet all the equipment needs of a major airline. Now Airbus is offering an increasingly broad range of up-to-date, high-performance aircraft and is making significant sales in the United States as well as abroad. Japanese companies are, for the first time, becoming a major factor in airliner manufacturing—although, so far, as partners rather than lead companies.

Manufacturers of aircraft and aircraft engines were among the earliest industrial companies to decide that they needed supercomputers. (Petroleum companies and aerospace firms remain the two largest industrial markets for supercomputers.) All major producers of high-performance aircraft and jet engines in the United States, Europe, and Japan operate supercomputers, are about to purchase systems, have access to supercomputer resources at government laboratories, are major purchasers of supercomputer time from service bureaus, or several of the above.

Fluid Dynamics: Difficult Equations and Tough Solutions

The Keys Were Locked Up

Why supercomputers? Why are other computers unable to do the job? Anyone who makes airplanes has to worry all the time about a branch of physics, fluid dynamics, which involves exceedingly complex, demanding mathematics.

Calculating the speed at which a space probe will enter the atmosphere of Jupiter, designing a radical new *America's* Cup yacht, analyzing the flow of fuel through the main motor of the space shuttle, attempting to decrease the drag caused by the hot gases leaving the jet engine of an airliner, speeding up the delivery of fuel oil through an underground pipeline, studying the reluctance of ketchup to leave its bottle, improving the silence of submarines, estimating accurately the rate at which blood is pumped through the heart—a very heterogenous set of investigations, but they all depend upon a single kind of physics: fluid dynamics.

This chapter focuses upon the application of supercomputers to problems of fluid dynamics in the aerospace industry (see Chapter Nine for applications to yacht design and Chapter Thirteen for studies of blood flow through the heart).

The keys to fluid dynamics were found 150 years ago, when the problems just listed were insoluble or would have been considered outright fantasy. The equations governing the flow of air, water, and other fluids were first published by Claude Louis M. H. Navier in 1823 and generalized by Sir George C. Stokes in 1840. Ever since, physicists and engineers have been seeking to make practical use of the Navier-Stokes equations, but the natural order has been frustratingly complex. Except in very simple conditions, the investigator must consider phenomena like turbulence—evident in water descending rapidly through rocky rapids, a flag flapping in a strong breeze, and the unruly flow from a bathtub faucet turned on full. An unaided researcher may obtain rough approximations of the true values for a simple case; for example, air flowing in straight lines at low speed past a cylinder.

If a shape is more complicated and the flow at higher speeds, the task has in the past been too difficult. The point at which smooth flow becomes turbulent was also defined in the nineteenth century, by the Irish-born English physicist Osborne Reynolds. The Reynolds number, derived by a formula that depends upon the speed, density, and viscosity of the flow, marks the onset of turbulence. For well over a century after Navier and Stokes published their work, and close to a 100 years after Reynolds' research in the 1880s, fairly complete solutions for more complicated situations were out of reach. Even now, with the high-performance computers of the 1980s, full-scale, three-dimensional solutions of the Navier-Stokes equations are just at the edge of possibility.

Researchers rely upon a simplified but nevertheless useful form known as Reynolds-averaged Navier-Stokes equations. It is estimated that computations providing complete Navier-Stokes solutions would require machines several million times more powerful than the supercomputers now in general use. Perhaps it will be accomplished before 2023, the bicentennial of Navier's publication. Even within present limitations, however, computational fluid dynamics is accepted as an essential tool for research in fluid dynamics.

Adding Simulation to Experimentation

Experimental methods in aerodynamics reached a high degree of sophistication before computers were first applied to fluid dynamics. The main tool is the wind tunnel, also a simulator. It imitates actual flight conditions in simplified form and gathers data through analog instruments. But there are major limitations. Wind tunnels cost a lot. Expansions or major changes can be very expensive or simply not practical. Large designs like transport aircraft must be studied in the form of smaller-scale models; extrapolations may be inaccurate.

Setting up experiments is time-consuming, and the capacity of a facility tends to become booked up quickly. A wind tunnel cannot simulate unearthly circumstances, like the entry of a space probe into the atmosphere of another planet.

The results of experimentation must be verified through actual use of full-scale operating prototypes—flight testing. The initial design and wind tunnel experiments establish presumed limits of performance for an aircraft—rate of climb, speed, susceptibility to stalls, maximum G forces during turns, and so on. Step by step, increasing by small increments, a test pilot checks performance within the "flight envelope" and may attempt to find out whether the envelope can safely be stretched.

This is a time-consuming process. Even for the most prudent test pilots, it is always dangerous. Flight testing may expose unanticipated design flaws: severe flutter that requires extensive changes in a control surface, poor engine performance due to inadequate air intake, and so on. Correcting these flaws late in the developmental process can cause costly fixes and long delays. The predictive powers of experimental methods in aerodynamics are limited. They can forecast the performance of a model that has been tested thoroughly, but they cannot say much about alternative designs. Thus, each design is usually an incremental change, an obvious descendant of the previous one.

A designer who wants to start from zero—define performance objectives and, free from the prejudice of past solutions, determine the best possible form for meeting those objectives—must go beyond experimental methods. This does not imply that wind tunnels are obsolete. They are essential, cost-effective tools and are the best way to obtain certain kinds of indispensable data. Prototypes must still be flight-tested.

Computational aerodynamics has joined the wind tunnel and flight testing as an essential instrument of aircraft design and development because of its ability to simulate and predict performance accurately, and with a quick turn around time. A dedicated advocate of computational aerodynamics, W.F. Ballhaus, Jr., chief of NASA's Ames Research Center, presented the case:

> Computational simulations are especially useful for the following applications: (1) making detailed fluid physics studies, such as simulations

designed to shed light on the basic structure of turbulent flows; (2) developing new design concepts, such as swept forward wings or jet flaps for lift augmentation; (3) sorting through many candidate configurations and eliminating all but the most promising before wind-tunnel testing; (4) assisting the aerodynamicist in instrumenting test models to improve resolution of the physical phenomena of interest; and (5) correcting wind-tunnel data for scaling and interference errors [due to extrapolation from smaller models and the effect of walls and supports upon the airflow within the wind tunnel].

From its beginnings in the 1960s and early 1970s, computational fluid dynamics has matured rapidly. In 1972, one of the first solutions for a wing in transonic flow required eight hours of computation on an IBM 360. In 1980, 15 minutes on a CDC 7600 computer produced results for flow around an entire KC-135 (a military predecessor of the Boeing 707) that had been modified by adding winglets. These were simplified solutions, setting aside the effects of viscosity (the tendency of a fluid to shape itself and adhere to other objects).

Early results could be compared to a sixteenth century map of the world, which gives only the rough shapes and approximate interrelations of the continents and main islands. The early days of computational aerodynamics were adequate for a small problem, like air flow around an airfoil. Similarly, sixteenth-century navigators provided much more complete renderings of limited, familiar waters like the English Channel and North Sea.

Transonic Flow and Nonlinearity

The territory now being explored through computational fluid dynamics is not inhabited by sea monsters or mermaids, and the areas marked "unknown" are being reduced rapidly. Attention is focused upon the characteristics of air flow in the vicinity of the speed of sound. At lower speeds, drag on a wing, for example, is essentially proportional to the speed—a linear progression. At supersonic speeds (the cruising speed of the Concorde, for example) the flow can also be reduced to a single linear equation. Problems arise at or around Mach 1 (the speed of sound) a region termed transonic. The airspeed indicator of the aircraft may show a speed below Mach 1, but drag may become extreme because the flow over parts of the aircraft may involve local mixtures of supersonic and subsonic speeds. Transonic flow is esentially nonlinear (see Chapter Four for a brief discussion of nonlinearity). Thus, a complete aerodynamic solution cannot be achieved by adding together a number of elementary solutions—an approach that suffices for subsonic speeds. Solution of these problems requires sophisticated grids, efficient algorithms, and very high computational capacity. The difficulty increases when the viscosity of the air is taken into consideration.

Researchers at Ames characterized the current situation: ". . . problems involving complex geometries can be treated with simple physics and those involving simple geometries can be treated with complex physics, but more powerful computers with larger memories are required to solve problems involving both complex geometries and complex physics." Advances since the beginning of the 1980s have been far-reaching. Costs have been reduced dramatically as increases in computer power have been accompanied by improvements in algorithms and other methods for deriving solutions. Ballhaus estimates that costs for carrying out a given computation have been reduced by a factor of about 10,000.

Nevertheless, aerodynamics confronts a recurrent paradox among users of supercomputers. Great progress is being made— dependent primarily upon the power provided by the latest supercomputers. That power is, however, far from sufficient—even when some applications are run for up to 20 hours on current machines.

Jet Engines: Propellers, Jets, Fans, and now . . . Propellers

In terms of fluid dynamics, the problems of studying flow inside a jet engine are not all that different from considering flow around an aircraft—except that temperatures are much higher, distances are much shorter, and tolerances are very fine. A jet engine is a turbine, not fundamentally different from the steam turbines that have been used for many years to propel ships and generate electricity. Rows of fixed blades direct flow past rotating blades that deliver power to a shaft, driving additional blades which compress air entering the system. Doing this right is even harder than describing it clearly.

Efficiency has been increased greatly since the early days during

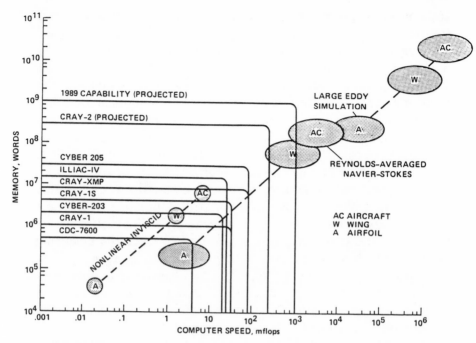

Unfinished Business. This chart depicts the gap between present and projected computational capabilities (lines) and requirements (shaded ovals) in computational aerodynamics. It was developed by Victor L. Peterson and James G. Arnold of NASA's Ames Research Center.

World War II. Advances were accomplished through repeated trial-and-error, supported by analysis. Now, analytical design using numerical simulation is becoming the major methodology for turbine design. Increasingly, numerical simulation is based upon the use of supercomputers. Reynolds-averaged Navier-Stokes equations are used. The usual approach has been to employ what is known as quasi-three-dimensional flow models, setting aside the effects of viscosity, analyzing flows through a single row of turbine blades. Three-dimensional codes including the effects of viscosity can be solved only on a very high-performance computer, such as a CRAY X-MP with an SSD storage option or a CRAY-2.

In recent years, improvements in thrust have been obtained in large part through the development of large fans, located in the upstream end of the engine duct, which drive air around the turbine itself. The next step is the so-called unducted fan: in effect, a multiblade propeller, or set of counter-rotating propellers, that is driven by the turbine and operates outside the engine.

Engine designers and airframe manufacturers are now testing a number of alternative forms of this concept. Boeing, McDonnell Douglas, and other companies anticipate that this will become the preferred aircraft propulsion system of the 1990s. Its advantage is greater fuel efficiency. The disadvantage is more noise than the most advanced fan-jets. Researchers have attacked both aspects with three-dimensional simulations that explore the subtle interactions between the two blades of a counter-rotating propeller system. The next problems are on the desks of publicists for engine companies, airframe manufacturers, and airlines. After decades of asserting that jet engines are more elegant than propellers, how are they going to explain that fashion has reversed itself? This is one problem for which supercomputers are not of much use.

What Are the Results?

Computational aerodynamics began to have a substantial impact upon the design of airliners in the latter part of the 1970s. Designs developed at that time which made extensive use of this technique included the Airbus A-310, the Boeing 757, and the Boeing 767. The A-310 achieved a substantial improvement in fuel economy over its predecessor, the A-300, designed with more conventional methods. This resulted in immediate savings, because wing designs required less wind tunnel testing. It also resulted in savings for operators of the A-310 that could total millions of dollars in fuel costs over the service life of each aircraft.

The wing of the original Boeing 747, which went into service before computational aerodynamics matured, has a total of four elements to increase lift during takeoff and landing: a leading-edge slat and a three-element flap. This represents a large investment in weight and structural complexity that is tucked away and unused during most of the flight, when the airliner is earning its keep. Boeing engineers estimate that, with the benefit of computational aerodynamics, the same results could have been accomplished with only three elements, bringing large savings. The new 747-400, now under development, features a redesigned wing that is the result of extensive application of computational simulation.

Ballhaus notes the value of computational simulation in recalling aircraft developed in the 1950s and later: "In spite of the use of the best simulation tools available at the time, [these designs] encountered major aerodynamic design problems that went undetected until flight testing. The consequences were severe penalties in cost, schedule, and/or performance. Several of these problems would have been detected early in the design cycle, and the consequent severe penalties avoided, with the computational capability available today."

The examples he mentions include the C-141, the C-5A, the F-111, and several civil airliners. Problems detected in one or another of these designs during flight testing included incorrectly predicted wing flow, incorrect predictions of transonic drag on the airframe, and unexpectedly severe interference between engine nacelles and the wings. Among the consequences: costly redesigns and modifications, shorter service life, and reduced performance.

More recently, researchers at Ames were asked to examine a problem that had arisen in the engine design for the space shuttle. Hydrogen fuel was brought to the combustion chamber through large pipes that look to a layman like the ducts emerging from a hot-air furnace. Because of space constraints, several angles were relatively acute. Analysis with supercomputers showed, in graphic form, the flow lines through these junctions. Workstations displayed the region of flow that was constraining fuel and reducing thrust. The system was redesigned with fewer pipes and shallower angles. This change could be considered a matter of common sense, but the simulation was able to demonstrate the optimum redesign.

Supercomputers are also being used to study one of the paradoxes of flight: a helicopter creates its own adverse environment. Like all wings, the main rotor of a helicopter leaves vortices of turbulence behind as it passes through the air. The slow-moving blades of a helicopter rotor encounter gnarls of their own turbulence as they swing around, reducing performance and adding to vibration. Detailed analysis of this phenomenon is leading toward improved rotor designs.

Ever since the first multi-engined jet aircraft, it has been standard practice for wing-mounted engines to be slung under the wing on pylons. This was considered necessary in order to avoid interference between the airflow over the wing and flow through the engine. In designing the 737, Boeing engineers determined that there would be many advantages to a direct engine attachment without a pylon. Among other things, this design would save money (and weight, which is the same thing) on landing gear. Careful studies on supercomputers determined a way in which this could be done without compromising performance of either the wing or the engines.

Rockwell International is examining design concepts for the National Aerospace Plane (a hybrid which would take off and land like a conventional aircraft and propel itself into orbit) and the U.S. Air Force's proposed Advanced Tactical Fighter. V.J. Shankar of Rockwell points out it would in effect be impossible to think about such concepts without supercomputers.

CHAPTER 8 _____

The Air, Sea, and Earth

Atmospheric sciences (including weather prediction and the study of the climate) were among the earliest applications of high-speed computers and continue to consume much supercomputer time. Geophysics (especially the application of seismology to exploration for fossil fuels) relies equally upon supercomputers. High-speed computers are also used for earthquake studies and for modeling oil fields in order to determine optimum extraction rates. Oceanography is now making use of supercomputing. Increasingly, the earth, sea, and air are beginning to be considered as a single unit, which creates additional demand for large-scale computing.

The National Center for Atmospheric Research (NCAR) lies at two boundaries. Its buildings stand on a mesa in the lee of the Rocky Mountains, high above Boulder, Colorado, at the point where the mountains end and the Great Plains begin. NCAR is also at another boundary. Like most other human activities, it stands where the land ends and the atmosphere begins. The Scripps Institution of Oceanography, perched on a cliff above the edge of the Pacific Ocean at La Jolla, California, is at a third boundary. The contrast

The National Center for Atmospheric Research, Boulder, Colorado. The building was designed by I.M. Pei. (*NCAR.*)

between sea and land is as consequential as the differences between either and the air.

Life came from the ocean and occupies the land as an uneasy tenant, surviving only because each living cell carries a tiny sea inside itself. The persistence of life in the sea and upon the land is possible because the air, sea, and land conspire to accomplish a reasonably even distribution of the energy that the sun delivers so unevenly upon this planet.

Atmospheric science, oceanography, and the earth sciences share the same fundamental unit of study, our planet. All possess another common factor: a voracious, growing appetite for computational capacity. Increasingly, each depends upon supercomputers to feed that appetite. Practitioners in these fields foresee an almost infinite need for greater computational power. This chapter recounts conversations with scientists at NCAR, Scripps, and elsewhere who are using supercomputers to understand this planet, and to harvest fossilized energy and other treasures.

Weather Forecasting: Making Better Sense out of the Data

Every once in a while, American science and the federal government stop muttering in one another's direction and come together in a genuinely fruitful collaboration. NCAR is a happy instance. It was launched in 1960 because scientists were concerned about the contrast between the widening opportunities for atmospheric research (based in large part upon new data-gathering techniques developed since the outbreak of World War II) and a shortage of meteorologists with full academic qualifications. Fourteen universities grouped together to form the University Corporation for Atmospheric Research, which still manages NCAR and now has more than 50 members, scattered all over North America. (Names of these institutions are listed, along with participants in other supercomputing programs, on the chart following Chapter Six.) Federal funding was arranged through the NSF, which continues to be the principal source of NCAR's budget.

Modern high technology and top-quality modern architecture started out in the same neighborhood but now, alas, usually walk along different streets. The main NCAR facility on the mesa is a delightful exception. It was one of the earlier, most influential works by I. M. Pei. Every detail reflects his originality and his respect for the site. Its dominant themes are rectilinear, but its pinkish ochre tint blends gracefully into the colors of the stony mountainsides behind it. On the site, deer wander close to the parking lot, and hikers pass by.

Too many pinch-penny legislators and administrators maintain that the flesh of scientific researchers should be lodged in ugliness, crowded together and otherwise mortified so that their souls will be purer and overhead will be reduced. They should visit NCAR to see the beneficial results of a civilized workplace.

For most people, the atmosphere is a problem to be deciphered, a game of chance, not an object of research. Will it rain this afternoon? Will there be good skiing at Squaw Valley when our turn comes up at the condominium next month? What are the chances of bad weather when Priscilla and Bob finally get themselves properly married next April?

NCAR does not produce weather forecasts, but its researchers are in close touch with people whose work shows up on the evening news and in the weather predictions used to brief airline pilots. Data about the weather are becoming more abundant all the time. Automated ground stations are more numerous and more accurate. Sounding balloons investigate high-altitude winds; aircraft in flight, ships at sea, satellites and radar add further information.

Nevertheless, specialists like Jim Hack, an atmospheric dy-namicist at NCAR, point out that data collection is far from adequate. "People live on a scale of less than 10 kilometers, and it is difficult to deliver that kind of precision." Even in the United States, ground stations are tens of kilometers apart on the average, or even more widely separated. Upper atmosphere probes are supposed to be made every 12 hours, but things go wrong; in any case the stations are perhaps 100 kilometers apart in North America. Weather is global; the distances between observations are even greater in most other countries, and especially so over the oceans.

Hack notes that the European Centre for Medium-range Weather Forecasts (ECMWF) in Reading, England works from one of the densest grids in general use. Even for ECMWF, however, the average distance between points on the global grid is about 110 kilometers. This represents an enormous volume of data. ECMWF has relied upon high-speed computations since its inception in 1975 and was the first overseas customer for a CRAY-1, in 1978. It has since installed a CRAY X-MP. The Canadian Meteorological Centre in Montreal also operates a Cray supercomputer, installed in 1983. For ECMWF, the supercomputers have made it possible to produce six-day winter forecasts as reliable as earlier two- or three-day winter forecasts. As the grid is refined, it produces surprises. Staff at ECMWF were puzzled by anomalies in their model. They guessed that it might be due to over-simplification of the Rocky Mountains and the Alps, both of which were treated as plateaus whose height equalled their average altitude. A more precise model of these mountains resulted in more accurate forecasts.

Ever since its founding, NCAR has used the fastest computers available. It was one of the earliest customers for a CRAY-1, in 1977, and added another later. A CRAY X-MP/48, with exceptionally large, fast memory, was installed in October 1986 (see Appendix II, Section 2).

Attention is now concentrated upon what meteorologists call meso-scale events. This is a technical term for weather on a smaller scale than full-scale storms or fronts but larger than a patchy summer shower that delivers dampness to a neighbor's parched lawn but passes up our own. Typical meso-scale phenomena include thunderstorms, tornados, squall-lines, and wind-shear. In conjunction with universities and federal agencies, NCAR is now focusing intensive attention upon wind-shear, which has caused several recent serious aircraft accidents.

Such localized, relatively small phenomena can have disproportionate impact upon human lives and livelihood. Jim Hack says that Doppler radar and other techniques are close to making it possible to obtain adequately precise measurements on this scale. Numerical simulation of such phenomena is within reach, but it requires a great deal of computer power as well as sufficient data. Hack anticipated that the new X-MP would become saturated within a few months after it went on line. "There is always more physics," he says. A shift from two-dimensional to three-dimensional models at the same resolution can increase the demand upon the computer 100 times.

A lot of people don't smoke or drink these days, a few don't eat very much, and some don't even watch TV or drive a car, but no one is able to get along without weather. What does all this mean for all of us?

Long-range and medium-range forecasts are improving steadily. These can have the greatest economic impact, affecting agriculture, power companies, and transportation. For example, more accurate forecasting of temperature enables power suppliers to determine peak loads more accurately and generate power more efficiently. Better forecasts of the jet stream and other high-altitude winds, as well as surface weather, make it possible for airliners to fly with more fuel efficiency as well as greater safety.

Will the 12-and-under soccer finals be rained out tomorrow afternoon so I can get my shopping done at last? Short-term forecasts with this kind of precision will require more detailed and complete data collection as well as improved modeling of meso-scale events. Forecasts of all levels will continue to depend upon increases in computational power. ECMWF's ten-day forecast, which is updated every day, requires about four hours of time on an X-MP. Jim Hack says that increases in computational capacity of 100 or 1000 times would be put to practical use right away.

Walter Washington, head of the Climate Research Section, National Center for Atmospheric Research. (*NCAR.*)

"The Weather Here Is Okay Sometimes, but the Climate Is Lousy"

Alligators at the North Pole

Climate is to weather as history is to the evening news. We are accustomed to assuming that climate, like the location of the continents and the polarity of the earth's magnetic field, is stable and at least reasonably consistent. In fact, all these apparently solid facts change a great deal, and climate is one of the most variable. The changes are not easy to discern because they take place in cycles measured in millions, thousands, and hundreds of years.

The causes of these alterations are only beginning to be understood, partly because the historical record is shallow and spotty. Fossil records, other geological evidence, and the studies of annual rings of long-lived trees like the Bristlecone Pine provide glimpses of different parts of the climatological past. Local records of first frost, the beginning of planting, the rice harvest, and so on have been kept in China for many hundreds of years. (This was not for scientific purposes: the data were forwarded to bureaucrats who checked to make sure that the taxes sent on by local magistrates matched up with the harvests that could be expected in good or bad years.) Under an arrangement with the Chinese, funded by the U.S. Department of Energy, these records were translated and made available to U.S. climatologists. They were delighted to find that the Chinese data also reflected a bitter summer in 1816, when dust thrown from a volcano in Indonesia caused summer frosts on Cape Cod.

Warren Washington, head of the Climate Research Section at NCAR, is one of the researchers who uses the Community Climate Model (CCM) which has required 10 to 15 man-years to develop. This is a model of the global climate at a relatively coarse resolution of about 2000 grid points, which means roughly that a single point represents the state of Colorado. (Finer resolutions exist that require much greater computational capacity, however, these are more readily available for day to day forecasting than climate simulation). The model enables researchers to probe into the past and forward into the future, modeling previous and anticipated climates. The CCM is not the only global climate model; more than 10 others are in use or being developed elsewhere, including the United States, Europe, China, the Soviet Union, and Japan. The CCM is used at about 40 universities in the United States.

The CCM should be considered as a basic model which can be modified to suit various research purposes. A few of the planned or on-going research topics involving the CCM are desertification in the Sahara (University of Alaska); El Niño and other ocean temperature anomalies (University of Utah); effects of equatorial Pacific ocean temperature anomalies on Brazilian rainfall (University of Miami); examination of the monsoons in the CCM (University of Washington); the role of Kelvin waves in the tropical stratosphere (Peking University); and paleoclimate simulations with coupled and uncoupled atmosphere-ocean models (Brown University and University of Washington).

Washington and an NCAR colleague, Eric J. Barron, have employed the CCM for paleoclimate research—studies of ancient climate. They examined the climate of the Cretaceous period, approximately 100 million years ago. A straightforward comparison is difficult, partly because the continents have moved from their present position a good deal. One observed fact is clear: the Cretaceous climate was significantly warmer. Barron shows that the average surface temperatures were warmer then than now. Increases for the polar regions were much greater—alligators lived near the North Pole. This does not necessarily mean that the Cretaceous equivalent of banana trees in the tropics curled up and died. Tropical temperatures then were not much different from present levels. They point out that the causes of these differences are complex. Changes in the geographic distribution of land masses and the absence of ice on Antarctica appear to be important factors, as shown by model experiments. They are sufficient to explain the warmness of that period. An additional factor that may be required to explain the warmer polar temperatures: there may have been much higher amounts of carbon dioxide in the atmosphere at that time.

Tomorrow's Climate: Policy Disputes and Models

The study of climate would seem at first glance to be a safely academic pastime far removed from controversy. In fact, climatologists have become involved repeatedly in disputes over public policy. These issues are likely to become more acute and probably more numerous.

Attention has been focused upon the chemistry of the atmosphere, as well as upon the atmosphere's main work of energy transfer. In the 1970's, the main issue was chlorofluorocarbons (CFCs—often lumped together under Dupont's trade name, Freon). It was feared that the release of these substances (especially from their use as propellants in aerosol cans) into the atmosphere might lead to the destruction of ozone and a consequent increase in ultraviolet radiation reaching the earth. This in turn could cause an increase in skin cancers and other damaging effects. Although uncertainties remained regarding the ozone depletion theory, 20 countries took action by 1982 to control release of CFC's.

Current issues in what is known as anthropogenic changes in atmospheric chemistry include increases in the carbon dioxide content of the air and nuclear winter. Atmospheric scientists are generally agreed that carbon dioxide in the air has been increasing steadily over the last 50 years or so. It is attributed to a large-scale increase in the burning of fossil fuels, the elimination of forests that would otherwise sop up carbon dioxide, and other activities of a human population much larger, and more extravagant with resources, than was the case earlier in this century. Climatic models show that if the atmospheric carbon dioxide were doubled, the upper atmosphere would retain heat more readily. The resulting "greenhouse effect" would cause a large increase in average temperature.

So far, however, there is much less agreement on a central fact: are temperatures going up? A few years' measurements don't mean much. Temperatures are known to rise and decline in cycles that remain poorly understood. Some specialists claim to see a definite increase. Others say that recent readings do not emerge clearly from the "noise" of annual and cyclical variations. Stephen H. Schneider, an NCAR climatologist who does not shrink from public controversy, thinks that the increase is taking place but is masked by the vast capacity of the oceans to soak up heat. Schneider calls for improved models that will take fully into consideration the interaction between the atmosphere and the oceans. Schneider also emphasizes the need for models that examine the present slow rate of increase in atmospheric carbon dioxide, rather than assuming a doubling, working back from that point, and drawing conclusions. He believes it is important to focus upon the considerations most important for human life—like the effect of climatic change on availability of water for agriculture—rather than talking about degrees of warming.

The findings of atmospheric scientists may be used and interpreted according to assumptions and positions about public policy. Advocates who are devoted to a lean, natural life-style based upon replaceable resources are more likely to dwell upon the disastrous effects of continuing the headlong consumption of fossil fuels and destruction of rain forests. Those who consider themselves realists may place their emphasis in the opposite direction. Both may offer computer models to justify their position. Because of the complexity of the problems, the most complete models are executed upon supercomputers. Yet the results—and often the policy implications which are drawn—may depend in turn upon the resolution, assumptions, and detail included in a particular computer model.

Nuclear winter is another example of a public controversy, based upon climatic analysis, which hinges upon computer models, contrasting assumptions, and policy preferences. The issue was first brought to public attention in late 1983 in an article by Richard Turco, O. Brian Toon, Thomas Ackerman, James Pollack and Carl Sagan. It said a widespread nuclear war would inject so much smoke into the atmosphere that energy from the sun would be blocked and catastrophic global cooling would take place. They employed a computer model called TTAPS (after the initials of the authors' surnames) that made drastic simplifying assumptions about the earth, taking it as a homogenous all-land sphere with no seasonal variations, and about the volume and characteristics of the smoke that would be injected.

Subsequent studies, using different models that included the oceans and a rough representation of actual geography, found that cooling would be neither as severe nor as universal. Temporary, localized effects in the interiors of continents might be severe, however, especially if the nuclear exchange took place in the summer. Later studies also emphasized the wide range of uncertainty, depending in part upon assumptions regarding the characteristics and quantity of the smoke thrown into the atmosphere. Stephen Schneider is among those who continue to attempt to refine the models being used.

Discussion of this issue has at times involved a degree of acrimony hypothetically avoided in scientific discourse. Attention in the news media and the impact upon public opinion were heightened by the implication that the words "based upon a computer projection" meant "scientific certainty." Subsequent differences were then discussed in terms of "which computer projection is right?" rather than in more realistic dimensions; that is, the limitations attached to any computer projection.

This book is not the place to attempt another judgment upon this serious, difficult issue. It is, however, important to remember that, even—or especially—in climatology, a good, neutral computer program is sometimes hard to find. And, at the same time, increasing computational power—including the use of supercomputers—is making it possible to reduce the limitations of simulations. This could narrow both the size and emotion of differences, making it less difficult to resolve such questions.

The Weather of the Ocean

The Scripps Institution of Oceanography is a part of the University of California at San Diego. It takes part in the Institute of Geophysics and Planetary Physics (IGPP), which links several campuses of the University of California (UCLA, San Diego, and Riverside) and the two national laboratories managed by the University (Los Alamos and Lawrence Livermore.)

As it happens, the building that houses the IGPP branch at Scripps is another agreeable piece of architecture, a graceful construct of unpainted wood that rests easily on a steep slope. No deer are evident, but plenty of squirrels occupy the pines at the brow of the cliffside.

Scientific oceanography began just over a hundred years ago, with the voyage of HMS *Challenger*, a steam corvette that made a round-the-world circuit of the oceans between 1872 and 1876, taking systematic samples of depth, temperature, salinity, and ocean currents. Walter Munk, a man with dense white hair and an abundance of middle-Europe charm, was formerly an Associate Director of the IGPP and head of the San Diego branch. He points out that in recent years, newer tools such as sonar and seismography have been added. Research submarines now plunge thousands of meters beneath the surface, but the principal research method is still that employed by the *Challenger*.

As a result, Munk says, scientists now have a vastly improved understanding of what he describes as the climate of the oceans: the average state over time of any particular portion of the seas. Munk, his colleagues at Scripps, and other researchers at MIT, the University of Michigan, Woods Hole Oceanographic Institution, and in France are beginning to understand the weather of the ocean as well.

Many people remember the Gulf Stream from geography classes and atlases—that bright blue band, pirouetting grandly around Florida, sweeping past the east coast of North America, and continuing firmly on to Europe. This was a simplified depiction of a much more complicated current. As shown by an artist in a geography book, the Gulf Stream would divide into a few clearly-depicted forks, breaking its dignified progress in order to bring fog and roses to England and encourage wild strawberries to flourish in Sweden.

This was a reasonable, if simplified, depiction of the climate of the North Atlantic, but the weather of that ocean is much more complicated. In fact, the Gulf Stream wanders a good deal; eddies separate and drift toward the east, apart from the main stream. In other oceans as well as the Atlantic, energy transport features like the Gulf Stream and the eddies that accompany it are most active at the western edges of the oceans and diminish in intensity toward the east.

Everything is slower in water than in air. A typical storm in the atmosphere may have a diameter of 1000 kilometers and an active lifetime of a few days. Comparable transient features (weather) of the ocean are smaller, perhaps 100 kilometers in diameter. They develop languidly, with a typical lifetime of 90 days. These phenomena are not caused by the wind or tides. They are, in fact, like the weather of the air, redistributing over the globe the solar energy that arrives unevenly upon the surface. The energy contained in surface eddies, re-radiated into the atmosphere, affects in turn the weather and climate of the air.

The slow development and relatively small size of eddies and other features of ocean weather account for its relatively late discovery. These features of oceanic weather are phenomena of the surface, and curiosity was concentrated upon what went on down below. This made it likely that measurements taken from a ship sailing on a fixed pattern would not reveal these phenomena—or might result in odd readings that would be thrown out as variants or obscured by being averaged in with the rest.

Oceanic weather is now being studied by a new technique called ocean acoustic tomography. Sound sources, which until now have been on buoys anchored to the ocean bottom, transmit at intervals. Arrays of receivers some distance away register the signals as they arrive. As in seismic explorations on land, several signals can be received from a single transmission. Analysis of these wave patterns—a very computer-intensive process—can provide profiles of the ocean. The technique and results are similar to a counterpart in medicine—computer-assisted tomography, the CAT scan. The surface eddies of oceanic weather differ in temperature from the water below and so transmit sound vibrations at different speeds. Thus, they can be revealed by ocean tomography. Warmer water in an eddy may result in a local increase in the elevation of the ocean by as much as 10 centimeters, which is detectable by radar altimeters on satellites.

So far, the analysis at Scripps of data gathered through ocean tomography has been carried out on a Prime minicomputer. The next step, according to Munk, is to make continuous observations from moving ships. This could provide much more detail but will increase the computational requirements greatly. A supercomputer will be needed, and Munk's group is already using the San Diego supercomputer to do preliminary studies. For example, the ideal pattern to be sailed by a survey ship engaged in ocean acoustic tomography is not self-evident; a straight course, circular, parabolic, or what?

What is it good for? Munk points out that fuller knowledge of eddies and other surface phenomena could have important implications for antisubmarine warfare and its counterpart, the art of hiding one's own submarines. It may have an impact, still far from completely understood, upon the distribution of biomass within the sea, and so upon fisheries, especially for pelagic species like tuna. Such research could also shed light on much larger question of the effects of the interactions between the oceans and the air upon global temperature, weather, and atmospheric chemistry.

Geophysics: Looking into the Earth

Global Rhythym

J. Freeman Gilbert, the current IGPP associate director at Scripps, is a quiet, friendly man, the kind of professor every graduate student would be glad to see on his dissertation committee. Gilbert is interested in the deep structure of the earth. When a large earthquake takes place, the whole globe vibrates—"like a gong," as Freeman puts it. Like a gong, the earth changes shape during the vibrations. The earth is of course never a perfect sphere, and when these vibrations take place, it deforms further. It may elongate—the "football" mode—return to a near-spherical shape, elongate in the other direction, and eventually resume its usual form.

In any percussion band, the earth would emit a very deep thrum indeed. These whole-earth oscillations take place at very low fre-

J. Freeman Gilbert, geophysicist at the Scripps Institution of Oceanography.
(*Scripps Institution of Oceanography.*)

quencies, with each cycle measured in minutes, and are difficult
to detect. In fact, the first oscillations were not observed until after
a very large earthquake in Chile in 1960.

Freeman and other investigators at Cal Tech, Harvard, and
elsewhere study these low-frequency oscillations in order to explore
puzzling observations about the composition of the earth. Are the
deep, inner workings of the planet in hydrostatic equilibrium? What
hypotheses about the internal composition of the earth best explain
its behavior when it vibrates?

As in so many other new fields, this one depends upon new
means for collecting data, combined with supercomputers that enable
scientists to interpret the data rapidly and efficiently. About twenty
long-period seismic sensors have been installed all around the world,
in a network called Project IDA. Freeman remarks that the complexity of the data "Make supercomputers practically a necessity
if any serious work is to be done." Work that would require months
on a minicomputer can be completed in a weekend on a Cray. A
year's research can be carried out in a month or two. This stimulates
serendipity. Young people take this for granted, he says. Freeman

is also a strong supporter of interactive operating systems like CTSS. These increase the productivity of engineers and scientists. "They are the ones who solve the problems," Freeman says, "not the machines that just perform algorithms."

Custom-designed Protection for Local Earthquake Risks

Especially in geophysics, the Scripps Institution decided long ago that it is artificial to separate the oceans from the land. Most areas with frequent, severe earthquakes and volcanos are not far from seacoasts. These events release energy built up by slow collisions of undersea tectonic plates with continental plates.

The need for improved earthquake-resistant building design (and the difficulty of doing it right) was demonstrated by the 1985 earthquake in Mexico. Seismologists, including some from Scripps, had been anticipating an early, severe earthquake along the coast west of Mexico City. A new array of sensors was being installed when the earthquake took place. Damage in the vicinity of the earthquake, where the ground motion was equivalent to about one-tenth of the force of gravity, was substantial but far from catastrophic.

Severe damage and loss of life occurred hundreds of kilometers away, in Mexico City. Tall buildings of 7 to 12 stories shook, split, and collapsed. Losses were concentrated in a portion of the city built upon an old lake. The vibrations set up by the earthquake in the sediments under the buildings coincided unhappily with the frequencies at which buildings of a certain height trembled and broke up—due to local ground motion that approached a full G, nearly equivalent to the force of gravity.

John Anderson and other researchers at Scripps study micro-seismology. They seek to predict, for specific locations, the probabilities and severity of ground motion, the acceleration that actually destroys buildings and so can take lives. Earthquake-resistant design of buildings has traditionally relied upon generalized principles. The Japanese have been dealing with frequent, severe earthquakes since the beginning of their civilization. Long ago, they evolved a simple, workable formula. Smaller buildings should be solid but flexible. The mortise-and-tenon structure of a traditional Japanese house, for example, is remarkably sturdy but possesses a lot of give. When an out-of-control truck smashes into a house like that, a lot of plaster is thrown around, but the structure yields, wobbles, and survives. A great deal of strength and mass were designed into larger Japanese buidings, and all structures were kept fairly close to the ground. Tall buildings of 30 stories or more are now commonplace in Japanese cities. They are built to different formulas, emphasizing flexibility as well as strength. None has yet been subjected to the full-scale effect of a major earthquake.

Extensive seismic data on southern California are available. If an investigator examines the data on all the faults in the area, including slip history and rupture spreads, it is possible to come up with fairly good predictions for a particular locality. Hospitals, police stations, and similar structures are required by building codes to meet stringent specifications for seismic survival. Studies based upon an examination of the local microseismology and dynamic building design can result in more efficient, cost-effective protection against earthquake damage by designing protection on a custom basis, rather than applying general standards that may not be suitable for a given situation.

Freeman Gilbert notes that the mathematics required for these analyses typically involves difficult, contrary equations that may require protracted calculations (up to months, in some cases) on conventional computers. Supercomputers can accomplish the same results within a few days. This also advances learning about problems like the dynamics of fault rupture which are now poorly understood.

Fossil Fuels: Looking for Oil with a Stethoscope

Supercomputers are almost as universal, and as fundamental a tool in the oil and gas industry as stethoscopes are in a hospital. The purposes are somewhat similar. A physician will tap the chest of a patient while listening through a stethoscope to determine whether the lungs are clear or clogged. Seismologists add another step. They thump the surface of the earth or ocean with explosive charges, sharp raps with a hydraulic vibrator, or air cannons discharged in the water. Sensors pick up the reflections of seismic waves from strata of rock deep within the earth.

An experienced physician can interpret the sounds heard in a stethoscope, but the data collected by multiple seismic shots are too complex for ready understanding. Supercomputers are used

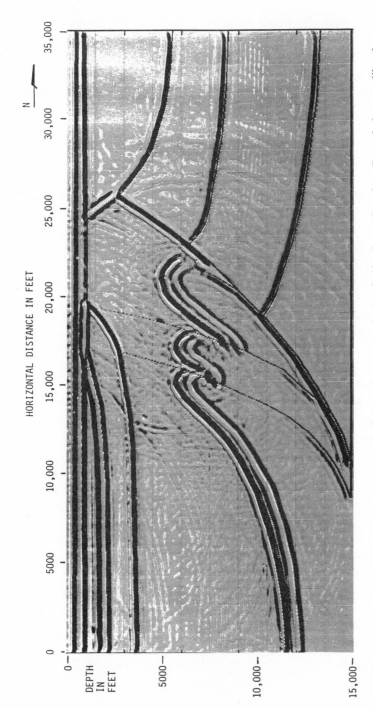

A cross-section of a geological feature, generalized by computer analysis of seismic exploration. Rounded strata like those in the center are of special interest as potential oil reservoirs—if they are large enough to contain enough petroleum to justify the cost of a test well. (*AMOCO Production Company.*)

for this purpose by fossil fuel companies and by service centers that do work for petroleum firms in the United Kingdom, France, the Federal Republic of Germany, the Netherlands, Saudi Arabia, Abu Dhabi, and Japan as well as in the United States. Oil exploration authorities in the Soviet Union use some of their most powerful computers: special purpose array processors. If all supercomputers in the world were to crash irrevocably tomorrow from some improbable epidemic of silicon fungus, the impact upon the oil and gas industry would be greater than upon any other—with the possible exception of the aerospace industry.

It would be difficult to find another industry in which the relation between computational power and profit is so intimate. Under the best of circumstances, a solid majority of test wells do not find enough oil or gas to make extraction worthwhile. A relatively simple test drilling costs several million dollars. Unusually deep holes and test drilling offshore can cost 10 or 20 times as much, or more. At the other extreme, a large, productive field with easily pumped oil, reasonably close to major markets, provides a return upon investment not available in any other honest business, and few dishonest ones. Few really big fields that fit this description remain to be found. This drives oil companies to risk more money under more difficult conditions with slimmer prospects of easy returns. Anything that raises the chance of a productive hole is worth using. Supercomputers are among the most cost-effective of those anythings.

Seismic exploration involves complexities from start to finish. The layers of rock that may contain oil are themselves complex, varying in density, composition, and thickness, often folded and turned upon themselves. The data-gathering process is complex. Shots are made at intervals (24 per mile, for instance) on a line that may continue for many miles. Many receivers are used—48, 96, and now 1000 or more. This makes it possible to obtain many images of each feature deep below. It also generates an enormous volume of raw data that must be resolved into decipherable images. A single seismic line may produce a billion or more values to be processed.

Reverberations, refractions, and ricochets must be filtered out. Data must be corrected for the distance between the source and

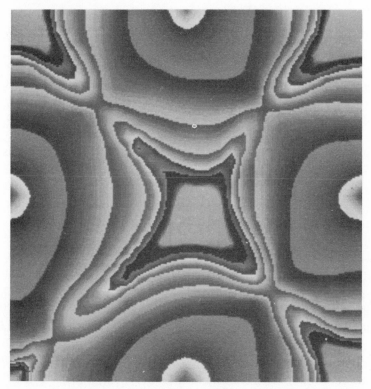

A computer simulation of a cross-section in depth on an oil reservoir. (*AMOCO Production Company.*)

each of very many receivers. An intermediate result is called a stack, which provides a simplified profile of the layers being explored. Dipping and other changes from the horizontal are considered through a process called migration, which requires the use of additional sophisticated algorithms.

Until recently, all this effort resulted in a two-dimensional profile. Improvements in the technology of data acquisition, as well as increases in the computational power available, are making it possible to conduct three-dimensional exploration. When shots are fired, receivers are placed in a rectangle rather than strung out on a line. The data collected reveal an area rather than a cross-section. The advantages are considerable, but the added complexity is intimidating.

Getting More of the Oil Out of the Ground

What happens when gasoline costs less than a dollar a gallon? The oil companies spend their money and use all their other resources very prudently. They keep on exploring, keep on risking tens of millions of dollars on test holes, because that is where their future lies. They also concentrate with redoubled intensity upon getting the most efficient returns from oil fields already in production.

An oil field is not some vast subterranean bucket waiting to be pumped dry. Typically, oil is found in porous rock, and it must be extracted with care. The physics are different, but the process is a little like siphoning a liquid. If you lose continuity of the liquid in the hose, you have to try again. In an oil field, the movement of oil through the rock toward a pumping well depends upon viscous connectivity. If the well is operated too greedily, connectivity may be lost. Orphaned deposits of oil may become separated from the rest of the oil reservoir and be left behind. Recovering them is costly and uncertain.

Under the best of circumstances, a majority of oil is left in the ground. In some fields, notably some very large ones in the Soviet Union, excessive pumping took place early in the lifetime of the reservoir in order to meet ambitious production and export quotas. Connectivity was lost, and future production will drop off earlier than necessary. Very careful study is required in order to achieve maximum recovery over the potential useful life of a field.

A pool of oil may be complex in shape and extend over a large area. Wells drilled into the field provide accurate data, but on a sampling basis. Accurate extrapolation and three-dimensional analysis are needed. Next to exploration, modeling the dynamics of subsurface reservoirs is the most important application of supercomputers in the petroleum industry. This is true for primary recovery (the initial pumping) and at least as important for secondary and tertiary recovery (which may involve injection of steam or other techniques to obtain oil missed the first time around). As the large, relatively easy fields are all found or approach the end of their most productive years, long-term optimization of recovery of the globe's limited fossil fuel resources will become a growing preoccupation.

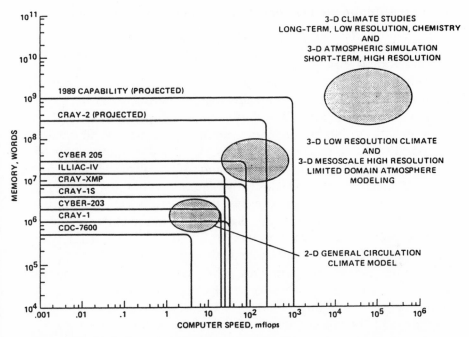

Unfinished Business. Present and projected computational capabilities (lines) and requirements in atmospheric science (shaded ovals) are depicted in this chart developed by Victor L. Peterson and James G. Arnold of NASA's Ames Research Center. These assume 15-minute runs with 1985 algorithms.

Eliminating the Boundaries: The Whole-Earth Approach

Atmospheric scientists, oceanographers, and earth scientists are recognizing that the boundaries between their academic disciplines, taken for granted a few decades ago when all were expanding so rapidly, are losing their significance. This was recognized long ago by institutions like NCAR and Scripps, which harbor and mix specialists in all three dimensions of inquiry.

Increased attention is also being given to the interaction between the biosphere—a fancy name for the totality of living things—and the other dynamics of the planet. At NCAR, for example, Steven Schneider heads the Natural Systems Group that considers broad-based problems. Another group in NCAR's Advanced Study Program, the Environmental and Societal Impacts Group, studies the effect of such studies upon people and their livelihood.

Satellites make it possible to see the earth as a whole—including the flares that burn gas around the clock on the edge of isolated oil fields, the empty areas left by widespread new tropical deforestation, and the fertile flood plains that are buried under headlong urbanization. Satellites show these things and provide much data about what is going on, but they cannot explain what it all means.

Are the actual consequences as serious as the emotions raised by the words used in the last paragraph? If so, what measures are needed? What are the most effective measures, not just action for action's sake? How much time do we have? How can that time— the most precious resource, but the one most likely to be wasted— best be used? The answers cannot be found just by retorting with other words. It will require patient, thorough interdisciplinary examination. Supercomputers and other computational resources cannot provide the answers by themselves, but they can play an important and sometimes central role in assisting investigators to comprehend the whole globe with adequate fidelity.

CHAPTER 9 _____

The Business of Creation and Other Diversions

> Supercomputers, like other computers, are in the end an extension of the user's imagination, creativity, and ambition. This chapter examines applications that demonstrate this explicitly: computer animation for television and films (which is also a business in itself and becoming a big business); the competition for the *America's* Cup; and computer chess.

Computer Animation: Good Enough for Disney, and Beyond

"Heavy trouble. Disney wants to move up the release date—from the seventeenth to the first."

"How can we get those sequences ready? Everything's been okayed, but it will take too long to do the computer runs."

"So use a faster computer."

"We don't have one. But waitaminit, where's that phone number . . . Damn . . . Gotcha. I think this'll do it. I'll call you back."

The preceding imaginary dialogue is not the lead-in copy for an advertisement in *Datamation* or *Computerworld*; it is the gist of an actual conversation that took place in spring 1986, in Studio G, on the old Paramount Pictures lot in Hollywood. Studio G houses the main West Coast operation of Omnibus, a computer graphics company based in Toronto. Omnibus was doing computer animation that was to be integrated into a Disney film, *Flight of the Navigator*. They were able to meet the accelerated release date by transferring processing of the sequences from an in-house special-purpose computer to the CRAY X-MP at San Diego.

Jeff Kleiser was in charge of the motion picture and television division of Omnibus when this interview took place and now heads an Omnibus subsidiary, Robert Abel Associates. Kleiser believes that computer animation is a "new tool with endless possibilities— anything but a fad." The need for the computational power made possible by supercomputers is growing. Computer graphics is a "wide-open medium. It provides control over so much of the image. Theoretically, it is possible to render anything and everything which can reach the eyes. It can all be simulated, using well-known mathematics—if you have the computer power."

Studio G is an old sound stage, one of a large number of indistinguishable buildings on the Paramount lot, painted the color of dirty sand, which look particularly faded and forlorn under an autumn rain. Visitors are directed to follow a dotted line on the pavement that ends in a large concrete-lined basin, the size of six or eight tennis courts. Parking slots are painted on the bottom of the basin, which has sloping sides and is perhaps 4 feet deep. A sky-and-clouds backdrop has been painted on a giant wall that rises 50 feet or more in the background and is about twice as wide.

A security guard splashing through the rain on a bicycle gives helpful directions to Studio G and confirms a visitor's fantasies. This is in fact the place where Moses parted the waters of the Red Sea, the Shogun's ships sailed, and the Battle of Midway was won in Herman Wouk's *The Winds of War*.

The mind recalls those illusions of the past. It was all so convincing. A real effort of skepticism was required to remind the movie goer or TV viewer that this was the result of sweaty work by technicians in wading boots, manipulating wind machines and smoke generators, enhanced later by visual effects and other fakery. Could computers produce equally convincing illusions of reality—

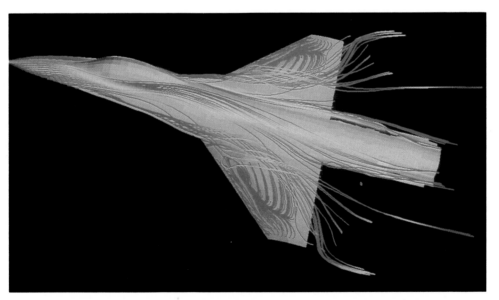

Supercomputers like this CRAY X-MP/48, top, at the San Diego Supercomputer Center are able to represent enormous quantities of data in readily-comprehensible form. The example, bottom, done on a CRAY-2 at NASA's Ames Research Center, simulates airflow over a simplified model of an F-16A fighter flying at Mach 0.6, somewhat below the speed of sound. Turbulence shows clearly over the wings.

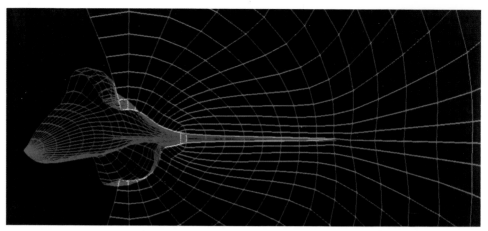

Making a Grid—and Using It. Even supercomputers cannot simulate everything that goes on in a complex natural event, like airflow around an aircraft in flight. To simplify the computations, programmers design grids, like the one above by Reese L. Sorenson of Ames. The grid varies in density according to the importance and variability of different areas of the phenomenon being simulated.

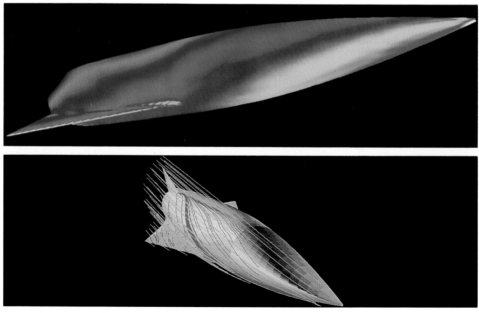

At very high supersonic speeds, turbulence is less than at speeds close to the speed of sound. This is a simulation, by Yehia Rizk of Ames, of a generic wing body (similar to possible designs for a hypersonic space plane) flying at Mach 25—over 12,000 miles per hour. It shows the anticipated surface pressure (top) and airflow (bottom).

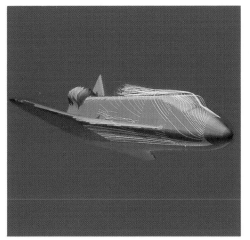

Using a supercomputer and powerful graphics workstations, it is possible to zoom in and out and view a simulated image from any direction. These images of the space shuttle, showing flow patterns at supersonic speeds, were done on a CRAY X-MP at NASA's Ames Research Center by Denny L. Chausee.

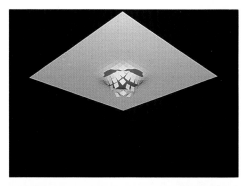

▲
Supercomputers are used by designers of memory chips to simulate extremely complex, very dense circuitry. Simulations are now moving from two dimensions to three dimensions. This chip, able to store one million bits of information, was designed on supercomputers at AT&T Bell Laboratories.

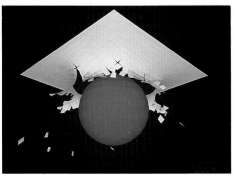

◄ Engineering programs for computer analysis usually divide actual surfaces into polygons in order to simplify the computation to a manageable level. The sequence at left is a demonstration of this principle: the computer sees the surface, impacted by a sphere, as breaking into flakes rather than small pieces. It looks simple but required careful programming and a great deal of supercomputer time at Lawrence Livermore National Laboratory.

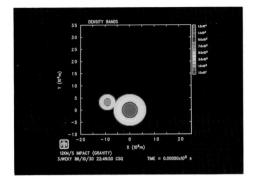

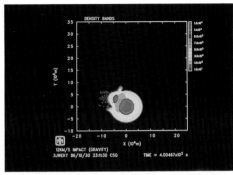

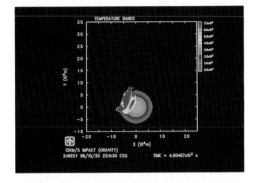

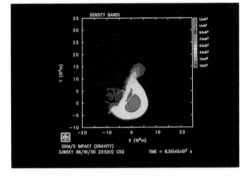

The Dimensions of Time. By showing the natural events in sequence, simulations using supercomputer graphics add the dimension of time. This simulation was created by M.E. Kipp of Sandia National Laboratories, Albuquerque, New Mexico, in conjunction with H.E. Melosh of the University of Arizona, and run on a CRAY X-MP. It shows about three very eventful minutes in the development of the earth. The simulation postulates that the still-molten proto-earth was struck about 4.5 billion years ago by a smaller proto-planet. The impact vaporized material from both objects, resulting in two jets of vaporized material that later coalesced to form the moon.

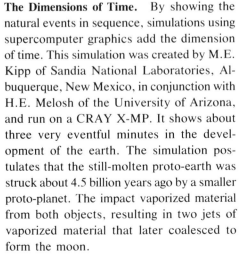

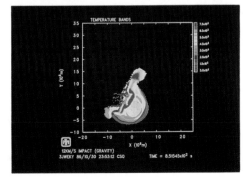

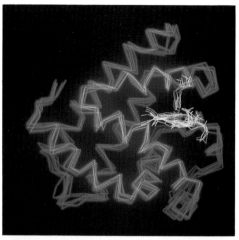

Computer Animation—From Animated Objects to Simulated Humans. Ever since its beginnings 10 years ago, computer animation has depended upon company logos and other advertising spots for its bread and butter. The technique has emphasized animation of inanimate objects, actual or imaginary. The sequence to the right, from a TV spot for Rockwell International by Robert Abel Associates, is typical.

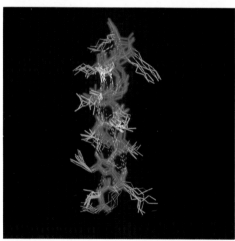

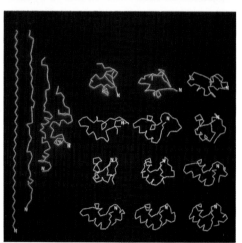

◄ **The Dance of Life.** Time is also an essential dimension for computer simulations of the molecular dynamics of proteins in living things. The two top pictures, by John Kuriyan of the Chemistry Department at Harvard University, based on a simulation of myoglobin, a substance that stores oxygen in the muscle, show intervals of 7 picoseconds, or trillionths of a second. The simulation below, by Axel T. Brünger, also in the Chemistry Department at Harvard, shows in full a sequence of 16 snapshots, at intervals of 1 picosecond, as a molecule of crambin folds from a slightly-kinked string into its usual shape, reminiscent of an exotic paperclip; NMR interproton distance data are used to induce the folding.

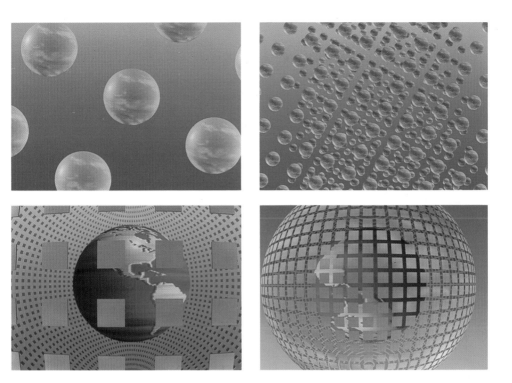

The current challenge is to represent human or human-like figures that look and move realistically. The picture on the left uses the algorithms and techniques of the 1970s and early 1980s—vector graphics. It generates the shape of a head, looking very much like an old-fashioned wicker dress form. The one on the right uses the techniques of the mid-1980s—more sophisticated algorithms and raster graphics. Not yet fully human, perhaps, but a large step in that direction. Both were developed by Robert Abel Associates for a commercial for TRW, Inc.

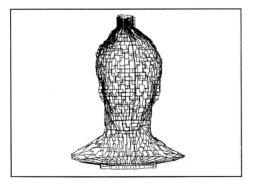

Understanding the World. Supercomputers are essential tools for scientists who seek to make sense out of the voluminous data collected about the complex interaction of the earth, its seas, and its atmosphere. This depicts a relatively simple model of the world climate developed at the National Center for Atmospheric Research. Much more detailed models will be needed to analyze the interaction of global phenomena. In order to make these analyses comprehensible, sophisticated graphical representations are required. (*National Center for Atmospheric Research.*)

or substitutes for reality that satisfy the expectations of the eye and mind?

For now, the answer seems to be "not yet," but the art (and, to a considerable extent, science) of computer image making is moving forward at a rate that amazes its own practioners and is not easy for outsiders to follow. As the horizons of creativity are expanding, the demand for increased computer power is becoming more imperative.

From Live Action, to Animation, to Computer Graphics, to . . .

Randy Rudd, creative director of the Omnibus operations in Studio G, was a late convert, as missionaries say, to computer graphics. He spent about five years doing live-action direction. Then he decided that there were more live-action directors than there was live action to direct, so he turned to what is now known as conventional animation. At that time, the first steps toward computer animation were tentative and limited. Much of it concentrated upon demonstrations of slick new capabilities, rather than integrating those capabilities into a rounded creative result.

Rudd turned to computers in 1982, when a great deal was happening, all at once. Earlier, *Star Wars* had generated an enormous market for special effects. The possibilities of conventional techniques were becoming exhausted—or too familiar. Customers for TV commercials were presenting story boards (visual concepts for a TV spot, presented as a sequence of frames) that could not be carried out through traditional animation. "If you were not able to do computer graphics, you had to let those story boards (and the business that meant) pass you by," Rudd recalls.

Computers, using vector graphics, had been employed as a side tool. A computer could help by speeding up the generation of outlines, which would be produced on printers. Colors and textures would then be filled in by hand. Then it changed. "No one was ready for the speed at which raster graphics came in," says Rudd. "Up until then, people were satisfied with wire grids—representing surfaces in a very sketchy way—and no textures. Then textures, rendering, lighting, and color shading—all of that became possible, all at once. New algorithms which made it possible to represent shape, motion, and light more effectively were even more important.''

Many individual artists and a number of firms, mostly small, came forward to explore and exploit these new possibilities. One of the earliest was Information International Incorporated (III, or 3-I) which developed special-purpose hardware as well as software and creative products. 3-I equipment is still chugging away at Studio G and many other places. Gary Demos and his associates split off to found Digital Productions, the first computer animation firm to acquire its own supercomputer. Robert Abel, another innovator, founded his own company which later, like Digital Productions, was acquired by Omnibus. Jeff Kleiser started out in computerized music at Colgate University, then moved on to graphics at Syracuse. He ended up at Digital Effects in New York City. Kleiser and his associates traded the software they had developed at Syracuse for computer time that could be used to produce their work.

The Pursuit of Imperfection

These artists, and many more, have spent the last three or four years adjusting to the Raster Revolution—and to other new developments in software and hardware. Representations of light have become more and more sophisticated. Kleiser points out that a spaceship in *Flight of the Navigator* was integrated into a live-action scene. The illusion of reality was heightened because the reflection of the ship could be shown, as well as a representation of the ship itself. Any texture can now be added to a surface. A recent innovation is called "bump mapping"—adding the appearance of imperfections to overcome the slick-surface look of prior computer graphics that looked too smooth to be believed.

The process is becoming much easier. Adjustments of lighting used to be an especially painstaking task. If the profile of a figure didn't look right when lit from over the right shoulder, it might take an hour or more to change the lighting to the other side. High performance workstations are now being used. (At Studio 8, Omnibus uses Silicon Graphics' potent IRIS Turbo.) Combined with advances in software (including some developed in-house at Omnibus) it is possible to consider essentially unlimited alternatives for lighting within an hour. Using a mouse, lighting and colors can be chosen,

Jeff Kleiser, head of Robert Abel Associates, a subsidiary of Omnibus Simulations, Inc., shown against a backdrop of some of his creations. (*Courtesy of Omnibus Simulations, Inc.*)

shown, and changed within a few seconds. In traditional animation, and in earlier days of computer images, the dialogue between a creative shop and a client took the form of an endless, time-consuming exchange. Pencil renderings, rough outlines, character sketches, and preliminary versions were shuttled back and forth by messenger or discussed at periodic meetings. Now a client can be sat down at a work station and shown everything on an interactive basis—"not so much green there . . . yeah, that backlighting is just right . . . speed up that movement a little . . ."—in a brief session.

In the mid-1980s, motion, especially motion by replicas of humans, is the challenge for computer animation—as it has always been for conventional animation. At first, movement was limited to rotating or turning objects, just as a mechanical device can turn a model of a new electric shaver or collapsible umbrella in a show window. At first, this was done with geometrical shapes or a customer's logo. Then Digital Productions did it with a glittering representation of a new Chevrolet van. Gary Demos and Digital Productions also produced the ultimate rock video: a rendering of the Rolling Stones' "Hard Woman." The human figures were still wire grids (or live inserts) but the movement was natural and attention-getting. Another computer animator, Randy Roberts, choreographed the flight of a paper glider in an apartment. Lucasfilm has turned out a dance by a family of lamps.

Here, also, imperfection is sought. Earlier, a ball would travel in a single, uniform movement. Now, movement is "tapered"— given a start, a main arc, and an end, each at appropriate speeds. Simulators are learning to imitate the lags and compensations produced by human camera operators. Randy Rudd believes that the influence of computer people—who like to obtain nice, sharp results—is being tempered by interaction with persons trained in traditional animation who have been coping with problems like this all along.

The great possibilities—and current limitations—of the present state of movement in computer animation were shown by an Omnibus-created TV commercial that Kleiser ran on a VCR in the Studio 8 conference room. It was a 60-second spot for a well-known brand of fruit-flavored soft drink which, at that time, had not yet been broadcast. From start to finish, the continuity consisted of constant, active, fluid motion. Robots with a humanoid appearance danced about, simultaneously a part of and product of some kind of assembly line. They quaffed frequently from cans of the soft drink, which energized them into more inventive, compelling motion. The robots had their own personalities, deriving from their shapes, but more distinctively defined—some tall and skinny, others shorter and squat. In fact, they had more individuality than the "grin chorus" of live actors who joined the action in the last few seconds. The latter were the standard mix of young-old, thin-fat, black-white, square-cool types who are shown getting a good clean boot out of the product in TV spots of this kind.

All in all, it was an amusing and brilliant piece of work. Kleiser described this as characteristic of the current phase of computer animation. The emphasis is on giving a human-like personality to non-human representations. The same tactic was employed by Disney when child-like cute squirrels and the Seven Dwarfs were given personalities which would have been less believable if Disney's artists had attempted to draw actual children. Kleiser says that it will be a long time before computer imaging will be able to create a credible imitation of an actual person. He is not sure that audiences would want it. Randy Rudd seems somewhat more optimistic. He notes that Robert Abel has produced a character referred to as the sexy robot, a Marilyn Monroe caricature. After all, fantasy in the onlooker's mind is the final product of illusion. Bystanders look longingly both at shopwindow models, obviously made of plaster, dressed in bathing suits and at photographs of lusciously live models wearing similar bathing suits on travel posters. Meanwhile, Abel and others develop software for the analysis and representation of human motion.

Now, Brothers and Sisters, We Will Read from Chapter 11

Making commercials for television is an expensive, highly competitive, uncertain business. Using computers to make commercials for television is all of the above. It is also more risky because it is necessary to support highly specialized creative people and expensive computers, rather than hiring camera talent by the day.

The going rate for computer images is, according to Randy Rudd, $3500 to $10,000 per second. The lower figure is sufficient for a relatively simple concept for which images are created at the lower level of definition acceptable on TV. This adds up to $80,000 to $100,000 for a 30-second spot. (The price for a commercial of equivalent quality using live action or traditional animation is in the same general range.) The higher figure is about right for a sequence in a feature film, which generally involves a "higher concept" and requires much higher, 3000-line resolution. An average spot requires six to eight weeks of work. A more complex one, like the soft-drink commercial just described, may take six months.

The firms that compete in this market are typically small, started by creator/entrepreneurs, generally under-capitalized, and inclined to turn pale and develop the croup during periods of low cash flow. An observer of similar companies engaged in a different kind of creativity in Silicon Valley has said that "Sooner or later, they find that the psalm of the day is Chapter 11." He was referring to the chapter of the bankruptcy code, much used for reorganizations which fall short of outright collapse or wrongdoing. This tendency has afflicted computer imaging. Jeff Kleiser's firm didn't make it.

Now that Digital Productions has been absorbed by Omnibus, the word out on the street is that Gary Demos is thinking of starting over again with a new firm of his own.

Omnibus appears to be an exception. It was started by a Toronto businessman named John C. Pennie, is listed on the Toronto stock market and is run like a regular business. There are operations in New York and Toronto as well as on the West Coast. Its number of employees and annual revenues are five or six times larger than that of any of its competitors. Jeff Kleiser is glad that he can draw upon the financial resources and equipment of Omnibus. He looks toward the creation of a network that could make it possible to run off a job on a supercomputer in Canada or at any of several sites in the United States. "Just place the work wherever they have some excess capacity, and then get back all the video direct, by satellite."

At the same time, Kleiser is acutely aware of the drawbacks of high overhead. Kleiser points out that a new entrant with the right experience and red-hot ideas can start for about $500,000. This buys a high-end workstation with full-bore graphics capabilities and a suite of software like Wavefront's Preview. Once a concept and the actual job are developed and finalized on the workstation, the new person on the block could buy time on a supercomputer and deliver the product, with high quality, quick turnaround, and modest cost.

While the entreprenerurs and creative artists of computer imaging consider these possibilities of the future, they are enthusiastic about the present. As Randy Rudd says, "It took films 30 years or so to get from the hand-cranked stage to sound movies and color. Computer simulation has come the same distance in less than 10 years. We are getting out of special effects and onto a much broader stage. Software is improving all the time, making it possible to get the same results with fewer polygons. But the most promising area for improvement is in CPUs. We really need the memory and computational power which supercomputers provide."

Advanced computer animation is not just a North American phenomenon. Seibu Promotion Network Company in Japan uses Cray equipment at the Mitsubishi Research Institute to develop products similar to those now standard on American TV, including animated lead-ins to news programs. Seibu artists also created an ethereal, glowing representation of a Buddhist mandala for Agama, a publication company. A mandala is both an object used to focus consciousness during meditation and a visual representation of a Buddhist worldview. Mandalas and rock videos are examples of a new language of images, a language that seems likely to grow richer in vocabularly and creative depth very rapidly.

The *America's* Cup: "How Much High Technology is Enough?"

Yacht design is an art of reluctant compromise, anxiously arrived at. The sea and winds are infinitely variable, while a boat design is perilously finite. Sails have been an arena for rapid technological advance, involving materials as well as aerodynamics, relying increasingly on computations. High-performance sails for world-class racing yachts are expensive and prone to lose an optimum shape in stiff winds, but sails can be changed. They only cost money. The syndicates of rich men (now more likely to be skilled men backed by rich corporations) that enter 12-meter yachts in *America's* Cup competition have money, although as in other competitions there rarely seems to be enough.

But the boats? A yacht is made, launched, and there it is, like a racehorse. It is possible (and indeed extremely necessary) to train crews exhaustively and fine-tune the rigging. An inch may be shaved off here or there, the distribution of weight may be changed, or the shape of keels or rudders may be adjusted. The basic design, once settled, is however a fixed investment. Not a trivial investment. The total cost of a single hull—including design costs, tests in a model basin (the marine equivalent of a wind tunnel) and computer time—is measured in the multiple millions of dollars. Several of the syndicates competing for the *America's* Cup in 1986-87 built and tested two or three different hulls.

Versatility is desirable, but not easily achieved. A design which does very well in light airs may be left behind in a 30-knot wind, and vice-versa. Both conditions may be encountered during the series of races sailed in a single competition. Rules governing 12-meter yachts add to the problem. A complicated formula requires

Heiner Meldner, a member of the design team for the *America's* Cup challenger *USA,* discusses conventional designs for 12-meter yachts. (*Lawrence Livermore National Laboratory.*)

that an attempt to gain in one characteristic (larger sail area, for example) must be compensated for by giving up something else.

Ironically, 12-meter yachts are not the fastest on the seas. Basic specifications governing hull length (especially on the waterline), weight, and other characteristics limit speeds to around 8.5 knots. Planing hulls (which, in effect, fly over the surface of the water instead of plowing through it) may be twice as speedy. Thus the

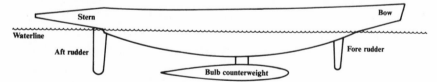

Schematic Drawing of Hull Design of *America's* **Cup Challenger** *USA.* A side view drawing of the *USA* shows its radical underwater elements: A long, thin rudder at each end of the boat and a bulb counterweight in place of the standard keel. The design separates and optimizes the two functions of a normal keel—boat stability and retarding sideways slip. (*Lawrence Livermore National Laboratory.*)

technological challenge is unusual. A designer is not seeking absolutes, but sufficient excellence within closely-defined constraints. Speed is only a means to the end of getting across the finish line before an opponent. Designers perform prodigies of effort to achieve improvements of one or two per cent—or even less.

The 1986-87 *America's* Cup competition, sailed in the unpredictable waters off Fremantle, Western Australia, demonstrated that intensive use of high-performance computers is essential in order to attain the narrow margins of hull speed which, combined with skilled helmsmanship and a first-class crew, mean success. The two American yachts which reached the quarterfinals of the challenge competition, *Stars and Stripes* from San Diego and *USA* from San Francisco, both made extensive use of supercomputers in developing hull designs. The San Francisco syndicate experimented briefly with an evolutionary design but chose to take a radical design to Australia. The San Diego entry, essentially evolutionary, dominated the later stages of the competition. *Stars and Stripes* decisively defeated *USA*, a strong New Zealand entry, and *Kookaburra II*, the yacht chosen to defend for Australia. The cup was returned to the United States.

In 1983, the Australians became the first to wrest the cup from American sailors. They possessed many strengths, including a skilfully-created aura of technological mystery around the winglet keel design which contributed to their victory. In 1986-87, virtually all the boats competing from seven countries used variations on the winglet keel—including *Stars and Stripes*.

USA was an exception. One of the principal designers of this radical entry was Heiner Meldner, a physicist at Lawrence Livermore National Laboratory. Meldner first became interested in sailing and the application of computers to yachting in the 1970's, when he taught at the University of California at San Diego.

When preparations began for the 1986-87 challenge, Meldner signed on to support the Golden Gate Challenge syndicate, sponsored by the St. Francis Yacht Club in San Francisco. He took leaves of absence from his regular work to concentrate on developing a new design. Other U.S. entries, including the San Diego syndicate, enlisted specialists in computations and fluid dynamics. Both the San Francisco and San Diego design teams ran their codes on CRAY X-MP's, utilizing facilities donated by Cray Research, which provided support valued at $1.4 million to the San Francisco syndicate.

The San Francisco group asked radical questions. They asked themselves, "What does a keel do?" which is like a car designer asking what wheels do. It turns out that a keel does several things. It serves as a counterweight, balancing the boat against the pressures exerted against the mast by the sails. The keel also resists lateral forces, especially important when sailing into the wind. The design of the keel affects maneuverability and stability and so has an important influence on performance during the complicated courses which must be sailed during a race.

Meldner and his associates decided to take a look at what happened if these functions were separated. Their large-scale simulations used 100 points in each dimension, amounting to roughly one cell for each six square inches of hull. This may seem a coarse mesh, but it ends up with one million points to describe the geometry of a single proposed hull shape. The addition of other factors, including velocity, boundary layer conditions, air-water and water-hull relationships, and the effects of heeling over, results in about 100 million calculations. In order to obtain reasonably accurate time-dependent Navier-Stokes calculations, each of these must be updated, or time-stepped, 1000 times. Many different possible hullforms were simulated in this way, adding up to a lot of computer time.

The keel proper was reduced to a thin blade ending in a heavy bulb or torpedo, serving primarily as a counterweight. Fishes do not need keels, but most have fins fore and aft to aid in steering and stability. The San Francisco group adopted the same approach. A steerable fin forward would be used in conjunction with the rudder in the rear (in effect another fin) to provide lateral stability as well as excellent maneuverability. Experts from Livermore donated their time to determine the best way to reduce drag around the keel and fins. In the calculations, performance was optimized for strong winds. In addition, the steerable fins could widen the range of circumstances in which the boat would sail well.

This unconventional hull was built and launched in time for hurried testing in San Francisco Bay before being christened *USA* and shipped to Australia. Meldner commented at that time that it would take a while before everyone got the hang of it; they would lose some races during the initial rounds of races among the challengers, but *USA* would make the quarterfinals. There was polite skepticism among knowledgeable people in the Bay Area. Such a specific prediction about untried technology could hardly turn out to be correct.

Meldner was right. *USA* lost races because of equipment failures, crew errors, and other problems arising from limited preparation, a thin budget, and a staff smaller than many other international entries. It also won races, including some crucial ones, and it ended up one of the four best boats among the challengers, along with *Stars and Stripes*.

At the least, *USA* demonstrated, with considerable success, an alternative to accepted 12-meter designs. It will be interesting to see whether future competitors (reportedly to include West Germany and Japan) will remain with the main stream or continue along the path pioneered by Meldner and his colleagues' *USA* design.

So far, the San Diego syndicate has revealed few details about their winning hull design. Glimpses suggest a somewhat flattened, turtle-shaped bulb keel with triangular winglets on the aft extremities of the bulb. During the later races of the 1986-87 challenge, *Stars and Stripes* also made use of another current development in fluid dynamics—"riblets," which are actually very fine scorings in the surface of plastic sheeting fixed to the hull. These tiny channels, now also being applied to experimental airfoil designs, reduce drag. The margin gained by this innovation may be only a tenth of a knot or less, but that may be sufficient. The riblets, also, are the product of extensive computational simulation. Two predictions can be made, even now, about the next competition for the *America's* Cup: a great deal of money will be spent, and a substantial part of that will be devoted to exhaustive computations.

Computer Chess: General-Purpose Supercomputers versus Chess Machines

Very soon after the first computers appeared, people began to wonder about using computers to play chess. After all, chess has specific rules and operates within a strictly bounded universe of its own. To an onlooker, at least, chess seems totally logical. These circumstances seem perfectly suited to computers. Some early enthusiasts foresaw an early chess victory by machine over man. It was proven long ago that reasonably well-prepared machines can defeat beginners and even middle-level players at chess. In challenges between highly ranked players and computers, however, the human being has the advantage, and there is no sign that this will change soon.

Nevertheless, an almost equally fascinating question remains: Whose chess-playing computer is best? This continues to fascinate computer specialists who take part in regional, national, and international competitions. Ordinary chess players watch with varying degrees of admiration and apprehension.

The would-be competitor at computer chess must make several choices. Is it better to use a general-purpose computer, for which only the program is chess-specific, or a computer designed specifically to play chess? Are there advantages in using a very powerful computer, even a supercomputer, as opposed to a more conventional machine? Does parallel processing help, or does it result in unproductive additional complication?

Thus far, these questions cannot be answered absolutely. In recent competitions, wins have alternated between general-purpose machines and special-purpose computers. HITECH, a special-purpose machine developed at Carnegie-Mellon University, defeated Cray Blitz, which runs on a CRAY X-MP/48, at the North American Computer Chess Championship matches in October 1985. Cray Blitz won, however, at the World Computer Chess Championship at Cologne in June 1986, retaining the international crown it won in 1983.

Competition at Cologne was evenly matched. Four teams (out of 22 entrants) tied for first place in terms of direct results. Cray Blitz won because it came out one point ahead on secondary scoring, which is based upon the standing of other entrants that each of the four tied teams had played during the match. It seems clear that a well-developed chess program run on a powerful general-purpose machine can at least hold its own against the best competition. It is equally evident that a well-developed program run on a specially designed machine with much less computing power

Harry Nelson, one of the members of the Cray Blitz computer chess team, holds the international computer chess championship trophy while standing in front of a cousin of the CRAY X-MP used in the 1986 competition at Cologne, West Germany. (*Lawrence Livermore National Laboratory.*)

(and costing much less than a supercomputer) can compete successfully at the same level.

Those who worry about humankind being taken over by computers will be reassured (for a while at least) to know that the machines competing at Cologne were not simply turned on and left alone gossiping with one another to play each round while their owners went out for a pilsner. Chess-playing computers are usually attended by teams consisting of chess experts, computer specialists, or people who are some of each. They inform their machine of its opponent's last move and watch for defects in the program. (International rules permit program changes between rounds of play but not in the middle of a game. The Cray Blitz team made such a change after a disappointing showing in the early rounds at Cologne.)

The computer itself need not be present. The X-MP used by the Cray Blitz team was the ultimate absentee chess-player, remaining at a Cray Research facility in Mendota Heights, Minnesota. Opponents' moves were typed in on a keyboard in Cologne by team member Harry Nelson. The message travelled via Sweden and Canada to a terminal in Birmingham, Alabama; team member Robert Hyatt then forwarded the information to Minnesota. The machine chose the next move and the cycle was repeated.

Whatever the hardware, programs are the heart of computer chess. A chess program has two principal parts. It needs a data base consisting of the vast compilation of openings and variations (known as the book) which all skilled chess players carry around in their heads. It also includes a capability to evaluate alternatives and make decisions. A flat-footed move-by-move evaluation/decision cycle gets nowhere in championship chess. The program must look ahead, considering the implications of each alternative move for a number of cycles into the future of the game. It must examine the possible arrangements of pieces on the board for each of the alternative futures. The Cray Blitz program is able to to look ahead for about eight steps and consider 100,000 alternative boards each second. HITECH is capable of a similar look-ahead and can contemplate 175,000 hypothetical boards each second.

HITECH accomplishes this through a specialized arrangement of modest hardware. This consists of a Sun workstation, essentially a powerful microcomputer, and an arrangement of 64 VLSI chips, one for each square of the board. Chips focus upon possible moves for the squares under their supervision but also evaluate all other squares. An umpire device chooses among the alternatives examined simultaneously by the 64 chips. A special module searches the future alternatives. This ingenious system, and HITECH's record in competition, persuaded an author in *Scientific American* to state that HITECH appeared to be the world's strongest chess-playing computer, and would be unstoppable at Cologne. Perhaps next time, but not quite yet.

Computer chess is not a casual recreation. Hyatt, a strong chess player himself, began the Cray Blitz program in 1976 while a student at the University of Southern Mississippi. He works with Albert Gower, a specialist in the opening moves of chess, and Nelson, a senior computer programmer at the Lawrence Livermore National Laboratory who started contributing to the program in 1980. Hyatt, who is working on a doctorate in artificial intelligence, is already considering the possibilities of the much faster Crays that can be expected before long.

Harry Nelson believes that the future of computer chess lies in multiprocessing or large-scale parallel processing. He points out that the first, second, and fourth-place teams at Cologne used multiprocessor or parallel machines.

New Creative Uses for Supercomputers—What Next?

What other expressions of human creativity and competitiveness will make use of high-performance computations? After all, computer chess has been around a long time, yachtsmen have been tinkering with computers for about 15 years, and serious computer animation is approaching its tenth birthday. It is not easy to predict specific fields, but it is reasonable to assume that many young people are now doing what Jeff Kleiser was doing at college in the late 1970s— poking around, finding out new ways to do things, getting fresh ideas, and then perhaps trading software for computer time. The results may not necessarily be of practical use, and it may not make anyone much money, but it could add surprise and pleasure to a lot of lives.

Larry Smarr, himself a scientist and now head of the NSF-supported center at the University of Illinois, has anticipated a future of this kind. He has called upon graphic artists and other creative people—who may not have much supercomputer experience—to join in the explorations at his center. Staff at the SDSC have discussed the potential for research programs, involving the possible use of supercomputers, with Harold Cohen of the University of California, San Diego art department. Programs in computer music as well as the visual arts are being examined. The next dramatic development in the application of supercomputers to the creative arts may take place in a formal academic setting. It is at least equally likely to happen in the corner of a rented loft, where a young person sitting at a borrowed workstation or a kludged-up machine tries out a new idea that just might possibly make him or her rich and famous.

CHAPTER 10 ⎯⎯⎯⎯⎯⎯⎯⎯⎯

Tomorrow's Revolution—
Accessibility:
Software, Workstations,
Networks, and Storage

Better software, more powerful workstations, and improved communications are raising the productivity of supercomputers and making them easier to use. During the next few years, as the supercomputer era becomes more mature, ease of access can be expected to accelerate, as steps are taken to reduce the barriers between different software, workstations become even more capable, the current tangle of networks is straightened out, and software productivity is enhanced.

Supercomputing began as a labor-intensive industry, like most other small-scale industries, and it remained that way for the first few decades. Operating and using supercomputing systems required the services of craftsmen—or, to avoid any injured pride of status, engineers and scientists who functioned like craftsmen. In particular, efficient use of a supercomputer required specialists who could produce optimal software for each application—often on what amounted to a custom basis.

Many scientists who used supercomputers ended up producing special software—writing their own code, as the jargon puts it. As in the old guilds of craftsmen, a long, arduous apprenticeship could be expected. Generally, this was accepted as part of the price for being at the frontiers of science. (If you choose to fly around in open-cockpit biplanes, you have to put up with the breeze.) As noted in Chapter Three, this has been a major barrier, causing many scientists and engineers to be reluctant to use supercomputers.

With this in mind, supercomputer manufacturers and specialists in high-performance computing are now concentrating their efforts upon making supercomputer resources more accessible. Software is the most important; competition from Japanese manufacturers is making sure that American makers pay attention. Rapid development in workstations (due to specialized manufacturers, not supercomputer companies) is adding greatly to the usefulness of high-performance computers. Networks and mass storage facilities are not advancing quite as fast as workstations but should improve greatly in the next few years. The benefits of these developments for supercomputer users will be far-reaching.

Software: Productivity, Transparency, and Interoperability

The main concerns of software developers are productivity, performance, transparency, interoperability, and interactivity. Interactivity involves software as well as hardware, and its most spectacular benefits involve output in the form of graphics. It is discussed a little later in the section on workstations.

In the early years, supercomputer manufacturers concentrated upon delivering hardware. Their software specialists had a great deal of ground to cover. Much of the work, especially on applications codes, was done by the the Programmers' Guild chapters at the national laboratories and other specialized users. The stock of standard programs adapted to supercomputers grew steadily, but a researcher with a new problem pretty much had to start from scratch and write code as best he or she could. Then, in the mid-1980s, the Japanese appeared in the market. In most respects, software development is one field in which American specialists maintain a substantial lead over their Japanese colleagues. For supercomputing, however, Japanese manufacturers, particularly

Fujitsu, offered software tools that made it much easier to adapt a code to supercomputers and maximize a program's efficiency. Now all manufacturers are emphasizing software tools that raise productivity and simplify access.

Transparency implies that a customer sitting at a workstation in an office (or, at the least, at the home campus) can input data for analysis by a supercomputer in the same way as a routine problem that would be processed within the workstation using its own resources. The system would route the project to the appropriate processors (which would not necessarily always be supercomputers), complete the solution, and then display the results upon the monitor. The user would not be aware of the specific machinery, circuits, and software that intervened to do this particular computation, and need not be concerned about it. Next, the user might make a telephone call to a colleague in England, again not knowing or caring how the conversation was routed and whether part of it went over microwave circuits or via an undersea cable. Those who seek transparency hope to offer a similar happy indifference to remote users of computers.

This goal—or ideal—goes beyond time-sharing, which was introduced for supercomputers in the 1960s. Time-sharing permits dozens or even hundreds of customers to use the same CPU simultaneously. A program is not necessarily equally busy all the time; there are pauses, roughly like the pauses in a piece of music or silences in a conversation. The operating system manages the multiple calculations so that all move forward, the CPU is used continuously, and users (wherever they may be) are not conscious of delays or, at the worst, are not delayed for significant periods.

In time-sharing the user must do a certain amount of work. It is necessary to input the correct commands to access a particular CPU. Often, this involves a series of commands, like checking in at a series of desks before being cleared to board an airline flight. If a particular user's program will not run on a specific machine, he must change the program or try somewhere else. Proponents of transparency wish to eliminate these barriers. The NSF-supported supercomputer centers, AT&T's Bell Laboratories, NASA research centers, and many other projects, especially at universities, are working vigorously toward this objective. Some computer specialists express reservations. In the realm of supercomputers, performance, the *raison d'être* of supercomputing, could easily be lost if transparency were to be taken as a goal rather than a means.

As in other crafts, each supercomputer specialist, or chapter of the guild, is inclined to favor a particular way of doing things. Traditionally, manufacturers of workstations, communications devices, and other components as well as supercomputers themselves have promoted their own operating system. Each has been incompatible with the machines of other manufacturers. Each claims that they do this because their system is best, but they also hope to obtain and protect a share of the market.

Efforts to correct this situation concentrate upon two strategies. The first is interoperability or compatibility. This emphasizes software that will permit front-end minicomputers and other intermediary equipment to translate information between one specific program and another. Such intermediary machines would act like simultaneous interpreters at the United Nations, passing data back and forth regardless of the pronunciation, grammar, and vocabulary of one language or another. Thus, a user might be able to use a variety of programs, whatever the operating system of a particular CPU. The process of interpretation may slow things down, but this can be tolerable if the alternative is the much more protracted task of writing or adapting software.

The second strategy is universality. This would establish a standard that would govern the entire traffic from workstation to central processing unit and back again—an Esperanto for scientific computing. Manufacturers and users alike recognize the importance of interoperability. There is less unanimity about the feasibility or desirability of a uniform standard, and differences as to what the standard should be. (The skeptics point out that Esperanto has been reduced to a hobby for eccentrics, while English, despite its lack of consistency and miserable spelling, is the closest approximation to a global language.)

UNIX is the most widely-advocated candidate. It was developed at AT&T Bell Laboratories and is used widely for research and teaching at universities. UNIX itself is not uniform. Variations and elaborations have been developed at the University of California at Berkeley and other universities and by computer manufacturers and software firms. Commercial software firms have designed proprietary versions for personal computers and other specialized applications.

The differences among supporters and opponents of UNIX are highly technical and very emotional. Some say that the advantages of UNIX are evident and should be obvious to anyone who is not deliberately prejudiced. Others dismiss UNIX as the creation of computer theorists who don't really know about making a real system work at peak capacity and ignore the importance of a secure system. Some strengths of UNIX are, however, generally recognized, including convenient input and output and the ability of different programs to communicate among themselves.

Increasingly, however, the arguments are leaving the coffee tables at conferences of computer scientists and systems managers and are entering the machine rooms. Manufacturers of CPUs are adding their substantial weight to the balance. Cray Research has adopted UNICOS, a variant of UNIX (*UNI*x plus *C*ray *O*perating *S*ystem, the earlier basic Cray system) for the CRAY-2. UNICOS is also being used on X-MP systems at AT&T Bell Laboratories, Apple Computer and the University of California at Berkeley. UNIX guests have been added to the main CTSS operating systems at the National Magnetic Fusion Energy Computer Center at Livermore and the NSF-supported centers at San Diego and the University of Illinois.

The first delivery of the ETA-10, for initial trials in an operating setting, was made to Florida State University in December, 1986. When software is fully operable, it will offer a dual-capability environment (the word preferred by ETA representatives): a UNIX variant and another that will permit users of the Cyber 205 (produced by ETA's parent corporation, Control Data) to adapt their codes to the ETA-10 with minimum pain. So far, IBM is staying with its proprietary operating systems, and the Japanese are using either their own or IBM's operating systems.

When will UNIX-based transparent systems be available? Nils-Peter Nelson of Bell Labs thinks it will take a couple of years. Other researchers quote similar periods of time. The critics are more skeptical, stressing the serious difficulties involved in managing a highly distributed system—one involving many computers of various sizes as well as large numbers of users. Those skeptical about UNIX do not offer alternatives; they anticipate what might be termed the "English outcome:" a continuation of the status quo, ameliorated by improvements in translator systems that will facilitate interoperability.

The signpost on the road leading toward more productive applications software for supercomputers reads "FORTRAN." It is not clear whether the pointer on the signpost aims only toward the past or also includes the future. This is not a new issue— FORTRAN (originally an acronym for "Formula Translator") has been old enough to vote for a long time, one of the most elderly computer languages still in active use. (COBOL, used primarily for business-related programs, is one of the others.)

There is no question about the importance of FORTRAN. It was introduced in 1957 and was one of the first "high-level languages." This software permitted programmers to write in a semi-human language. Many of the rules are arbitrary, and the vocabulary is limited, often frustrating, but FORTRAN is far easier than machine language, or machine codes, required to communicate with a processing unit on its own terms. It is the principal language for scientific work on computers, especially for large-scale, mathematics-intensive tasks.

Scientists and computer specialists regard FORTRAN the way a duck hunter thinks about an old water dog. It is ancient, slow, often irritating, stubborn, and sometimes smells bad, but it still brings in the birds. And it would take too much time and trouble to find a new dog, train it, and get it familiar with all the best shooting marshes. Others think we should leave the birds alone and just go fishing.

FORTRAN-based codes for many applications have been under development for 20 years or more. NASTRAN, used by engineers doing structural analysis, and the various generations of SPICE, used for circuit design, are among the most familiar examples. These programs are run on many levels of computers, not only on supercomputers. Changes, additions, and improvements have accumulated over the years. They can be compared to WordStar (with which most of this book is being written)—not the simplest or most modern word processing system for PCs, sometimes frustrating and abritrary, but a hard habit to break. The English analogy is also applied to FORTRAN. Its richness makes up for a lack of elegance.

In recent years, attention has focused upon new software tools: compilers, optimizers and vectorizers which make it easier to obtain efficient performance from programs written in FORTRAN. Present-day supercomputers work best when maximum use is made of their high vector speed. These new tools make it easier to identify portions of a program that are running slowly because of inadequate vectorization; the most versatile utilities (notably one offered by Amdahl/Fujitsu) suggest corrections.

As in so many other issues in computing, there is some agreement that something needs to be done but much less unanimity about tactics. Critics of present supercomputer software say that FORTRAN should be left to doze by the fire while developers chart new ways to productivity. Others say that the need for practical, productive software is so pressing and immediate that it is better to build upon existing foundations.

In any event, the transition from single processors to multiple and parallel processors that is already under way (see Chapter Eleven) may require far-ranging changes in operating systems and other software. (Companies, including minisupercomputer makers, whose products have several processors, nevertheless emphasize that their software utilities make it possible to run FORTRAN programs efficiently.)

Workstations: One Picture Is Worth Ten Million Digits

Rapid improvements in power at the other end of the line—workstations—are among the most impressive and important developments in supercomputer systems. Personal computers and for that matter old-fashioned dumb terminals can be used to access supercomputer systems. Indeed, better accessibility through available, inexpensive equipment is one of the objectives of current efforts to improve access. Supercomputer centers and individual users make extensive use of both the major variants of personal computers: the IBM PC, its numerous cousins and natural children, and PC's based upon the technology initially elaborated by Xerox's Palo Alto Research Center, notably the Apple Macintosh.

The rise of the PC has been paralleled by the development of compact, extremely powerful workstations, intended primarily for engineering, computer assisted design (CAD), and other work requiring high-quality graphics. These machines make use of the advances in microprocessors, storage media, and software that have contributed to the growth of the PC—but at much higher levels of performance. Sun, Apollo, and Silicon Graphics' IRIS workstations are among the best known of the many entries that compete energetically. All three are in use at the SDSC. DEC and IBM are also aiming at this market, which includes stand-alone applications and networking with more conventional computers as well as use with supercomputers. The race to improve performance, add enticing new options, and reduce prices is intense. Prices range from $6000 or $7000 to $100,000. The deals are getting better all the time as competition heats up and the cost per unit of output plummets steadily.

Workstations offer a versatile solution to one of the most vexatious problems created by supercomputers. What do you do with all that output? How do you digest a 6-foot stack of printout, containing nothing but numbers? The answer: translate the numbers into shapes and colors. Supercomputers are not very good at doing that all by themselves. Workstations that include special graphics co-processors and graphics software can summarize thousands of pages of output in displays of flow-lines, color-coded depictions of heat or pressure, and indications of stress, flexing, and imminent shattering. Highpowered workstations are an essential tool of animation artists, who use them for most of the work involved in designing, lighting, coloring, choreographing and applying texture to an image before a computer adds movement and turns out the final image on videotape or film. Researchers in fields as widely separated as molecular dynamics and violent, localized storms use essentially the same techniques to produce visible simulations of their subjects.

The objective of transparency is made much more achievable by taking full advantage of the growing capabilities of the newer generations of workstations. The grail now being sought by many searchers is full real-time interactivity—accompanied by full transparency. The user sets up a simulation with certain assumptions of temperature, shape, velocity, and so on. The computer does its calculations, which are translated into graphics at the workstation. Then the user finds that the initial assumptions do not provide the results sought. He or she may want to investigate in more detail a selected area of the graphics display where interesting and unexpected things are happening. Moving a mouse or changing a few numbers alters the display to zoom in on the preferred detail.

This goal has not yet been reached. It is being approached by experimenters at NASA and elsewhere, however, and significant progress is being made. Meanwhile, high-performance graphics workstations are becoming an indispensable part of supercomputing systems and are making enormous contributions to the overall capability and usefulness of entire systems.

Networks: Make Enough Roads, Decide Which Side to Drive On

Everyone knows how to communicate quickly with someone else, but how you do it depends a lot on where you are. In China, in small towns in Thailand, and in most of the rest of the world, you go to the post office and send a telegram or book a telephone call and settle down to wait for it to be set up. In India, you pray, attempt to make the telephone work, curse, and send a runner. In Japan, North America, and Western Europe (even in France now) you dial a few numbers, or a lot of numbers, and get through on the telephone.

The apparent simplicity of these familiar procedures—which, incidentally, are remarkably transparent to the user when they work right—obscures the difficulty of moving large quantitites of information reliably through space or over conduits of metal or glass fiber. Americans had a small taste of these complexities when the dissolution of the Bell system revealed some of the seams.

It is much more difficult to accommodate the enormous input and output capacity of a supercomputer. There are two alternatives. The entire capacity of a circuit (which may accomodate thousands or tens of thousands of ordinary voice messages) may be reserved. Or the data is communicated at a rate much slower than it is processed by the computer, like a powerful pump on a fire engine attempting to deliver water through a straw. As noted in Chapter Two, the protocols (software managing the flow of messages) are as critical as the capacity of the circuits. At a minimum, everyone on the network must be using the same or compatible protocols. Some experts doubt that protocols now in use are sufficient to use efficiently the full capacity of circuits with very high band-widths.

Many aspects of modern supercomputer technology originated in defense-related programs, and networking is no exception. In 1969, the U.S. Department of Defense's venture-capital window, the Defense Advanced Research Projects Agency (DARPA), inaugurated a research and development project called ARPANET. The objective was to establish dedicated, reliable communications links among computer users in academic, industrial, and government research laboratories. The circuits were to have a band-width of 56 kilobits (56,000 bits) per second, which in those days seemed an entirely adequate fire hose. ARPANET also developed improved network protocols. In 1981, a protocol named TCP/IP was introduced. This protocol became widely used in the academic community.

In 1969, the state of networking in the United States was comparable to the U.S. highway network in the early 1920s. There weren't many good roads, driving was slow and often uncertain, and the roads didn't always lead where people wanted them to go. At least one key point was settled. Napoleon decided that his armies would go along the right side of the road. Most Europeans, and nearly all the rest of the world, decided that was a good idea. (The prominent holdouts were England, which was spared the arrival of the Napoleonic forces, and Sweden, which took one of Napoleon's marshals, Bernadotte, as king but delayed switching to the right side of the road until a few years ago.) For computer networks, the rules of the road have not been resolved. TCP/IP intended to make sure that the roadway could serve cities and towns of all kinds and sizes, regardless of the political affiliation of the mayors. It also made it possible to create a network of networks. ARPANET underscored another point. Scientists communicate a lot, and if they rely upon computers they like to use them as means of communication. ARPANET did not always work very well as a means to move large blocks of data, but it did a good job as a mechanism for information sharing.

During the 1970s, other networks—using other protocols—were established. Greater emphasis was placed upon sharing time on remote computers in order to do heavyweight computations. MFENET, based upon the Department of Energy's National Magnetic Fusion Energy Computer Center, developed a national and eventually international network emphasizing satellite communications at 112 and 56 kilobits per second. Boeing Computer Services and other companies established their own networks. BITNET provided an economical, easily used network for computer-assisted communications among scholars at universities spread all over North America. By the end of 1985, BITNET had expanded to include over 175 institutions, serving more than 600 computers. It relies primarily upon 9.6 kilobit per second leased lines.

Meanwhile, the appetite—and output—of supercomputers was growing steadily. A 9.6 kilobit line might be all right for electronic mail, but for supercomputers it looks like a very constricted garden hose. The 56-kilobit circuits pioneered by DARPA and used by the MFENET were reliable and substantial but began to look a little small.

In 1984 and 1985, when the NSF found itself committed to large-scale support of improved supercomputer utilization in the United States, it was recognized that network development must be a central part of the overall strategy. Two of the new NSF-supported centers, at San Diego and Princeton, placed special emphasis on networking. San Diego, which had made a basic decision to stick to systems that had proven themselves, emphasized 56-kilobit circuits and the MFENET protocols. The von Neumann center at Princeton decided upon the band-width that is now becoming the mid-term ideal for supercomputer networks. This is the T1 circuit, theoretically capable of transferring 1.544 *million* bits per second. The von Neumann network, which expects to provide T1 circuits to most of the members of its consortium, became operational in summer, 1986.

Other networks, most of them local or regional, are planned or in various stages of creation. These include the Merit Computer Network, linking campuses in Michigan; a similar network in Georgia; NYSERNet in New York State; SURANET, servicing universities in the Southeastern United States; and the Bay Area network in Northern California. Some, like NYSERNet and portions of the

Bay Area network, are aiming at the T1 standard. Most will be, in effect, like commuter airlines, providing local services at relatively low speeds and feeding into the main trunk channels.

As of now, the highest capacity coast-to-coast circuits servicing scientific and engineering users are 100 kilobit channels operated by MFE, the NSF, the SDSC, and ARPA. TCP/IP appears to be gaining ground, but protocol issues remain unresolved. As noted in Chapter Twelve, the situation is worse in Europe. There is a wide-reaching effort to develop protocols which meet criteria defined by the International Standards Organization (ISO—the criteria themselves are known, perversely, as OSI, for Open Systems Interconnect). In the United States, and especially in Europe, the ISO's OSI is seen as the ultimate solution, but its implementations remains to be elaborated and agreed upon. Meanwhile, it is at times as if a ticket for travel from Tallahassee to Tacoma was not honored beyond the first major airline hub at Atlanta.

The NSF is among those seeking solutions. It is working toward the establishment of NSFnet, whose basic resource is a backbone network linking the five NSF-supported supercomputer centers and the National Center for Atmospheric Research in Boulder, Colorado (also supported by the NSF). Initially, it is to operate through 56 kilobit circuits, which in time are to be upgraded to the T1 level and beyond. It will use the TCP/IP protocols at first, with a view to switching to the OSI when that standard becomes a reality. The trunk line is to be interconnected with regional networks and the systems operated by the various NSF-supported centers.

Every air traveller has found himself outside the terminal with no taxis in sight, confronting buses that seem to be headed for every destination but his own. This also afflicts supercomputer networks. What happens when the data arrives at the user's campus or research center. How does it reach the user's workstation?

Some networks, like San Diego's and the system being established by the Houston Area Research Center, provide for user access stations that assure linkage with the network and may be used for pre-processing and other services. That is not quite enough, however, for the researcher who likes to do everything in his or her own office. Many university campuses and other research institutions operate local area networks, typically at nominal capacities of 10 megabits per second, which can tie together a wide range of hardware, including minicomputers, graphics workstations, and PCs. Other installations use higher-capacity circuits for short- or medium-range communication, like the T1 circuit between the National Cancer Institute supercomputer in Frederick, Maryland and the main campus of the National Institutes of Health 30 miles away in Bethesda. Still others depend upon regular telephone wiring (known in the jargon as a twisted pair, which is a physical description of the simplest form of the wiring, not a commentary on marriage) and chunk away at a few thousand bits per second.

It is not impossible to tie all this together, and it is certainly possible to improve it a great deal. The NSF is dedicating substantial resources to the development of improved software and the standardization of protocols. In the short run, the situation will be complicated and occasionally frustrating. The ideal is a national network—more accurately, a hierarchy of interconnected networks—that offers supercomputer users the same versatility and ease of use that are now expected from other networks, such as voice communication and the travel system. Like these other systems, users may have to put up with uncertainty, redundancy, and occasional delays, Costs per unit of service will drop steadily but will never be low enough to offset fully each user's appetite for moving more data over longer distances.

Storage

Adam: "Where are you going to put all that stuff, now that you've bought it?"

Eve: "Oh, there's still some space in the closet."

Adam: "Once it's in there, how will you find it?"

Eve: "I remember exactly where everything is."

This conversation, perhaps the second oldest in human history, illustrates a serious problem for supercomputer systems. What can be done with the enormous output of a supercomputer? For example, the Octopus internal network serving researchers at Lawrence Livermore National Laboratory handles 250,000 files each day. Of these, 8000 are archived (placed in long-term storage), 4000 of which are accessed at some later time. The entire central facility has a capacity of many hundreds of billion bytes.

The vast quantities of data accumulated during seismic exploration for fossil fuels occupy row upon row of tapes shelved within large, closely guarded vaults. At Livermore, valuable Cray time is used each night for data compression (which reduces demand for storagebysqueezingthingstogether) to save space taken up in the long-term files. The users of a supercomputer system—even someone who logs in for a few minutes every month or so—expect that their stored data be on hand for the next calculation, and they expect that it be made available promptly. Typically, files placed in storage are moved ("migrated") at fixed intervals from rapid-access storage systems (usally high-speed disks) to slower means of storage. Some systems (the San Diego center is one) eliminate a file from short-term storage within a stated number of hours unless it is collected by its user or dispatched to slower-access storage.

In practice, most users are not bothered too seriously by delay, but storage remains a headache for systems managers (especially far sighted ones who worry about the much greater volumes of output to be created in due course by the more powerful machines of the future). The accepted practice has been to tuck files away on reels of tape. These objects are awkward to handle, and it takes a fair amount of time to spin the tape through to the location of the desired file. Supercomputer operators are turning to the IBM 3480. This machine handles tape cartridges whose appearance is similar to the videocassettes rented out by an adult movie outlet. Systems managers are also concerned about the fundamental fragility of information stored upon a magnetic medium. The quality of the tape itself and of the magnetic media have been improved greatly, but uncertainties remain about the long-term survival of the information.

Here again, better methods are not too distant—although a real solution for the storage problem may take longer than some of the other issues involved in improved access. The present hope is that optical recording (presumably using laser technology similar to that now used for super high-fidelity compact disks) could provide a satisfactory answer. This technology is developing rapidly and is in experimental usage at many facilities. For widespread usage, however, it remains in the "not-quite-yet" category. NEC has built optical disk storage for supercomputer systems sold in Japan, but—

because of reported quality-control problems—has not offered them with systems sold abroad.

The history of computing is not long, but long enough for certain things to repeat themselves. In the late 1950s, IBM developed an optical mass storage system, code-named "Walnut" within the corporation. It was too early for lasers, so information was coded into plastic strips by another process. Few customers required the vast capacity of the system or could afford the expense. Old hands at Livermore still recall fondly its giant capacity and total reliability. Once encoded, data was immune to magnetic mishaps and essentially beyond the reach of time. Walnut was set aside as magnetic media became the solution of choice.

CHAPTER 11 ───────────────

The Day After Tomorrow:
The Next Generations
of Supercomputer Hardware

The next major stage in the supercomputer era will depend upon substantial technological change. For a decade, super-computer power has increased primarily through higher clock speeds, more efficient chips, larger memories, and efficient vector calculations. They remained single-processor machines like the first computer. These designs are now approaching the limits imposed by the speed of electricity and problems of cooling. Manufacturers are turning to multiple processors: several or very many processors operating on a problem at the same time. This places severe new demands upon software developers.

In 1944, the boys under draft age and ageless mountain men cutting up logs at a camp on the western slopes of the Sierra Nevada relied upon a primitive ancestor of the chain saw. The saw blade was conventional—a somewhat shorter, stiffer version of the familiar two-man cross-cut. It was powered by a massive, cast iron engine, with a single sparkplug and a piston about the size of a wash bucket, which operated at somewhere between 30 and 40 revolutions per

VON NEUMANN ARCHITECTURE

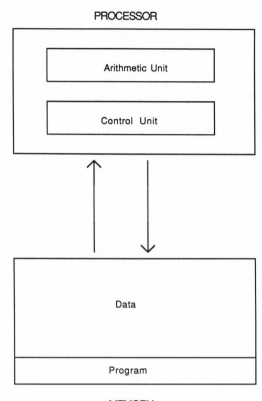

Von Neumann Architecture. (*Richard Freund, SDSC.*)

minute. Keeping it in good humor was almost a full-time job, but it got all the attention it needed because it was all there was.

The principle of the computer, laid down by John von Neumann not long after those logs were being cut up, was not too different from that old one-banger. The central processor is unary, so that the program that tells the dumb metal what to do can keep track of what is going on. It is much easier for the shepherd to count the sheep if all of them pass through the same opening in the fence.

For decades, this did not create insoluble problems. Every year, people found ways to make the metal much smarter and to run the machine at higher and higher speeds. The rapid and enormous improvements in the capacity and density of computer chips accounted for a lot of this. Denser, more efficient, cheaper chips also made it possible to add memory—more stalls in which to lodge the sheep while they were waiting to be counted, more space to store the results of the sheep counting, and more space to store the names, quirks, and medical histories of the sheep.

Now, however, unary processors appear to be approaching their limits. Chapter Two described the limits that are being approached due to the boundaries defined by the laws of physics rather than human inadequacies. As a result, components must be packed in very tightly. The entire machinery of a CRAY-2 could be mistaken for an eccentric custom-designed household refrigerator. If circuits are packed so closely, however, where does the heat go? No matter how clever the design, electrons rushing around create heat—which is, in the most basic sense, a measure of motion. More heat arises when the electrons bump into other things. Sophisticated cooling systems are now being used. Chips made of substances like gallium arsenide generate less heat. Josephson junctions and other exotic devices may reduce the heat generated within the circuits, but it has proven very difficult to make them work. Such measures stretch the limits but involve knotty technological challenges and appear much more costly than silicon- based devices. Optical circuits based upon devices that switch light rather than electricity are also a possibility, but so far seem a distant one. Thus, it appears that the physical limits on a single unary processor will be reached before too long.

Many Hands Make Fast Work

An outsider might point out that multicylinder internal combustion engines have been in use for a century: that old single-cylinder oil-spitter was obsolete even in 1944. Why not do the same for computers? Multiple processors are indeed the solution being explored by manufacturers of supercomputers. Some are doing so conservatively, starting out with relatively small numbers of processsors. Many others, in universities and in industry, are experimenting with parallelism on a much larger scale.

In order to grasp the issues involved in parallel processing, it may be useful to consider a few metaphors. Parallel processing architectures would herd the sheep through a number of gaps simultaneously. A cheering section in a sports stadium can spell out slogans and create pictures if each of several hundred persons is issued a number of large colored cards to be displayed according to a programmed design or sequence. A band of musicians all playing sousaphones while marching during halftime could provide another example. It would be a better parallel if each musician were asked to play the music at any preferred speed and rhythm as long as everyone finished at the same time. It might sound funny, but it sure would produce a lot of music.

Using a number of processors to achieve high performance computing has appealed to many investigators for a long time. In fact, computer designers experimented with this approach before the vector processor became the *de facto* preferred method for achieving extremely high computational speeds. The ILLIAC IV used at NASA's Ames Research Center in the mid-1970s was a multiple processor. It was difficult to program, however, and this approach was set aside when vector-intensive machines reached the market a little later.

In recent years, interest in multiple processors has become intense once again. By the mid-1980s, more than 100 parallel-processing projects were being pursued at universities (including places like Cal Tech and MIT) or under development by industry. Most of the companies are small start-ups spun off from university research. Large companies like Intel and established manufacturers like Floating Point Systems also offer parallel machines. Since 1983, NASA has been using a large parallel machine for image processing at the Space and Earth Sciences Computing Center at the Goddard Space Flight Center in Maryland (see Appendix II, Section 2). Several minisupercomputer designs rely upon parallelism as well as relatively high clock speeds and other features to achieve high capacity.

Multiple processors are already taking a place in the mainstream of supercomputer development. The separate vector pipelines as well as the vectors themselves, characteristic of the present generation of computers are a form of parallelism, although the term is usually reserved for machines that have separate full-scale processors. The CRAY X-MP is available with one, two, or four processors. The CRAY-2 has two or four processors. The ETA-10 will be offered with up to eight central processing units. Regular versions of the upper-end models of IBM's 3090—the 3090-200, 3090-400 and 3090-600—have two, four, and six processing units, respectively. Vector processors are added to give this machine performance at supercomputer levels.

A machine like the X-MP can be used in two modes. It can be treated as if it were several CPUs that happen to be in the same shed and share the same memory. A user's program is allocated to one processor or handed around among the processors. The multiple processors also can be used in an oxen-yoked-together mode, with all devoted to a single problem. Supercomputer managers at facilities as distant in concept and functions as Apple Computer and the San Diego Supercomputer Center use almost identical words to describe these alternatives: For very large problems that require massive quantities of computer time and have very high priority (like calculations of flow efficiency for a new jet aircraft engine) it makes sense to use all processors in parallel. If, however, there are many users with programs of moderate lengths and similar priorities, it makes more sense to stay with the multiple-but-separate processor mode.

According to Robert H. Ewald, a Cray Research vice president, Cray intends to take further steps toward parallelism during the next few years. He anticipates that Cray machines in use in the 1990s will have 32 to 64 processors. Ewald did not say whether the processors in those new designs would share a memory, possess individual memories, or some of each.

Coarse-grained and Fine-grained Systems

Displaying once again the talent of scientists for using familiar words in ways that puzzle the uninitiated, systems that use a relatively small number of full-scale processors (the Cray approach) are called "coarse-grained" systems. A design which utilizes larger numbers of less powerful processors is "fine-grained." The Connection Machine, made by an MIT spinoff in Cambridge, Massachusetts called Thinking Machines Corporation, is very fine-grained indeed. It

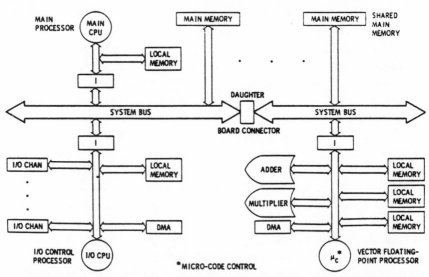

Parallel Processing Architectures—The Cal Tech Mark III. Architectures of parallel processing computers vary widely. The Cal Tech Mark III is a hypercube machine. (*Don Callahan, University of Michigan.*)

consists of 64,000 processors, each processing one bit of information at a time. Such systems typically distribute memory among all these units as well as distributing processing.

The T-series, announced in spring 1986 by Floating Point Systems (FPS), offers options which extend from the coarse to the super-fine. It can be purchased in escalating numbers of identical modules, with totals ranging from a few processors to more than 16,000. FPS reports sales of the T/20 version (at the lower, coarser end of the spectrum) to the Northrop Research and Technology Center and Michigan Technological University. Prices range from less than $500,000 at the lowest end to multiple millions for a large herd of modules.

Another parallel entry, the Butterfly from Bolt, Beranek & Newman, Inc. (BBN), can package configurations extending from four processing units ($40,000) to 32 ($375,000) and on up to 256. In mid-1986, BBN changed to more powerful processing chips and added memory for each of its processors. It reports sales of 63 systems, primarily to universities and other laboratories experimenting with parallel processing.

To return to the sheep counting analogy, the matrix of fences needed to run sheep through 64,000 gaps would be exceedingly complicated. It would be somewhat easier if the counting were done in a multi-storey building, providing a three-dimensional system. In either case, a lot of time would be spent rushing sheep around a complex system, and a lot of heat and other by-products would be generated. This would detract—somewhat, at least, and perhaps a great deal—from the theoretical speed advantage gained by putting the sheep through many openings simultaneously. These disadvantages might be reduced if the geometry of the ramps and design of other features of the building were optimized for sheep counting and the sheep-dogs were drilled carefully.

If the solution is roughed out on a napkin from a takeout taco shop, it appears simple: Four processors give four times the performance, 16 increase it 16 times, 32,000 gives you . . . and so on. In practice, the gains have been less than proportional to the increase in the number of processors. Experiments at Lawrence Livermore National Laboratory and elsewhere have achieved improvements of about 3.7 times from simultaneous use of four processors (at Livermore, on a CRAY X-MP). Refinements in software are steadily improving the gain in efficiency. When the number of processors goes up, however, the proportionate increase in performance sometimes goes down.

The reasons for this are not difficult to understand, but solutions will not be easy to find. Military officers at staff colleges spend a great deal of time at sand tables learning how to avoid obvious mistakes in coordinating an attack, especially an attack that requires several columns to move separately and arrive at predetermined jump-off points at predetermined times. (The troops rarely move along parallel paths, but then information in a multiple-processor system doesn't, either. Parallelism is itself a metaphor). A bad map, a broken down tank, an underestimation of difficult terrain, or just plain mistakes usually foul things up in maneuvers, and always do so in real combat.

One solution is communications-intensive. An American infantry battalion in the field during the Vietnam War could generate more continuing exchanges over field radios and walkie-talkies than the total of telephone conversations among the members of a high school senior class during the weeks before the prom. Another solution is the general staff approach: Allow plenty of time for the unavoidable delays, and hold each column when they reach the objective until all are ready.

These martial examples may appear distant from computers but are nevertheless to the point. A design that coordinates the many processors by constant exchange of messages diverts part of the attention of each processor from manipulating numbers. (As snipers are aware, a lieutenant who is talking into a field telephone or radio mike instead of watching for movement in the underbrush is an easy target.) The result: a decrease in the computing power obtained from each processor, and so a loss in overall capacity. The alternative (or general staff) approach means that some (or perhaps most) processors may complete their job and then sit around sulking while the rest finish up. This also means that results are short of optimum.

The Brain Does It; Why Can't a Machine Do It?

Advocates of parallel processing cite a distinguished example that has performed reliably over the years: the brain. Each neuron has limited capacity and processes information relatively slowly, yet the entire system is linked together so efficiently that its total power remains far beyond the ambition of even the most optimistic computer designer. (Almost beyond the claims of the most enthusiastic supercomputer publicist.) It can be answered that human cultures and the lessons acquired during evolution have been programmed into the brain for millions of years. Fully effective fine-grained parallel processing should not take quite so long, although, like the brain, it will require a lot of programming time.

A communications design that emulates (however distantly) the efficiency of the brain is one way to achieve a useful level of productivity for parallel processors. Several options are being explored. One is a high-speed switching system (the one used by BBN runs at 32 million bits per second). Bus linkages, a familiar feature of computer design, and various cube geometries are also

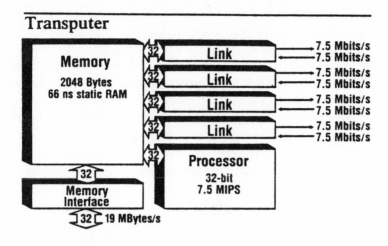

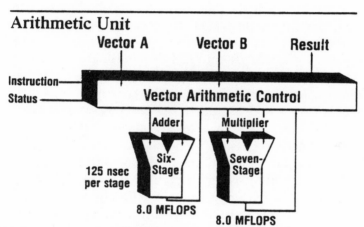

Parallel Processing Architectures—The Floating Point Systems T-Series. The FPS T-Series is composed of modules that can be linked together in a wide range of sizes, from 20 processors up to thousands. It is also a hypercube machine. (*Don Callahan, University of Michigan.*)

used. One variant, the hypercube, designed by Charles Seitz of Cal Tech (favored by FPS and others), attempts to strike the best balance between the unproductive complexity of a fully-connected system and busy-signal delays caused by excessively sparse linkages.

The relatively cheap chips and simple, repetitive designs of fine-grain systems can result in low system prices, generally much less than the cost of a more conventional general-purpose super-computer. At lower systems costs, it makes sense for some users to choose a system optimized and programmed for a specific application. This was the philosophy behind the Massively Parallel Processor (MPP), produced by Goodyear and in operation for several years at NASA's Goddard Space Flight Center in suburban Maryland, outside Washington, D.C. The MPP is used for processing images obtained by satellites in space, a task that adapts well to the capabilities of parallel systems.

Operating systems remain far from standardization. Occam, developed in 1983 at Oxford University, is intended for use on any conceivable network of processors, whether operating in serial or parallel. FPS includes Occam as a standard feature with its T-series. Cornell is providing a more standard operating system and language environment for the T-series. They have contracted for a compiler for the C programming language, with FORTRAN to follow. Their Trillium message-passing operating system, now in development, is a follow-on to Cal Tech designs. Programmers at universities, the NSF-supported supercomputer centers, the national laboratories, and elsewhere are working away on compilers and other tools that would make it possible to adapt well-established programs in FORTRAN to take advantage of the potential performance of multiprocessor and parallel designs.

It may take some time. Kenneth Wilson of the Cornell Theory Center, a persistent advocate of parallel systems, has said that if a team of software developers push hard on one specific program for use on a large-scale parallel machine, a workable solution could be achieved within two years. Asked about the time required to make full utilization for multiple applications of the capabilities of a system like the FPS T-series (available at Cornell) Wilson said that it might await major new developments, and it is difficult to predict where the market will lead.

The entire issue remains in the state at which problems and objections can be defined easily, while solutions remain to be demonstrated—a familiar condition in the history of science. This chapter reflects that situation. The mainstream in the development of supercomputer hardware over the next few years seems most likely to be dominated by step-by-step experimentation with coarse-grained multiprocessing by established manufacturers of supercomputers.

Fine-grained systems may find specialized applications or begin to compete in some sectors of the general-purpose market on the basis of low cost. Concentrated effort by software developers at these manufacturers and at large-scale users as well as universities may find ways out of the thickets that now appear so confining.

In the past, start-up companies making personal computers and other computer hardware have emerged dramatically from a large pack of competitors. They found a better way to do something or found a way to market their product successfully. So far, none of the contenders in the fine-grained parallel computing market has shown an evident advantage over the others. The conservative choice remains with the main-stream manufacturers that are moving into multiple processing more cautiously. Striking success by an aggressive design could accelerate the process. The breakout in the production of parallel systems for high-performance scientific computing has not happened yet, but this does not prove that it can't happen.

It must also be remembered that the performance of a high-speed computer does not depend solely upon the CPU (or CPUs). An impressive proportion of recent buyers of the CRAY X-MP have gone for the multi-million dollar option of a solid-state storage device. This re-emphasizes the adage that for many computationally-intense applications, a large, fast memory can be at least as important as computational power. Even though the physical limits to von Neumann architecture may be close at hand, substantial impovements in actual results can be achieved through more efficient software.

As suggested in Chapter Five, the coming period of the supercomputer era—the rest of the 1980s—may see a broadening of the market, with minisupercomputers, specialized fine-grained systems, lower-end systems like the IBM 3090 and some Japanese products, and full-bore general-purpose supercomputers (at several levels of performance) sharing the marketplace. Customers whose requirements emphasize some straightforward applications could choose a suitable dish from this cafeteria. If their choice is a little faster or a little slower than some other machine the job will still get done.

This does not do much for the heavy users: the chemists, molecular dynamics people, aerodynamicists, astro- and miscellaneous physicists, atmospheric scientists, animators, and others who don't want steady, incremental improvements in computational power. They want improvements of orders of magnitude, preferably several orders of magnitude, and preferably right now. These are not greedy, unreasonable people. They can cite very good reasons for their ambitions and very significant potential results if these ambitions are satisfied. More-of-the-same-ism based on von Neumann architecture or small-scale multiprocessing will have a tough time meeting these objectives. The advances of supercomputing, so steady and impressive for so many years, could be slowed if software development (and, perhaps, breakthroughs in hardware) are unable to satisfy these expectations.

During the early months of 1987, scientists all over the world have been fascinated by dramatic developments in superconductivity. Until now, superconductivity (enormous reductions in electrical resistance) has been possible only at extremely low temperatures, close to absolute zero, which can be attained only at great expense, using liquid helium. Recent developments indicate that superconductivity can be accomplished at higher temperatures—possible, for example, through cooling in liquid nitrogen, which is relatively inexpensive.

The potential implications for supercomputing could be far-reaching. New technologies like the Josephson junction, which depends upon superconductivity, could become practical. Despite the recent headlong pace of discoveries in superconductivity, however, large-scale production of actual components will require protracted development. Meanwhile, supercomputers will be at work, exploring new superconducting materials and designing circuits making full use of the new technology.

CHAPTER 12

The International Dimensions of Supercomputing

More than 70 supercomputers are in use or on order outside the United States—roughly 30% of the total. Almost all are in Europe, Japan, and Canada. Supercomputers have become the subjects of international disputes: a trade argument between the United States and Japan and an effort by the Soviet Union to win out over the United States as a supplier of high performance computer technology to India. The Soviet Union lags behind Japan and the United States in supercomputing. U.S. attempts to control exports and prevent supercomputer use by Soviet or Eastern European nationals have been disputed by other countries and by scientists arguing that this is incompatible with academic freedom. Japan is an important market for supercomputers and seeks to become a major supplier. China is another possible future entry in the supercomputer stakes.

If international contention in the midst of a widespread international market is a measure of the significance of a technology, supercomputing certainly qualifies. In a new chapter in the long story of computer-related trade disputes between the United States and Japan, Washington has accused the Japanese of unfair competition in supercomputers and an alleged attempt to protect domination of Japan's domestic market by Japanese manufacturers of supercomputers. The agenda for Soviet Communist Party head Mikhail Gorbachev's state visit to India in late 1986 included an offer to supply India with the technology for high-performance scientific computers, free of the restrictions on use which the United States had advocated for U.S. supercomputers. The United Kingdom and the United States have also differed over proposed limits on the use of supercomputers made in the United States.

At the same time, supercomputers are being put to use by universities and business firms throughout the advanced industrialized countries of the Northern Hemisphere. The rate of increase in supercomputer use in Europe, Canada, and Japan has been roughly the same as in the United States. The applications are also similar. The Soviet Union and the People's Republic of China are designing and making their own high performance computers, but so far it appears that they have been unable to equal the performance achieved in the United States and Japan.

The supercomputer era is not yet worldwide. A country considering the acquisition of a supercomputer needs a substantial technological sector, qualified operators, and cash. Two oil-producing states of the Arabian Peninsula (Saudi Arabia and Abu Dhabi) have bought supercomputers to assist in managing their petroleum resources. India has sought to obtain supercomputers, for meteorological studies (especially the monsoon) and other purposes. Taiwan has reportedly purchased a supercomputer for meteorological applications. Elsewhere in the developing countries, direct participation in the supercomputer era lies in the future. Economies at every stage of development will, however, be able to share in the scientific and technological advances made possible by the use of supercomputers. After all, improved meteorology and more fuel-efficient aircraft—to mention only two examples—are already having a worldwide impact.

Supercomputing in Western Europe and Canada

Europeans like to point out that scientific computing, like so many other aspects of modern technology, began in Europe. In the seventeenth century, both Leibnitz and Pascal invented calculating machines. Wilhelm Schickard of Tübingen developed a mechanical computer 20 years before Pascal; a modified version was used by Kepler to help him calculate the elliptical paths of the planets. In the nineteenth century, Charles Babbage of England was the first recorded computer entrepreneur/inventor to be abandoned by his venture capitalist (in this case, the British exchequer) when he was on the edge of an absolutely decisive breakthrough which would revolutionize the state of the art. His associate, Ada (Countess Lovelace) is often described as the first programmer.

In the final quarter of the twentieth century, Europeans concerned with supercomputing policy have decided to concentrate upon advanced computer applications rather than attempting to keep up with the United States and Japan in supercomputing technology. France is an exception. The French firm Compagnie des Machines Bull (also known by a corporate designation, Groupe Bull) is reported to be working on a high-performance computer. It is described as a high-speed vector machine that would be used primarily for military and related applications in France. In addition, Machines Bull is taking the leading role in joining the Japanese firm NEC, which makes supercomputers, and the U.S. company Honeywell in a joint enterprise to manage the computer business that Honeywell is spinning off. The possible impact of these projects upon the worldwide market for supercomputers is speculative. Siemens, a large German electrical firm, markets supercomputers manufactured by Fujitsu.

Who buys supercomputers outside the United States, and for what? The answer is straightforward: pretty much the same kind of people who buy and use supercomputers in the United States. The pattern of adoption for supercomputers, as marketing textbooks put it, has been remarkably consistent in Europe and Canada as well as in the United States.

In 1977, when the marketplace in contemporary supercomputers was just being established, the first sale to an institution outside the United States was concluded: a CRAY-1 to the European Centre for Medium-Range Weather Forecasts (ECMWF) in Reading, England. In 1979, Cray made additional sales to the British Atomic Weapons Research Establishment in Aldermaston and to the Max Planck Institute for Physics in Garching, West Germany.

As in the U.S., the well-established intensive government users of high-performance computing were in the lead, especially weapons development and atmospheric research. In addition, supercomputer installations at universities and at institutions devoted to academic research developed somewhat more rapidly than in the United States, especially in proportion to Europe's smaller populations of graduate students and other researchers. France began to purchase U.S. supercomputers two or three years after Britain and the Federal Republic of Germany. Once again, the first customer, in 1982, was the Commission for Atomic Energy. A supercomputer center serving French university research, in Paliseau, and a supercomputer service bureau at Gif sur Yvette followed in 1983 and 1984, respectively.

European industrial firms and central research institutes in the aerospace and petroleum industries were prominent in the second wave of supercomputer purchases—just as in the United States. So far, supercomputers devoted full-time to other industrial applications remain fewer. Adam Opel, the West German subsidiary of General Motors, operates a CRAY-1/S at Ruesselsheim. A CRAY-1/A is in use by SAAB-Scania, in Sweden. Its primary use is presumably for aircraft design, but the firm is also a leading international producer of cars and trucks. Daimler-Benz, a formidable producer of trucks and buses as well as upscale automobiles, is reported to be considering a supercomputer purchase. Many other European firms use time on supercomputers in government-operated service centers.

In Europe as elsewhere, supercomputing is developing so swiftly that it is not easy to keep track of orders and deliveries. The following count is at least indicative of the present state of supercomputer installations in Europe.

The larger economies operate most of the continent's supercomputers: 10 in the Federal Republic of Germany, 10 in the United Kingdom (one serving a Europeanwide service, the ECMWF), and 6 in France. Facilities are also operated in the Netherlands (at Shell Oil and the University of Amsterdam), Italy (the University of Bologna), Switzerland (the Ecole Federal Polytechnique in Lausanne, which also services other Swiss universities) and the SAAB-Scania installation in Sweden.

It is worth noting that 11 of the roughly 30 supercomputer installations in Western Europe are at universities or are intended primarily to provide service for scientific research conducted by academics. All but the Swiss facility were installed or on order before the beginning of the NSF supercomputer initiative in the United States. Until then, supercomputer facilities for academic use in the U.S. were significantly fewer than in Europe.

Sales by supercomputer manufacturer are roughly the same as in the United States: 8 Cyber 205s, 4 Fujitsus, with Crays accounting for about two-thirds of the total. IBM is receiving orders and beginning to make installations of its 3090 machines with vector attachments. This could have a substantial impact upon total numbers as well as market share. So far, Cray dominates the replacement market: a number of X-MPs have been installed or are on order, and three CRAY-2 systems (one each in West Germany, France, and the United Kingdom) are at various stages of the procurement/ installation/initial run cycle.

In one respect, supercomputing in Europe remains at a decisive disadvantage. European political leaders and the bureaucrats of the European Economic Community have trudged persistently for many years in the direction of greater unification and fewer internal barriers. Along with agriculture, the governmental PTT (Post, Telegraph, Telephone) monopolies remain among the most tenacious examples of restrictive economic protectionism disguised as patriotism. The PTTs have used finicky technical standards, punitive rates, preferences for locally produced equipment, concerns about security and protection of data integrity, and other devices to slow the establishment of a flexible, responsive, and efficient European-wide communications system.

Users of supercomputers in Europe are thus isolated within their own institution or within a network largely limited to a single country. (Supercomputer specialists in the U.S. who have over the years remarked about deficiencies in enterprises like ARPANET and MFENET return home chastened after trips to consult with colleagues in Europe—an ARPANET which doesn't do everything asked of it is better than none at all). Limitations in networking also influence the prevalence of interactivity and time-sharing. None of the Cray facilities in Europe uses the CTSS operating system; until recently, all have operated on the COS system, limited largely to batch processing. The new CRAY-2 installations will, however, use the UNICOS system, which permits time-sharing.

In 1984, the European Academic Research Network (EARN) was founded with support from 21 countries (including the Persian Gulf states and Israel as well as sponsors in Europe). This network is similar to the U.S. BITNET in capacity and objectives. Thus, it is limited to the exchange of messages among researchers and the transmission of data in relatively small quantities at low speeds. Plans call for the creation of a network based upon the OSI standard proposed by the International Standards Organization. For essentially political questions of PTT sovereignty, however, this is not an early goal. Meanwhile, some countries are experimenting with high-capacity domestic channels for computer data, including the pilot installation of a fiber optic circuit between Hamburg and Munich and a high-speed circuit linking Karlsruhe and Stuttgart.

Eureka may come to the rescue. This project aims at a broad-based effort to improve Europe's competitiveness in high technology. Specific projects approved at a ministerial meeting in late summer 1986 included a proposal for a wideband telecommunications system. The objective is to develop a wideband interconnection module that would form the basis for a future capability meeting international standards. The duration of the project is to be five years. Expenditures of over $150 million (primarily from industry, with some government support) are contemplated. If the centralized bureaucracies of the EEC and the Eureka program can out spend, out persuade, and out wait the bureaucrats in local PTTs, this could bring great benefits to supercomputing in Europe. France, Italy, and Britain are to be the main participants.

Supercomputing facilities in Europe are as sophisticated as those in the United States. The Regional Computer Center of the University of Stuttgart, for example, installed one of the first real scientific supercomputers, the CDC 6600, in 1968. In 1983, a CRAY-1/M was purchased. A CRAY-2, replacing the CRAY-1/M, was brought on line during the second half of 1986. It serves other universities within Baden-Wurttemberg and outside it as well as customers in research institutes at Stuttgart. The configuration, including VAX 11/780s, PDP-11s, an IBM 3083 storage system, HYPERchannel local circuits, and high-performance workstations, would seem familiar to an American system specialist. Research topics using center facilities include nonlinear structural analysis, fluid mechanics, molecular structure, nuclear reactor safety, plasma physics, and crash analysis. High-quality graphics are emphasized.

The use of contemporary supercomputers began in Canada in the early 1980's, when the Canadian Meteorological Center (CMC) in Montreal acquired a CRAY-1. In Canada, the weather is vigorous and variable, the winters severe. The CMC, which supports Canada's Atmospheric Environment Services, has employed computers for weather prediction for more than twenty years. It uses the Cray for weather forecasts disseminated across Canada. A supercomputer has also been in use at the department of national defence.

Canadian researchers have long been able to use supercomputer facilities in the United States. Most Canadian universities subscribe to the North American BITNET network. Boeing and other U.S. supercomputer service bureaus have merchandised their services to Canadian customers. In addition, in Canada itself, the University of Calgary has been operating a Cyber 205.

More recently, Canada has been participating in the general North American tendency toward rapid development of local and regional supercomputing centers, often supported by local governments. The Province of Ontario appropriated Can.$10 million toward the establishment of a supercomputing facility at the University of Toronto whose capacity would be shared on a 50-50 basis with Ontario University. A CRAY X-MP/22, operating COS, was installed in 1986.

Universities in the Maritime Provinces, long sensitive to indications of neglect by Canada's Midwestern power centers, are asking for supercomputing resources, and a national network has been discussed. Canada is also the home of an unusual private venture in supercomputing. Two businessmen in Toronto, brothers named Gary and William Madriga, have taken advantage of tax credits for research equipment to purchase two Cyber 205's that are being used for research by their separate high-technology companies.

Toronto is the headquarters and principal source of financing for Omnibus, a large computer animation firm which operates all over North America. Omnibus seeks to consolidate a position as the most powerful company in this volatile, rapidly expanding field (see Chapter Nine).

High-performance Scientific Computing in the Soviet Union

In computer technology, the Soviet Union sails in the wake of the United States and has also been overtaken by Japan. This is especially true of supercomputing. Foreign visitors to the Soviet Union have been impressed by the elegant, thorough preparation of problems for computer runs, contrasting with the frequent American practice of stick it on and see what happens. This reflects a distinguished tradition of high quality mathematics—beginning long before the October Revolution—as well as a chronic shortage of computer time.

In computers, as in so many other fields in the Soviet Union, technology and production (especially quality control) are far behind theory. They can design it, but frequently they can't make it. This is not due to national incapacity but to a wide range of causes that include isolation and compartmentalization of academic institutions (even more extreme than in the United States); low productivity and poor workplace discipline; inefficient transfer of technology from academies to industry; rigid, bureaucratic allocation of resources; inflexibility in adjusting priorities; and management of research on the basis of seniority and conformity. These deficiencies are damaging to any industry; especially so to a rapidly evolving industry like computing; and devastating to supercomputing, which by definition requires the fullest use of the most advanced technology and the highest-quality components.

It is not difficult to imagine reasons for the Soviet Union's determined opposition to the U.S. Strategic Defense Initiative (SDI or "Star Wars") proposal. One of these reasons is the Soviet reluctance to take part in yet another military-technological competition, especially one in which the United States may possess so many advantages. The U.S. advantage in computations is one of the most significant. The computational requirements of any large-scale strategic defense system will be formidable in the extreme, so much so that a debate continues, especially among software experts, regarding the fundamental feasibility of a workable SDI computational system. The SDI developmental organization believes that its goal can be met but has made what is known as "battle-management" (dependent primarily upon computing) a central focus for funding and special research effort. A challenge that causes so much concern to American computer scientists would certainly appear even more intimidating to their Soviet counterparts, who possess much more limited resources. This is not specifically a supercomputer issue, but the technology and programming capability needed for advanced supercomputers would also be involved in solutions to SDI requirements.

There is no evidence that the USSR has placed in serial production supercomputers capable of performance equivalent to the CPUs introduced in the United States in the mid-1970s or the lower end of the current Japanese supercomputer product lines. They appear even more distant from more advanced machines, like the CRAY X-MP, CRAY-2 or NEC SX-2. Ambitious projects like the ETA-10 seem to be well beyond current Soviet reach. Deficiencies in memory, other peripherals, input/output capacity, and work-stations are at least as serious as those in CPUs.

The higher-end computers in wide use in the USSR reflect these limitations. The BESM-6 (Large Electronic Digital Computing Machine), introduced around 1966, is still relied upon extensively. Its performance is in the range of one million operations per second, several orders of magnitude slower than current models used in Japan and the West. The Elbrus series of multiprocessor computers, first introduced in 1971, exists in a number of configurations. For example, models with single, double, or ten processors have been produced. Speeds range from 1.5 to 12 million operations per second. Little information is available about the rate of production. Array processors and other add-on devices are used for seismic research and similar specialized purposes.

Discussions of Soviet technological capabilities must be aster-isked with an important qualification. Despite the deficiencies of their system, the Soviets have demonstrated an impressive capacity to concentrate resources and talent on high priority projects, es-pecially those of military significance. Supercomputing is eminently well qualified for this kind of attention. This is demonstrated by the early origins of supercomputing in nuclear weapons design and cryptography and its current importance for aircraft design and many other advanced military technologies. Prototypes kludged up in the laboratory or assembled as Skunk Works special projects could be employed to meet the most pressing military requirements. There are indications of the existence of such machines, perhaps including the M-10 announced in 1979.

China: Really as Cost-Effective as the Abacus?

Three scientific traditions intersect and often conflict in China. The Chinese are fiercely proud of their own long history of science and technology. They feel it has long been undervalued by westerners who assume that technology began in China in the nineteenth century, or with the arrival of Jesuit missionary-philosopher-artificers in the sixteenth century. A second scientific stream was added by the Chinese who studied abroad, especially in the United States, during the nineteenth century and, on a wider scale, during the first half of the twentieth century. Universities and scientific research of high quality, especially in physics, mathematics, medicine and public health, began to strike root in China. The final dimension was added during the relatively brief but intense period of Soviet tutelage from 1949 to the early 1960s. The Soviets did their best to replicate in China their structure of specialized trade school higher education and compartmentalized, seniority-bound research institutes under a national academy of sciences. As in the Soviet Union, this became a heavy burden upon technological advance. In China, it was made worse by the damages done to all science by the excesses of the cultural revolution of the 1960s and early 1970s.

This brief capsule of history illuminates the present state of supercomputing in China. Since 1978, the Chinese have been seeking to rebuild the scientific base that was begun earlier in the century and to modify the more noxious features of the research and educational system grafted on China by Soviet advisors. The importance of computing to modern advanced technology is well understood in China, and progress in computing is given very high priority.

China is able to buy computers and components openly from the United States, Japan, and other sources. U.S. export controls on exports to China are less restrictive than those on sales to the

Soviet Union, but high-performance computers (including the more capable mainframes as well as supercomputers) remain on the restricted list. The Japanese, who also belong to the Coordinating Committee on Export Controls (COCOM), the international body regulating trade in items of potential military importance, have adhered to these restrictions.

Substantial resources are also available close at hand. The border between Austria and Hungary—and other East-West boundaries in Europe—are highly permeable to circuit chips, other components, and whole lower-end computer systems. In Asia, the Chinese have even easier access—through Hong Kong or directly—to a wide range of electronic components and whole systems. Taiwan, South Korea, Hong Kong and Singapore are becoming significant manufacturers of low-end systems as well as parts and components. Taiwan and South Korea conduct a thriving—if officially discountenanced—trade with China. It would be surprising if computer technology was not represented in the "dark-of-the-moon" trade (actually often carried out openly) between fishing vessels from China and Taiwan.

Chips and other items obtained in this way can be applied to high-performance computers, but for high-speed systems the Chinese have found it necessary to rely upon their own resources. Models that have been reported in Chinese periodicals or oberved by visiting foreigners include the 757, developed by the Institute of Computer Technology and inaugurated in 1975, and the Yinhe (Silver River, the Chinese name for the Milky Way; also translated as "Galaxy"), a project begun in 1978 at the Defense University of Science and Technology. Following the Soviet practice, major new designs of advanced technology are generally developed—and often prototyped or even manufactured—at specialized institutes of the national academy or at universities rather than industrial production firms.

Both designs are laid out in the C cross-section introduced by Seymour Cray; the Yinhe looks like a somewhat oversized CRAY-1. The 757 is a pipelined vector-processing mainframe, cooled by forced air, has a magnetic core main memory, operates at a clock time in excess of one microsecond, and is reported to perform at a rate of 2.8 million operations per second on scalar operations and up to 10 million operations per second on problems suitable for pipelining. The Yinhe appears to be aimed at defense applications and has received less detailed mention in Chinese publications. Its performance is reported to be much superior to the 757: rates of 100 million operations per second have been claimed. The 757 relies upon an adaptation of the FORTRAN-77 language.

In computing, as in many other areas of technology, the Chinese possess (although usually in relatively small numbers) very talented, highly-trained specialists—including many well-qualified programmers. Major problems include quality control, workplace discipline and productivity, effective use of specialists trained abroad, more rational sharing of effort among institutes and other facilities (many of which often pursue similar or even identical R&D programs), and coordination between R&D facilities and production plants.

These are problems of organization rather than basic capability or national priorities. If these are overcome, the Chinese may create a role for themselves in computing comparable to the niche they are seeking to occupy in aircraft production and in space-launch facilities—basic, low-end, low-cost technology aimed primarily at customers who care a lot about price and are willing to accept performance levels that are modest in comparison to world standards but are nevertheless adequate for many purposes.

Export Controls and Restrictions on Supercomputer Use

Hundreds of years before the October Revolution, the Russian empire laid down a tradition of obtaining advanced technology from abroad. In addition to aboveboard commercial transactions, the Soviet Union has an undisguised appetite for the acquisition of examples of foreign technology and design details that can be analyzed and imitated. This is often done through midnight procurements and bogus shipping documents. It is reasonable to assume that anything relating to supercomputing is high on the wish list.

In the United States, there is a long tradition of trying to frustrate Soviet efforts to lay hands on advanced technology, a policy which has been applied with particular vigor to supercomputing. Supercomputers are large, conspicuous, relatively few in number, and would seem an easy candidate for export controls. In fact, this U.S. policy has proven contentious, and difficult to carry out.

Controls have not only been placed upon the *sale* of super-computers abroad; they have also been applied to the *use* of su-percomputers. The presumption is that a Soviet researcher abroad on an exchange project at a foreign institution could learn a great deal about supercomputing simply by using a supercomputer for his research. There may also be the fear that a hostile user might be able to slip a problem with potential military applications into his code.

Critics of this policy consider these concerns far-fetched. They also note that the technology is not secret. A great deal of technical information can be obtained from publicly available manuals issued by the manufacturers. Furthermore, the U.S. monopoly on su-percomputers is now history. Indeed, the Soviet Union is a member in long standing of the league of IBM admirers. It has imitated earlier IBM mainframes and would find it relatively easy to follow the path pursued by Fujitsu and Hitachi. They could add perfor-mance, especially in vector processing, to a proven, familiar IBM-style mainframe, and thus obtain perfectly serviceable CPUs without embarking upon the inconveniences of imitating Seymour Cray's unusual designs and complex cooling systems.

In any event, the tradition of "If it works, put a lock on it and stamp it secret" persists at the U.S. Department of Defense and other corners of the federal establishment, including parts of the Department of Commerce, which has immediate responsibility for enforcing export controls. This policy led to controversy in 1985 and 1986.The issue most fundamental to U.S. science was raised after the NSF launched its computer initative. The initial presumption was that the capacity of the new centers would be available to all qualified researchers and students at U.S. institutions, with access based solely upon scientific and educational merit. Then it was realized that a great many foreigners are working at all levels of academic life in the United States. These include many thousands of scientists and students from China and a smaller scattering of Soviets and persons from Eastern Europe who may find it dangerous to ignore Soviet suggestions. An effort was made to draw up rules that would control access by such persons to the new NSF-sponsored supercomputers. A rapid, united reaction from the U.S. scientific establishment stressed that such restrictions violated academic freedom, were not compatible with America's long-established practice of an open welcome to talent from abroad, and would moreover be extremely difficult to administer. In addition, it was pointed out that such restrictions would slow U.S. scientific progress—perhaps more than they might slow the Soviets. The effort at control was withdrawn but may only be dormant.

These issues remain a cause of friction outside the United States. The British government held title to a CRAY-1 at a defense research establishment, the Harwell Laboratory, which was being replaced by a more advanced machine. It was proposed that the CRAY-1 would be moved to the University of London Computer Center (ULCC). Another Cray was already in use at the ULCC, serving about 2000 scientists, and other American-made supercomputers are in service at British universities. The U.S. authorities asked that persons from certain (mainly Communist) countries be denied access, and that the CRAY-1 could not be networked with telecommunications systems in certain countries. Members of Parliament and officials of university teachers' organizations complained about these restrictions. Contention also arose about proposed restrictions on the use of a new CRAY X-MP/48 that the British Science and Engineering Research Council was purchasing for installation in its Atlas Computer Center, at the Rutherford and Appleton Laboratory. The new machine is intended to support universities and research councils.

Another case involved the proposed sale of an IBM 3090 to an institution in Finland. The Finns wished to add vector processors. It is reported that U.S. authorities concluded that this would constitute a supercomputer and must be the subject of restrictive agreements on access. Presumably those seeking this were not ignorant enough to believe that Finns love Russians, but it may have been thought that any Soviet pressure to pierce the secrets of the 3090 might be difficult to resist.

India is in a special category. High levels of scientific sophistication and technological competence are found in India, although often in isolated institutions and on a small scale that does not translate easily into competitive production. Prime Minister Rajiv Gandhi, an airline pilot before being called tragically to assume his dynastic duties, believes strongly that India's future development depends upon energetic, systematic application of advanced technology. Despite periodic episodes of coolness between India and the United States, the Prime Minister has made it clear that he is interested primarily in U.S. technology.

The Indians are understandably preoccupied with study of the monsoon, an extremely complex, poorly understood phenomenon that has enormous implications for the livelihood of India's population as well as its ability to develop a more productive economy. Indian atmospheric specialists are active in cooperative research and exchanges with the National Center for Atmospheric Research in the United States (see Chapter Eight) and other institutions around the world.

The Indians use conventional computers for their monsoon research and forecasting, but they realize the advantages of a supercomputer and are willing to invest the money and skilled staff needed to make a supercomputer work. India has also expresssed interested in supercomputers for general use at its Institute of Science and Technology. Indian representatives have met with supercomputer makers in the United States and Japan. Reports state that eventual acquisition plans may total four machines.

Official U.S. concerns about a possible sale to India emphasize India's ambiguous status. It has exploded a nuclear device, clearly possesses the capability to make and deliver nuclear weapons, but is not a signatory of the non-proliferation treaty aimed at preventing additions to the list of nations able to wage nuclear warfare. It is feared that India might use a supercomputer to solve the complex, computationally intensive problems of nuclear weapons design as well as explore the delicate balance of the monsoon. In addition, concerns have been expressed about India's close defense relationship with the Soviet Union, which supplies India with advanced fighter aircraft and other war material.

The next development came at the end of 1986, during Soviet Party Chairman Mikhail Gorbachev's state visit to India. In addition to the high questions of peace and politics usually discussed when two heads of government meet, Gorbachev and Gandhi also talked about supercomputers. The Soviets offered India the technology for supercomputers, remarking pointedly that they would not impose the restrictions demanded by the United States. Two very senior officials of the Soviet Academy of Sciences, including President Juri Morchuk, are to visit India to explore the matter further.

Indian scientists are no doubt aware that the Soviet technology is not up to Japanese or American levels, but they are also throughly capable of learning a good deal from the Soviet offer and, indeed, producing quietly a Soviet-derived machine superior to anything made in the Soviet Union. Some of the issues which have just been discussed appeared close to resolution as this book went to press. The U.S. government was preparing to reduce export controls, which had damaged the U.S. ability to compete. Approval of the sale of a U.S. supercomputer to India appeared close. Over the longer term, however, supercomputers were likely to remain a frequent and occasionally acute issue of international contention.

Supercomputing in Japan

Japan, with more than 30 supercomputers in operation, is the largest single supercomputer market after the United States. If growth in supercomputer use continues at its present rate, the total in Japan will be roughly proportional to the relative size of the U.S. and Japanese economies, when allowance is made for U.S. defense-related supercomputer installations which have no counterparts in Japan.

The Japanese market is not as protected as it used to be—a reflection of changing attitudes toward foreign products and foreign suppliers as well as new regulations, although both still have a long way to go to equal the accessibility of the U.S. market. Cray sales in Japan total seven, more than the total supercomputer population of France. Cray customers include Toshiba, Nippon Telephone and Telegraph, Mitsubishi Research, and Nissan.

Nevertheless, the expansion of Japanese supercomputing facilities in the mid-1980's has consisted primarily of Japanese-made machines. The mix of government agencies, universities, and industries using supercomputers has not differed greatly from the pattern in North America and Western Europe. Japanese governmental customers have included the National Weather Bureau, the Meteorological Research Institute, the National Aerospace Laboratory, the Japan Atomic Energy Research Institute, and the Japanese space agency. Japanese manufacturers, like their counterparts in the United States, have provided equipment on favorable terms to universities in order to establish market recognition as well as to benefit from the talents and patience of academic specialists. Supercomputers have been provided for general-purpose and specialized uses (plasma physics, for example) to universities and research institutes in Tokyo, Nagoya, Osaka, Tsukuba, and elsewhere. Industrial users are somewhat more numerous in Japan than in the United States or Europe. For starters, each of the three supercomputer manufacturers uses its own products as in-house resources for a broad range of product-development requirements.

Japan: Competing with the World—Even with IBM

Japan's first steps toward recovery of international competitiveness in the 1950's coincided with the introduction of electronic computers to world commerce. The Japanese started with a strong sense that they were inferior technologically and at a profound disadvantage in terms of worldwide marketing. Like the Europeans, they were intimidated by the U.S. advantage in computers. Like computer makers everywhere, they were perpetually dismayed by IBM's overall strength and dominance of so much of the world computer market.

The Japanese applied the talented stubbornness of a dedicated bureaucracy to the protection of their newer industries. Computers retained protection later than most. Even inside that fence, however, the most powerful company was IBM Japan, one of the few wholly-owned foreign subsidiaries in Japan. Sperry/Univac, NCR, and other outsiders had a strong presence.

Japan's electrical and electronics industry is dominated by about a half-dozen powerful diversified companies. Some, like Hitachi, compete across virtually the entire range of electrical manufacturing, plus heavy industry like shipbuilding. Others, like Fujitsu and NEC, are more concentrated, but they make their own chips and carry on other lines of business which in the United States are limited to companies like IBM and AT&T. All struggle continually with one another in order to preserve—or gain—market share across broad ranges of products. The most important arena of mutual competition is Japan's domestic market—a large market for almost everything, especially so for high technology. Exports come next. Computers are only one battlefield in this protracted combat, but possess special prestige and visibility. (It is interesting to recall that General Electric, the closest U.S. counterpart to the Japanese electrical giants, fumbled a discouraging early effort to make computers. NEC, one of the most aggressive and innovative Japanese computer makers, was one of the inheritors of GE technology.)

Over the years, Japanese companies, especially Fujitsu, NEC, and Hitachi, gained domestic market share at the expense of IBM and eventually accounted collectively for a majority of the Japanese computer market. These companies—and most Japanese computers—sold sluggishly abroad. This poor showing was especially painful when compared with the enormous worldwide successes that Japanese companies achieved with most other electronic products.

In the early 1980s, the Japanese launched two of their noted joint initiatives to correct this disadvantage in computers. One project was visionary, has received widespread publicity, and has been the subject of much anxiety and imitation abroad. It is intended to create Fifth Generation computers that would process knowledge, not just information. These were to be fast computers with a great deal of memory, but performance at the supercomputer level was not a major objective. The other project, launched in January 1982, was the high-speed computer initative, officially the High-speed Computing System for Scientific and Technological Use. It aims at developing technology and software that would permit Japanese firms to compete on a footing of equality with (and, perhaps, surpass) the rest of the world.

The supercomputer market may be much smaller than the market for mainframes and other categories of computer, but it is growing faster than most other categories. Making the fastest and fanciest attracts attention. Indirectly, Maserati and Ferrari help Alfa-Romeo and Fiat to sell cars. A convincing showing with supercomputers makes it easier to gain access to a substantial, growing market among universities and other research laboratories—a market that also buys lots of minicomputers and mainframes. As the altitude of high technology rises and the world enters the era of information-based industries (a prospect which has spilled enormous quantities of ink in Japan) this market gains concrete influence as well as prestige.

Both computer initiatives were joint efforts of the Japanese government, industry, and universities and were fuelled by substantial but not massive contributions of government funds. The Fifth Generation remains an uncertain hope, surrounded by a good deal of international enthusiasm. The fruits of the high-speed computer initiative could be more tangible.

Ten Gigaflops by 1990

The High-Speed Computing System (HSCS) project is budgeted at roughly $100 million over its seven-year life (compared with about $200 million in federal funds for supercomputing from the NSF over a shorter period). The NSF initiative is, however, a multi-dimensional program, supporting networking and training as well as the establishment of centers and research on software and hardware. HSCS is directed squarely at increased performance: a goal of 1 to 10 gigaflops (10,000 million floating point operations per second) by the end of Japan's fiscal 1989 in March, 1990. It emphasizes three key activities: R&D of parallel architecture and software; R&D of new devices, with attention given to Josephson junctions, high mobility electron transistors, and gallium-arsenide (GaAs) devices; and integration and evaluation of actual systems. It intends to advance by a classic Japanese R&D strategy—combining ambitious, specific nailed-to-the-flagpole goals with much more pragmatic step-by-step development based upon existing technology.

Japanese government bodies (and some government money) are joined with private industry in a unique combination which excites the envy and alarm of foreign competitors. The organizational chart for the HSCS looks like the impractical vision of a steadfast bureaucrat, but it reflects the complex relationships among Japanese universities, government agencies, and private firms. The Council for Industrial Technology, the Committee of National Development Programs, the Ministry of International Trade and Industry (the renowned MITI, object of much devout demonology in the United States), the Agency of Industrial Science and Technology, and the Electrotechnical Laboratory at Tsukuba Science City in principle all have spoons stirring the broth at the same time. These government or quasi-governmental bodies support and guide actual R&D through a research contract with the Scientific Computer Research Association, composed of private firms: Oki, Toshiba, NEC, Fujitsu, and Mitsubishi Electric (which also contribute R&D funds).

The Japanese are able to make peculiar organizations like this operate, and at times achieve remarkable success. (Often, they serve as "outside" organizations; an "inside structure," composed of a few key figures, resolves disputes and makes it work. The best American parallel is an old-fashioned farmhouse. There was a front door and a formal parlor, but these were used only by preachers and strangers. Real folks went through the back door, and all the business was done in the kitchen. Foreigners who attempt to emulate such organizations are copying only half of the reality—at best.) The HSCS serves as a vehicle for coordination, definition of objectives and as an umbrella over separate but related individual R&D projects by the participating companies.

Japanese progress reports on the HSCS program indicate that the toughest questions it confronts are the same ones preoccupying U.S. supercomputer developers. Points which the HSCS emphasizes are: selection and then reliable production of the next generation of basic devices at reasonable cost; solving problems of logic design and cooling; and developing efficient software and suitable algorithms for parallel processing. Japanese reports suggest that, like their foreign competitors, they find efficient parallel processing the most intimidating challenge.

Japanese-United States Competition in a
"Hollowing Out" World: A Supercomputer Threat?

The HSCS builds deliberately upon current supercomputing designs in Japan, but models now offered for sale by Japanese manufacturers began development before the HSCS began. Initial product announcements of supercomputers were made by Fujitsu in July 1982, Hitachi in August 1982, and NEC in April 1983. Actual shipments followed 12 to 24 months later. (Specifications and performance of these designs as well as other supercomputers are reviewed in Appendix I.)

A chill breeze swept through the American supercomputing

community in the mid-1980s when U.S. specialists made the pilgrimage to Japan, carrying benchmarking tapes in their luggage, and returned to report that the upper-end Japanese models were capable of benchmark performance higher than the U.S. machines then in use. In addition, the Japanese manufacturers, notably Fujitsu and Hitachi, accustomed to a strategy of being more blue than IBM itself, based their supercomputer designs upon existing mainframe models, making it easy to run familiar IBM software on the Japanese multi-pipeline vector machines. This opened a potential market of IBM users seeking relatively painless supercomputing which at that time (prior to the introduction of the IBM vector-added 3090) had not been tapped. Finally, the Japanese, who are in general behind the United States in software development, reversed the balance in supercomputing. The Japanese manufacturers, especially Fujitsu, introduced software tools that made it easier to optimize a program for productive runs on a vector machine. American manufacturers have doubled their efforts to catch up, but this Japanese advantage is not yet erased.

The Japanese have been formidable potential competitors in supercomputers, as in other aspects of electronics and, increasingly, in other fields of computing. Now, however, the Japanese find themselves in disturbing new circumstances. Due primarily to a stronger yen and sharp reductions in sales to several markets, Japanese manufacturers discovered during 1986 that they were no longer so competitive. They had observed (and benefitted from) this phenomenon in England and the rust belt of midwestern America, but it was happening in Japan. Not only in older industries like steel, aluminum, and textiles, but in high-technology manufacturing as well. Jobs are going abroad or simply vanishing. The Japanese news media are avid trendmongers, and they have applied the word *kudoka* to this trend. It is usually translated in English as "hollowing out," which simply sounds spooky. In Japanese, the resonance is much more desolate—the basic meaning of the root characters is "vacant cave." "Emptying" conveys the implications somewhat better. The fundamental meaning is clear in any case. If this trend lasts, the relatively easy times are past, in Japan as in other industrialized countries that have sought endless prosperity through an endless progression of high technology.

The effects in Japan have been surprise, alarm, and action.

The Japanese economy and individual Japanese firms may be weakening their grip on overseas markets, but they are still formidable. In recent years, the Americans have developed the habit of running the government and everything else at a deficit, and Japan has acquired a large part of the resulting outflow of dollars. Many companies are using this money to move more of their manufacturing overseas or buy foreign firms outright. They also concentrate with fiercer dedication upon applying even better the traditional virtues—constantly improved technology, higher efficiency, and relentless pursuit of market share. Even large, famous firms are reducing costs by cutting back on expenditures, including employment—an especially painful step in Japan. Like feudal lords (a comparison which most Japanese consider perfectly natural) powerful employers have taken pride in rewarding the loyalty of their employees with a commitment to long-term security.

The effect upon competition in supercomputers is not yet evident. It is worth noting, however, that NEC took only a modest share in the three-way deal for Honeywell's computer business, leaving the lead to the French firm Machines Bull. The three Japanese firms making supercomputers are exceptionally strong ones. A great deal depends upon whether "hollowing out" is perceived as the future of Japanese high technology or is just another trend-word to be discarded when another comes along. The Japanese may also be noting that AT&T and even IBM have been doing some hollowing out of their own in 1986, reducing expenditures and employment on a substantial scale.

It is equally plausible that one or more of the Japanese supercomputer producers may decide that the potential returns do not justify the effort. The supercomputer market may be substantial and growing, but it seems unlikely that in a foreseeable future it could be genuinely profitable for six manufacturers. Moreover, these competitors are not small, feisty startups, but companies which have appeared for years on Fortune magazine's listings of the mighty. Except for the Japanese domestic market, the Japanese makers contemplate a world dominated by the Americans, especially by Cray.

A decisive technological leap might do it. The world market for supercomputers remains unusually preoccupied with high performance. A powerful new machine that leaves the competition behind will fascinate potential customers, whatever its country of origin. The HSCS may enable Japanese manufacturers to achieve dramatic results of this kind. Meanwhile, the Americans are not idle. ETA is pressing forward. The shape of the CRAY Y-MP is taking form under a dustcover that is likely to be pulled away before long. Who knows what prodigies Seymour Cray may bring forth with the CRAY-3? The Japanese machines that will keep up in this race must be in development now, not dependent upon the achievement of 1990 goals.

The U.S. complaints to Japan over supercomputers have stressed the lack of U.S. sales to Japanese government bodies (including public universities) unfair price competition, and specifications which allegedly favored Japanese manufacturers. As this book went to press, the Japanese government was moving toward purchases of U.S. supercomputers, in an attempt to calm U.S.-Japan relations exacerbated by a much more conspicuous dispute over semi-conductors.

As the computer era leaves its initial stages and becomes more mature, the chief danger to the U.S. supercomputer industry is complacency, not external threats. As long as no one dozes off, the United States possesses a running start and a solid position from which to maintain a competitive advantage in most of the other components of supercomputer systems as well as CPUs. Especially with IBM in the market, total expenditures by U.S. companies for R&D of advanced supercomputer designs and technology between now and 1990 will be much greater than the $100 million kitty available from the HSCS. Americans should remember this in order to maintain perspective on the the international dimensions of the supercomputer era.

CHAPTER 13 _____

The Future of the Supercomputer Era

The people—from high school seniors to tenured professors—who are now beginning to become involved in supercomputing offer the best indication of the future of the supercomputer era. A continuing increase and broadening in demand for supercomputer capabilities will shape the development of supercomputing; this could be a more powerful influence than technological changes. New, even experimental applications of supercomputers to civil engineering, geophysics, statistics, archaeology, fisheries management, public health, the physiology of the heart, animal breeding, human genetics, and astronomy are examples of this future. Applications which no one can now imagine are likely to play even more important roles as the supercomputer era evolves.

Technology—more ingenious chips and better ways to obtain full performance from a large stable of processors—will be only one of the forces shaping the supercomputer era. The people who will be using supercomputers in 10 or 15 years will be an equally important—and perhaps more decisive—influence on the future of supercomputing. It is possible to gain a preliminary impression of these supercomputer users of the future: many of them have already discovered supercomputing and are beginning to learn the skills of supercomputer programming.

The panels of great names in science and computing whose recommendations helped bring about the NSF initiative in supercomputing emphasized that the needs go beyond hardware. Not enough people in the United States knew enough about supercomputers. There was a shortage of informed potential users as well as qualified systems operators.

From the start, training was an integral part of the program. The first summer institutes, aimed primarily at graduate students and postdoctoral researchers from a broad range of academic disciplines, began in 1985 (see Chapter Six and Appendix II, Section 1 for specifics). At the same time, the Department of Energy's (DOE) Office of Energy Research began the High School Supercomputing Honors Program. Students—most of them graduating seniors, some a little younger—were selected by the governors of the states, Puerto Rico, and the District of Columbia on the basis of scholastic aptitude and accomplishments in mathematics and computation. Participants spent two weeks at a DOE-sponsored laboratory, learning more about computations in general and, in particular, were able to gain first hand experience with supercomputers. In the summer of 1986, the authors of this book were able to meet participants at two of these sessions, the NSF-sponsored summer institute at SDSC and the DOE's high school honors program at Lawrence Livermore National Laboratory.

These sessions led to an important conclusion: The next decades of the supercomputing era are in good hands, certainly in hands that adapt to supercomputers very readily. Curiosity tinged with awe was the predominant initial reaction of the high school students, most of whom had no experience with anything more powerful than a personal computer. The participants at SDSC had previous experience with scientific computing, at least on the minicomputer level. Some had had a taste of supercomputers and were eager to make the most of the one hour of CPU time on a CRAY X-MP/48 allocated to each student. (It lasted the full two weeks for almost all of them; and many hurried home to make full use of the remainder before their accounts expired.)

In both programs, the participants learned quickly, were soon

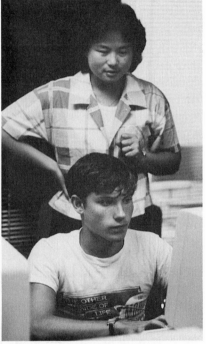

Participants in the Department of Energy's High School Supercomputing Honors Program, held at the National Magnetic Fusion Energy Computing Center, Lawrence Livermore National Laboratory. They are, from top left: Todd Trygier, Michigan; Wendell Thomas, District of Columbia; Amy Bustte, South Carolina; Keith MacKay, New Hampshire (Emily Yim of the NMFECC is in the background). (*Lawrence Livermore National Laboratory.*)

making effective use of supercomputer resources, and above all were not intimidated. Although supercomputers could be difficult and frustrating, they were accepted as just another computational tool. As at any summer seminar (or summer camp, for that matter) participants played obscure in-jokes on one another and made every effort to appear supremely cool and unbothered while accomplishing some difficult computational maneuver. Participants in both programs liked to talk about computers, but their preferred posture was in front of a workstation, doing something with computers.

What kind of people will do supercomputing in the 1990's and beyond? If these not necessarily representative samples are an indication, people very much like those who are doing it now. Most are male; the proportion of females taking part in these two sessions—about 10% per cent in each—was perhaps slightly larger than the proportion of women now active as professionals in supercomputing, but not by much. Women are becoming more numerous and more visible in computing as well as in the sciences that use supercomputers. In another two or three years, the proportion of women should be higher. The number of blacks and Hispanics of either sex was small. The number of Asians—from South and West Asia as well as persons of Chinese, Japanese, and Korean descent—was substantial. In both cases this, also, reflected the current composition of professionals involved in advanced computing. Foreigners are at least as interested in supercomputing as Americans. (In its second year, the DOE high school program at Livermore included students from Canada, France, and Great Britain, and discussions at the SDSC summer institute were carried out in a rich plaid of accents.)

The fields of study represented at the SDSC institute did not differ much from the areas in which supercomputing is an established tool: physics (including fluid dynamics), chemistry, biology, earth sciences, computer science, and astronomy. There was an unusually high percentage of persons working in engineering and mechanics, but it is difficult to tell whether this was a statistical accident or the beginning of a trend. Active interest in increasing familiarity with supercomputing is not limited to graduate students; a quarter of the SDSC participants held appointments as assistant professor or above.

Many of those who attended the institute at SDSC were exploring

Kirby Fong of NMFECC (standing), a guest lecturer at the SDSC 1986 summer institute, talks with participants Channon Price (University of Maryland) and Maria Perkins (Vanderbilt University.) (*SDSC/GA Technologies.*)

unusual areas within these academic disciplines or approaching their topics in an particularly interesting way. Two of their projects are outlined in the next few pages. Other new or experimental uses of supercomputers are described in the rest of the chapter.

Controlling the Floodwaters of Alabama

Harold R. Henry is balding and much inclined to smile. If he put his mind to it, he could do pretty well on television, playing parts as mayor or banker in a small southern town or as Scarlett's kindly uncle.

In fact, he is a professor of civil engineering at the University of Alabama. He served as chairman of the department for 14 years and now concentrates on teaching and research. He has been working with computers for many years. Now he is using high-performance computers, including supercomputers, to develop a system aimed at several objectives: to protect people from potential floods, assure adequate water for recreational and other purposes, and make the most efficient use of water to generate electric power. This, in turn, lowers the total cost of electricity and also reduces burning of fossil fuels and the inevitable release of pollutants into the atmosphere.

The project that Professor Henry has been working on makes use of a system for measuring stream flow that has been in operation for some time. Automatic measuring stations all over the drainage basin relay information to a central monitoring point. In the past, the use of this information has depended upon an expert system lodged in the heads of experienced operators: "Hey, number two on Crimmins Creek is going up fast. We better do something about it, you remember year before last." Doing something about it may involve releasing water from a dam downstream so that excessive runoff can be contained. If, however, the flow has been overestimated and too much water is released, water discharged for precautionary reasons is not available for later power generation.

Professor Henry has been working with an IBM mainframe to analyze the data from these multiple sources and provide accurate, timely predictions to the managers and operators who must make the decisions. These are, however, complex calculations that require a good deal of time. In Alabama, many of the problems arise from intense, localized storms and relatively small streams. Distances may be fairly short, and a lot can happen in the hour or so that a mainframe can require to come up with a solution to be communicated to the control room.

Henry sought to provide more immediate feedback. Under a grant from the NSF, he was able to work on a Cyber 205 at Purdue University. The model he was using responded very well to vectorization. Henry attended the 1986 SDSC summer institute in order to see how his code might run on the CRAY X-MP. Adapting his code from one machine to the other involved some frustrations, but he found that performance and ease of use were improved on the X-MP. Problems that required an hour on the IBM mainframe could be run in one minute on the Cray.

Computerized prediction of river runoff and flood risk is nothing new, Henry says. The National Weather Service issues bulletins that estimate future downstream flows and potential risk for systems like the Missouri and Mississippi. He believes that he is exploring new ground, however, in developing real-time interactive feedback and by considering in detail the smaller streams and localized phenomena of the kind found in Alabama. Henry works closely with the Alabama Power Company, which provides support for his research. He has discussed his work with the U.S. Army Corps of Engineers, which has supervisory authority over stream flow regulation. Professor Henry is pleased with his progress so far and confident that he can achieve marked improvements over previous practices. He says that he does not intend to quit until he reaches mandatory retirement, "and that is a long, long way ahead."

The Hole in the Bottom of the Sea

Every few years, the editors who try to explain the latest developments in science to general audiences discover a "genuine gee-whiz." This possesses the proper combination of wonderment, understandability, and striking, comprehensible visuals that guarantee popular interest. Strange, cute creatures add to the appeal.

The discovery of fissures issuing dark, very hot clouds of sulphurous compounds in the deepest depths of the sea produced a genuine gee-whiz of the first order—especially when reports were accompanied by pictures of worms, crabs, tiny pale shrimp, and other creatures who thrive in these remote, inhospitable environments. It was one of those rare occasions when the sense of excitement and discovery felt by scientists could be communicated readily to the general public—genuine gee-whizzes have their uses.

For Tom Brikowski, a research associate at the University of Arizona, a quiet young man with luminous eyes, these are interesting but marginal phenomena. The heat and nutrients that support these deep-ocean ecologies are produced when the movement of tectonic plates opens rifts in the rock which lies at the bottom of the seas. This permits seawater to come in contact with hot, molten rock from the magma underneath. This process affects heat flow and petrology (the composition of the rocks that solidify as this process goes on). Brikowski uses computers to perform hydrothermal modeling of this process.

Field geologists, the rock tappers who remain the popular image of a geologist, have found examples of seabottom fissures cast up and made accessible by earlier upheavals and erosion. They are inclined to believe that the chamber of hot magma under one of these midocean splits is very large. Seismologists have also studied these phenomona by analyzing the patterns created by pounding on the surface of the sea with special apparatus on ships sailing a precise course. Their tentative conclusion is that the magma reservoirs that supply heat and chemicals to the fissures are relatively small.

This difference has far-reaching implications for the understanding of the relatively unfamiliar phenomenon of midocean rifts. Brikowski is one of a few researchers (about five, he estimates) who are seeking to resolve this question through computer simulation. He uses a finite element code that requires a great deal of memory. So far, he has been using a Cyber 175 at the University of Arizona, but he yearns for more power. Arizona is acquiring a Scientific Computer Systems SCS-40 minisupercomputer that should permit efficient vectorization of Brikowski's codes. He enjoyed his two weeks at the SDSC institute and is still looking around for enough computer time to make some real progress with his project.

Have Code, Will Travel

Kenneth J. Berry could also probably find a place on the "A" list of a Hollywood casting director. A solid man with short-cut, greying hair and a calm manner, he would fit in perfectly as the Marine sergeant who provides a combination of firm discipline and sympathetic encouragement to the hero, who progresses from uncertain adolescence to winning the Battle of Tarawa in the final reel.

Berry is, however, too busy to spare time for the cameras. Although he was trained as a sociologist and teaches in the Department of Sociology of Colorado State University, he describes himself as a statistician. During his career, he has focused increasingly upon using computers to broaden the reach of classical statistics. Berry describes classical statistics as "very robust" and by no means out of date, but he stresses that the statistical techniques developed during the first quarter of the twentieth century rest upon the assumption of a normal distribution. This finds its most familiar expression in the bell-shaped curve, equally beloved by the makers of IQ tests and by stern chemistry professors issuing grades to their students.

It is presumed that any population of natural phenomena—whether the heights of athletes, the selling-prices of houses, or the noisiness of bluejays—will tend to peak around a median point and tail off at a fairly smooth rates toward the two extremes. Basketball players will be taller than jockeys, and residential prices in Boston will be higher than in Rapid City. Within each class, however, the distribution will follow the general pattern—although some curves will be flatter or fatter than others.

What about phenomena which don't follow this pattern, but are skewed in one way or another? Berry has been working for years, first on various mainframes and, for the last two years, on the Cyber 205 supercomputer at Colorado State University, to develop programs which deal with these maverick cases. It is not easy to explain to the statistically illiterate. Terms like "permutation technique" and "non-asympotitic inferences" appear in the papers that Berry and his colleagues have published.

Most developers of supercomputer applications plow a single academic furrow, or at most cultivate a relatively small field. Berry's method has been in demand for an extraordinarily wide range of problems. For example:

- Fisheries experts were studying the effects of competition between trout species native to Colorado and the brook trout, a foreign species introduced into Colorado streams. They tagged 1200 fish of both species with tiny transmitters that identified the species and sex of each individual as well as its motion. Berry points out that "All those fish swimming around generated a great deal of data pretty quick." The researchers had analyzed their data using conventional statistical methods, but they came to Berry for confirmation. Once Berry had set up the problem for the Cyber 205, it ran in about 150 seconds of CPU time. The result (about the same as that arrived at through other methods) was that the native trout were being placed at a competitive disadvantage. The brook trout were able to monopolize the regions of slower stream flow and reduced turbulence, forcing the native trout to stay out where it was harder work, requiring more energy output, to keep up the daily grind.

The balance could be improved by putting rocks, logs and other barriers into the streams to give the native trout more space to lurk and live easy.

- Cases closer to sociology—and more difficult to solve through classical statistics—included a study of the concentration of lead and other metals in the back yards and kitchen gardens of Baltimore. This has important implications for public health, especially for children who play outdoors and may ingest contaminated dust or dirt. High concentrations of lead and other metals can have serious neurological consequences and other adverse affects upon growth and health, especially for children exposed while very young. Samples were taken over a wide area of Baltimore city, the suburbs in Baltimore County, and adjacent areas. (Baltimore is of particular interest because older buildings covered with many layers of peeling, flaking lead paint have been considered a major source of urban lead contamination—but the overwhelming majority of downtown structures in Baltimore are unpainted brick buildings.) Berry's method demonstrated that sites in the central part of the city predominated clearly among examples of higher concentrations of lead. Average concentrations in the suburbs were much lower. Because external paint could not be a significant cause, this pointed toward other alternatives, including lead deposition from motor fuel and earlier industrial uses of the land over Baltimore's long history.

- Archaeologists sifting through sites in Israel sought to analyze the significance of the spatial distribution of scrapers and other tools found in a particular location. Painstaking excavation and careful record keeping provide a complete, accurate set of data, but what next? A specialist could page through the data or sketch out a map, noting that there were a lot of these items here and lots of those over there, but it was difficult to be more precise. The approach of Berry and his colleagues permitted a much more exact, quantified, three-dimensional analysis of the distribution of artifacts. This makes it possible to establish a better understanding of how those tools were used, and hence to comprehend the life of those who lived at this site long ago.

Ken Berry describes himself as a mainframe man. (He says that he has never used a personal computer and isn't sure how he would start. He uses an archaic terminal which he describes as "very dumb.") He was not by any means an early adopter of the services available when CSU installed its Cyber 205 in 1982. Then he discovered that compilers like the FORTRAN-77 programs, although not all that hot at the beginning, made it possible to give supercomputing a crack.

He says that his code is not an obvious match for supercomputers—not like Fast Fourier Transforms, for example. Nevertheless, he has achieved a high degree of vectorization and is satisfied with the results he obtains. It isn't really easy. He saves the 205 for problems with about 100 cases or more, but a supercomputer is needed for the big problems. For sociological applications, he estimates that the current limit would be in the range of 10,000 to 20,000 cases.

A lot of people all over the world are showing interest in this addition to statistical techniques. Berry receives inquiries from psychologists and many other academic specialties. He has responded to requests for examples of his program from Czechoslovakia, Hungary, the Soviet Union, and many other places. Berry is of course gratified by this attention. He also enjoys the diversity. "You learn a lot by taking a try at something new," he says.

Pipes and Fluids That Live: Blood Flow within the Heart

Studies of the flow through pipes and more complex systems (like the engine of the space shuttle mentioned in Chapter Seven) are an established subfield within computational fluid dynamics. In ordinary engineering, however, the pipes or combustion chambers just sit there, or perhaps deform a little under heat and stress. The air, petroleum products, fuel mixtures or other fluids passing through may be flammable or toxic but are not fragile.

David M. McQueen is a mechanical engineer, a research scientist at the Courant Institute of Mathematical Sciences of New York University. He and his colleague at Courant, Charles S. Peskin, apply the mathematics and techniques of computational fluid dynamics in an extraordinarily demanding environment: the heart.

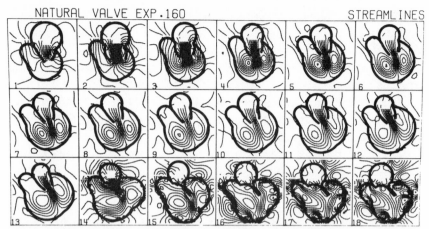

How the Heart Works: A Computer Simulation. These computer simulations by Charles S. Peskin and David M. McQueen show the cycle of the natural heartbeat, beginning at number 1 with the upper chamber full of oxygenated blood received from the lungs. The mitral valve between the chamber opens, and the upper chamber squeezes a solid stream of blood into the lower chamber. Then the mitral valve closes, and the lower chamber prepares to send the blood throughout the body.

The heart is dynamic, flexible, living, and in constant movement in every dimension. It is not just a mechanical component but monitors and directs its own actions. It pumps a fluid filled with living cells. If the rate of flow slacks off too far, thrombosis may develop. Clots may be sent out to do deadly damage elsewhere in the body, including the brain.

Most of the heart consists of solid, strong muscles that carry out the actual work of pumping. They can be vulnerable if deprived of their own blood supply or if the electric messages that control the pumping cycles lose their rhythym. If these perils are avoided the heart muscles are remarkably enduring.

The heart's valves are much more delicate and subtle. They can be damaged by disease. Physicians looking for ways to repair damaged hearts generally prefer to look first at possible replacements for the valves rather than the risky, still highly experimental, and extraordinarily expensive replacement of the entire heart with an artificial substitute. Hearts from human donors are less risky but always in short supply.

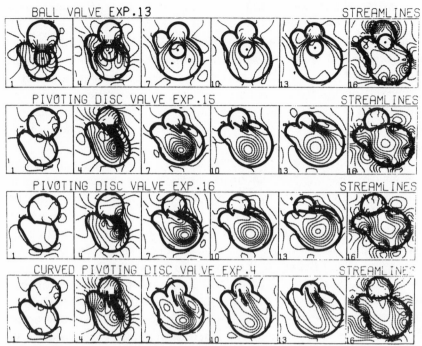

How Artificial Valve Designs Affect Flow Patterns. None of the potential valve designs delivers the solid, straight stream of blood, with balanced flow into both sides of the lower chamber, possible with a healthy natural mitral valve. These computer simulations by Peskin and McQueen suggest that, among these alternatives, a curved pivoting disk comes closest to the action of a natural valve.

McQueen and his associates have been supporting research and experimentation in this field by developing computer simulations that display, in graphic form, the flow through the normal heart and through hearts in which various designs of artificial valves have been inserted. The natural mitral consists of two thin, flexible, curved membranes, looking somewhat like a partially-collapsed parachute, as seen from below by an anxious jumper. The panels of membrane slap together to close the flow. When opened, they deliver a compact stream of blood from the upper chamber, which receives oxygenated blood from the lungs, into the lower one which supplies blood to the rest of the body. Symmetrical eddies spread off to each side.

Artificial substitutes cause different flow patterns. A ball valve results in a more widely scattered, turbulent flow. Valves with single, pivoting discs divert the main stream to one side or another, resulting in eddy patterns which differ markedly from those created by a natural valve. Studies at Courant have suggested a possible preferred design for replacements of the mitral valve between the upper and lower chambers. A two-leaflet butterfly valve shaped, in the researchers' term, like two parentheses back to back—) (— seems a promising shape.

In a 1985 paper reporting their work, McQueen and Peskin emphasize that "these conclusions are, in fact, *predictions* made with the help of a computer model. Such predictions must be checked by experiment. This paper will have served its purpose if it points the experimenter in the right direction. In particular, we hope that predictions concerning the beneficial effects of occluder curvature [the) (idea] will turn out to be useful."

Until recently, the investigators at Courant have used conventional computers. Forty minutes of computer time may be required to model a single heartbeat. Their preferred product is a graphic depiction in real time (a movie) of the beating heart, so a lot of computer time is required. They have also been limited to two-dimensional studies—cross-sections of the flow pattern.

McQueen reports that they are now using the CRAY-2 at the University of Minnesota. It has the computational power and memory to handle the massive calculations required for three-dimensional simulations. The only problem is familiar. The only communications available run at a few thousand bits per second, causing long, frustrating waits while data seep back and forth. "It's like a three-hour commute each way every day to do work which takes only five minutes," McQueen remarked. He and his colleagues are looking for a way to patch into a higher-capacity circuit.

These investigators at New York University are not alone in using computers to study and simulate the heart at work. Research into fibrillation (uneven heart rhythms that can often be fatal) is being carried out at many institutions, including the University of Arizona, Harvard Medical School, the Duke University Medical Center, and McGill University in Montreal. This new work is another example of a tendency that shows up in many other applications of scientific computations. Persons with diverse specialties, or ed-

Charles S. Peskin (right) and David M. McQueen of the Courant Institute of Mathematical Sciences at New York University examine computer simulations of the operation of the heart. (*Courtesy NYU/L. Pellettieri photo.*)

ucations that involve some unusual combinations of disciplines, are working together. McQueen's doctoral dissertation in mechanical engineering was on the mechanics and other technical aspects of one of the most common procedures of clinical medicine, taking a blood pressure reading by applying a confining cuff to the arm. Peskin is a mathematician with a physiology degree from Albert Einstein College of Medicine.

Computerized Stud-books? What's Next? Robot Cowboys?

Cattle raising is a tough business in good times, a miserable one when times are bad. It depends upon contrary and variable resources—including the land, often arid and marginal, and animals who can be almost as unpredictable and vulnerable as people. The product cycle is measured in years and includes segments like gestation time which do not respond to attempts at acceleration.

Long ago, however, cattle raisers learned to reduce their risks somewhat by improving the genetic potential of their herds. They focussed upon bulls whose progeny were more healthy, gained weight faster, were more fertile, and had other desirable characteristics. Bulls received more attention because each cow has only one calf each year, while a sire can have much more widespread influence upon a herd. As artificial insemination came into widespread use after World War II, a single sire of proven ability to transmit desirable traits could produce many thousands, rather than dozens or hundreds, of descendants.

Bruce Golden grew up on his family's cattle ranch in California, accustomed to these basic principles of cattle raising. Now, as a graduate student at Colorado State University, he is applying them in a new way. He uses a supercomputer to provide much more complete analyses of genetic potential and more accurate predictions of the outcome of matings between a specific bull and a particular cow.

The application of computers to data sets compiled by the breed associations which collect records of the genetic performance of beef cattle has been going on for some years. Research has been done at Cornell University, the University of Illinois, the University of Georgia, and elsewhere. These efforts have, however, been constrained so far by computer power which limited analysis to a relatively restricted number of desirable traits.

At CSU, however, Professor Rick Borden and Professor Jim Brinks, supported by Golden's programming skills, have been able to carry out much more comprehensive analysis on the Cyber 205. It is possible to analyze very large populations—5.5 million individual data points for the Polled (hornless) Hereford breed, for example—and consider a number of traits, including birth weight (which should not be too high, to prevent difficult deliveries), weaning weight, yearling weight (the higher the better) and the onset of fertility in heifers (the earlier the better). The program does not limit its attention to the record of a particular animal. It takes into consideration the genetic implications of an entire ancestry—the cows as well as the bulls. On one occasion, the stock of data was so large that the analysis could not be completed at CSU. The run was transferred to a Cyber 205 at the University of Minnesota which has a larger memory.

CSU does this work on behalf of the breed associations, including Charolais, Gelbvieh and others which are not household words among the ordinary buyers of the weekend special on chopped beef in five-pound packages. In turn, the breed associations publish catalogs for their members which list the characteristics and records of sires whose semen is available. It is not simply a matter of picking "the best" sires. A breeder can select for optimum effect upon the weaknesses, strengths, and specific requirements of his herd. Other traits which may have a beneficial influence upon a breeding program are being examined. One of these is what is delicately referred to as the "scrotal circumference" of a bull. A larger-than-usual measurement appears to have a favorable impact upon the age of fertility of that bull's daughters.

Golden is already contemplating new ranges. These include comparable studies for sheep and the most glamorous arena of animal breeding, racehorses. Golden says that Illinois has already done work on quarter horses. He has given thought to the special problems involved in becoming Bespoke Programmer to the Jockey Club. The racing ages of thoroughbreds are arbitrary, because all birth-dates are adjusted to a common date. How does one allow for variable influences, like jockeys and trainers? Golden recognizes that racing is a sport wrapped in tradition and mystery. Breeders, trainers, and for that matter bettors may not welcome the prospect of seeing their personal expertise being usurped by a machine. If, however, that machine could give an absolutely reliable tip for the fifth at Aqueduct . . .

How about people? A sure-thing computer installed in a singles bar would be fed a lot of quarters, if only out of curiosity. Humans are even more complicated than horses. There would be much uncertainty because much more accurate records are kept about cattle and horses than about people. Human breeding lines are very mixed, and getting more so. How would desirable traits be defined, and by whom?

Billions of Human Genes:
Sequence Them, Map Them, or What?

Bruce Golden practices applied genetics for practical ends which bring definable benefits to specific customers. Much larger and more contentious issues are taking shape in human genetics. Any scientific research device that requires many millions of dollars rather than thousands or a few millions is big science (although the threshold, as in so many other things, keeps rising). Thus a supercomputer facility is big science; a research project requiring many hundreds or thousands of hours on supercomputers can itself be big science. Furthermore, supercomputers, because of their exceptional computational power, often tend to become associated in one way or another with other big science projects, like large optical or radio telescopes.

Everyone is in favor of big science as long as it does not take money away from other projects, especially modest ones that have been surviving on relatively small grants and the hope of more. Funds are not drawn from a bottomless pot, however, especially in these days when rapid technological change is accompanied by equally rapid economic transitions and fiscal indigestion all over the world. A's gain can mean B's loss, belt-tightening for X, and a total close down for Y. Even when everyone agrees that the objectives are meritorious, big science can stir strong emotions. (The implications of this for the NSF supercomputing initiative are touched upon in Chapter Six.)

A full-scale example of the potential reverberations of big science arose in 1986. Genetics, like astronomy, is becoming overwhelmed with data. The human genome—the total information coded in the DNA of the 25 human chromosomes—contains three billion nucleotides, or fragments of information. It is now becoming possible to produce a complete nucleotide sequence—a description of the specific mix of DNA in each portion, known as a base—for the entire genome. Researchers all over the world are developing data about specific DNA sequences at an enormous rate. The two designated data bases, at Los Alamos National Laboratory in the United States and the European Molecular Biology Laboratory in Heidelberg, West Germany, have been hard-pressed to keep up.

The proposal: to sequence the entire human genome within the next few years. Most instances of big science arise from changes in technological capability, the sight of scientific opportunity or, much of the time, both. In the case of the human genome, supercomputers were not involved directly in the technological change. It arose from new procedures that determine sequences more rapidly and more cheaply, and the prospect of even better, less expensive methods in the near future.

Proponents and critics discussed this project at several meetings during 1986. Those in favor said that it could now be carried out with reasonable effort and would lay an essential foundation for future research in genetics. About 1000 human genetic diseases have been identified. Other diseases now the subject of intense public interest, including Alzheimer's disease, may have genetic origins. Opponents granted that a complete sequencing could be valuable but thought it would cost far too much—figures in the billions of dollars were mentioned—and could not be done very efficiently with current technology. Whatever the cost, an all-out effort could divert funds from other research in genetics or elsewhere in biology.

Other participants at these meetings wondered whether sequencing was the appropriate objective at this point in the development of genetics. They urged that attention be focused upon mapping the genome. This involves less detailed snapshots of the total genome. Genomic DNA would be fragmented into segments, perhaps each several tens of thousands of bases in length. The locations of these segments in the chromosomes and their functions could be identified. Segments with a known special interest might then be sequenced. As of the the end of 1986, it appeared that emphasis was to be placed upon mapping, while the proposal for all-out total sequencing would be set aside.

This short account is not intended to cover this issue adequately, nor to predict its outcome. It is relevant to this book because many observers believe that supercomputers will be required, sooner or later, in order to deal with the enormous data bases that would be generated by any variant of these proposals. Jacob Maizel is chief of the National Cancer Institute's Laboratory of Mathematical Biology at Frederick, Maryland. This old town is in an area of soft, rolling fields and low mountains, much fought over during the Civil War. It is rapidly becoming an outlying suburb of Washington. One symbol of this is the installation at Dr. Maizel's laboratory of a CRAY X-MP, linked by a high-capacity T1 circuit to the main laboratories of the National Institutes of Health in Bethesda, 30 miles to the south (see Appendix II, Section 2).

Dr. Maizel says that the prospects of involvement in the management of the data generated by sequencing was one of the reasons weighed before the Department of Health and Human Services decided to install the supercomputer. Geneticists are already making use of his Advanced Scientific Computing Laboratory. A study of RNA structure which would require 1200 minutes on a VAX 750 can be completed in five seconds on the X-MP, he says. The best algorithm for working with the human genetic data base requires tens of thousands of hours on a VAX and can be run in a small fraction of that on a supercomputer.

Planetary Fender-benders: The Origin of the Moon

"Where did the moon come from, Daddy?"

"I don't know, Bianca. Maybe it broke off from the earth, very long ago. Or it was just passing by, and it got caught by the gravity of the earth. Or it formed, out of junk in space, when the earth did."

"That was about what Ms. Gomez told us, in school."

"You sound like you think that's a dumb answer."

"Well, yeah. Didn't astronauts go up there, and drive around, when you were just a kid, and bring rocks back? Couldn't they find out *anything*?"

"I guess not. And, anyway, I was just starting college."

"Whatever."

For a long time, scientific theories about the origin of the moon did not advance markedly beyond the level of understanding implied in the preceding little dialogue. There were sound reasons for doubting any of the obvious possibilities (including differences between rocks on the earth and rocks recovered from the moon by visiting astronauts; the trip was not in vain). Until recently, there were no definitive arguments in favor of any of the main plausible hypotheses.

Once in a while, someone might suggest that the moon was the result of collision. As a consequence, perhaps, of some galactic miscue, an object of planetary dimensions intersected the earth's orbit, caromed off the earth, and then remained thereafter as a decoration lodged in the earth's gravitational field. Such proposals were considered thoroughly hypothetical, perhaps downright crackpot.

In 1984, however, a new theory was advanced at a conference on the origin of the moon at Kona, Hawaii. It was a collision theory but did not hypothesize an incident of galactic billiards, in which some object whizzing in from deepest space just happened to take an interest in the earth. The new theory postulates a planetary fender-bender.

About four and one-half billion years ago, the earth was mostly molten, just beginning to develop a rocky crust. Professor George Wetherill of the Department of Terrestrial Magnetism at the Carnegie Institution in Washington, D.C. explains that the space around the sun that now accomodates the inner planets was then a more crowded and disorderly neighborhood. Objects known as planetesimals in a wide range of sizes had condensed from the original cloud of dust surrounding the sun. Mutual gravitational attraction caused uneven orbits. Collisions took place, and smaller planetesimals were absorbed into larger ones. Relatively large planetesimals began to account for a greater and greater proportion of the total mass hanging out near the sun.

Professor H.J. Melosh, of the Lunar and Plantetary Laboratory at the University of Arizona, believes that the known facts can best be explained if it is assumed that a proto-planet around 3000 kilometers in diameter (one-seventh the size of the earth, or approximately the size of Mars) struck the proto-earth at a minimum speed of 12 kilometers per second—roughly 25,000 miles per hour. The surfaces of both objects crushed together. The enormous force of the impact caused the creation of two plumes of hot vapor which jetted away from the earth. The vapor consisted of material from the proto-earth as well as material from the visitor.

The vapor coalesced within hours. It began to develop into a dust ring and eventually into the the moon in its present state. The magnitude of the impact can be indicated by noting that the largest impacts that created the lunar mare, or "seas," were caused by latter-day planetesimals whose maximum diameter was on the order of only 50 kilometers.

Professor Melosh and the other scientists working in this field do not base these specifics upon a celestial traffic-ticket that has just been discovered. The new theory of the origin of the moon is based upon computer simulations. Professor Wetherill's work with planetesimals was carried out on a VAX. Professor Melosh and his colleagues developed their reconstruction, embodied in eye-catching graphics, on supercomputers at Sandia National Laboratory. Melosh has brought the scenario up to the dust-ring stage. So far, a lack of sufficient computer time—he needs about 200 hours—has kept him from going further. Scientists at Los Alamos National Laboratory have used somewhat different basic assumptions and a different computer code on supercomputers at their laboratory. Their results are not identical but do not cast doubt on the basic assumption that a collision of this kind took place.

Within a few years, this new theory about the moon may be generally accepted, or it may be abandoned in favor of some other. For a student of supercomputing, the key fact is that the use of supercomputers, running very sophisticated three-dimensional codes, played a direct part in sharpening academic debate about a long-standing unresolved scientific issue.

"Do I Hear You Correctly, Dr. Becker: Two Thousand Hours?"

Robert Becker, of the University of California at Davis, used to be an X-ray astronomer. Then the instrument that provided the best X-ray data, a NASA satellite, ran down. Now he describes himself in broad terms as an observational (as opposed to theoretical) astronomer, concentrating on radio astronomy.

The Milky Way Galaxy, which includes our solar system, is shaped like an enormous Frisbee. (We see the galaxy edgewise, from a point somewhere under the label part-way out from the center of the Frisbee that says it is the genuine article, made by a company named Wham-O, and woe betide anyone who tries to counterfeit one.)

Becker proposes to carry out a complete survey, in the radiowave portion of the spectrum, of the galactic plane: the portion (about two-thirds) of the edge-on view of the Milky Way galaxy visible from southern latitudes of the United States. Surveys have been done before, but they were carried out on single-antenna radio telescopes at relatively low levels of resolution. He anticipates that a survey at a higher level of resolution would discover many heretofore unknown radio-emitting objects that could have great scientific significance.

He wishes to use the multiple-antenna Very Large Array (VLA) radio telescope near Socorro (see Chapter Four) and to process the data on powerful computers like the CRAY X-MP. He anticipates that a galactic plane survey consisting of 90 minutes of VLA time per observation would require a total of about 300 hours of observation time—a substantial but not overwhelming portion of the VLA's annual round-the-clock observational capacity. In order to process the data, however, Becker will need about 2000 hours of time on supercomputers—close to 30% of the annual capacity of a single-processor machine, almost seven per cent of the annual capacity of a four-processor X-MP. Depending on the source of the computer time, the price on the open market would be between one and two million dollars. In any event, a commitment of a great deal of valuable processing time to a single project.

For the moment, Becker is working with programmers at Lawrence Livermore National Laboratory, adapting Socorro's basic image-processing code to a Cray operating under the CTSS operating system. Beyond that, he is caught in an Alphonse-Gaston dilemma. The managers of the VLA are reluctant to commit observational time until Becker is assured of computational time. He has received support for his program adaption from the Institute of Geophysics and Planetary Physics, a joint project of a number of University of California campuses and the national laboratories that are managed by the university (see Chapter Eight). He hopes for additional support.

Around the Bend in the Road

The medium-term outlook of the supercomputer era is fairly easy to discern in strategic dimensions, but the timing and specifics are murky. Technology is the least uncertain aspect. Computational power available in the marketplace will grow rapidly. The only question is whether it will grow extremely rapidly or only very rapidly. The problems of software and hardware involved in large-scale multitasking and then in massively parallel systems will be solved in a satisfactory way before long. The questions are: what is the definition of "before long?" A few years, 5 years, 10 years? What is the definition of "satisfactory fashion?" In any event, for most users, the availability and accessibility of supercomputers will continue to be a more widespread problem than the peak capacity of the most powerful machines.

Supercomputer may become a forgotton term. Or, like an old football which has abused and stretched too severely for too long, it may lose any usefulness and deserve to be set aside. It is to be hoped that the term could be retained for computers which are not just powerful but more powerful than all the rest. Other terms might be developed for different segments of a range of powerful machines which serve many important scientific and industrial purposes cost-effectively but are not at the extreme peak of performance. Science will always generate requirements that require the fullest measure of computational performance. Once these scientists obtain that, they will demand more. There should be an unequivocal label for machines that deliver that kind of performance at any given time, rather than smudging a name like supercomputer across a broad range of worthy performers.

In the shorter run, improving the accessibility of existing machines, especially in software development and networking, will have greater immediate impact upon overall utility to the scientific and business communities than breakthroughs in hardware.

Growth in the supply of high-performance computational capacity will continue to be accompanied by a reduction in the cost per calculation—although, as solutions become more complicated and materials become more exotic, the curve of improvement may flatten out. Demand will continue to grow more rapidly than supply. Researchers in other fields will become aware that studies as diverse as the design of heart valves and the origin of the moon have been stimulated or transformed by the results of supercomputer simulations. There will be additional stimuli from work like Harold Henry's, who applies supercomputers to problems of water runoff which preoccupied the engineers of ancient Babylon and China, and Tom Brikowski's, who explores phenomena discovered only a few years ago. Ways must be found to accomodate 2000-hour projects like Bob Becker's, and 200-hour projects like H.J. Melosh's. More of them will turn up, pursuing important scientific goals attainable only upon a supercomputer.

This tendency will be accelerated as people at every level from high-school students to professors become accustomed to the capabilities of supercomputers and consider them something to be expected, like electricity, just another tool of computations and of their own disciplines. This attitude contributed to a rapid expansion in the use of minicomputers and then the even more rapid adoption of personal computers and workstations in the 1980's. A similar impact upon the high-performance end of the scale seems inevitable. Effective, widespread training in the use of high-speed computing will accelerate this trend. Supercomputer training on a broad scale will also be a very wise investment for the institution or country that chooses to pay for it.

During the mid-1980s, supercomputing has done extremely well in terms of attracting federal and state support. There is no guarantee that this will continue. The newspapers, popular magazines, and television will discover other genuine gee-whizzes. Other big science projects will compete for attention from funding agencies and Congress. An inevitable question will be asked: "We put all that money into your supercomputers, but what have you done for the real problems? I still can't shake this damned cold, and why does commuting get worse every year?" Supercomputing is particularly vulnerable to this kind of query because supercomputers are not like dams. A model which served very well five years earlier may no longer do the job.

It seems certain that the internationalization of supercomputing, or at any rate of high-performance scientific computing, will continue. The Soviet Union will have a tough time catching up, by fair means or otherwise. The Japanese are powerful competitors in the marketplace as well as major, growing, and imaginative users of supercomputers.

In Western Europe, extensive use for diverse applications is already well established, and European production may become significant. The international character of science and the rapid, irresistible diffusion of powerful smaller computers will soon give other countries substantial computational capability. The countries acquiring these new capabilities are likely to include some which dismay officials in Washington who would prefer to control dissemination of this technology more closely.

As the supercomputer era begins to become established, a question mark remains. How soon will supercomputing emerge from laboratories into a production environment? There has been a very significant beginning, in Europe and especially Japan as well as in the United States, but it is not yet far advanced. Unless a great deal is hidden behind the walls of proprietary research, original and imaginative uses of supercomputers are still concentrated in research facilities.

If there is a Japanese threat in high-performance computing, imaginative, persistent applications of supercomputers to a wide range of practical technological problems could turn out to be more serious arena than the production of supercomputer systems. If U.S. private businesses across the full spectrum of industry establish and sustain a lead in the applications of high-performance computing, this could add significantly to the overall competitive strength of the United States. This is an entirely practical objective for the United States, which is after all the birthplace of the supercomputer and leads in most areas of advanced computational technology.

Supercomputer Hardware: Makers, Models, and Options

The six manufacturers now making supercomputers offer a bewildering variety of models and options. This section reviews models now in the market, including the ETA-10, now in the initial phases of operation. It also provides information about models no longer manufactured but available on the resale market. Brief descriptions of products offered by three mini-supercomputer manufacturers are also provided.

Cray Research, Incorporated

Cray Research offers two separate, distinctive basic designs, the CRAY X-MP and the CRAY-2.

CRAY X-MP

Introduced in 1982, the X-MP was the first mainline supercomputer model offering multiprocessing. As of February, 1987, the X-MP is available in two versions and eleven different options. Ten of these options operate at a clock speed of 8.5 nanoseconds (an

245

improvement in speed from the 9.5 nanoseconds that was offered until 1986). These main line options use the same basic chassis, and single-processor versions can be upgraded to two processors on the user's site.

Single-processor models are available with memories of four, eight, or 16 million words. Double-processor options include memories of two, four, eight and 16 million words. Four-processor X/MP systems can be ordered with four, eight, or 16 million-word memories. Prices include $5.5 million for an X-MP/14 (reduced from an earlier price of $6 million); $8.5 million for the X-MP/116, a new model; $6 million for the X-MP/22 (down from $7 million), $14 million for an X-MP/48, and $16 million for an X-MP/416. On-line solid-state storage devices (SSD), composed of MOS semiconductors, are available in five options, ranging in size from 32 to 512 million words.

A February, 1987, product announcement also inaugurated a new option, the CRAY X-MPse, a single processor unit with four million words of central memory, operating at a slower clock speed (about ten nanoseconds), and not upgradable to other X-MP systems. It is offered at $2.5 million, slightly less than half the price of the least expensive of the main line CRAY X-MP options. The CRAY X-MPse also features simpler installation requirements and a lower monthly maintenance fee. A Cray Research announcement states that the CRAY X-MPse delivers approximately 80% of the performance of a CRAY X-MP/14.

Multiple processor options of the X-MP are capable of multitasking (dividing a program to be executed in parallel). The standard operating system is COS, with UNICOS to become the standard operating system in the future. CTSS, which is optimized for time-sharing by multiple users, is also used. Basic software tools include a FORTRAN compiler, an assembler, a C compiler, and a Pascal compiler. A broad range of applications software is available. (See Chapter Two for additional information on the CRAY X-MP.)

CRAY-2

The CRAY-2, introduced in 1985, has several distinctive features: a 4.2 nanosecond clock time, a maximum of a 256 million word common memory serving two or four processors, and immersion cooling, using an inert fluorocarbon liquid. The CPU is also exceptionally small, a circular shape 45 inches high and 53 inches in diameter, containing memory and all processors. The footprint of occupied space is 16 square feet (1.5 square meters) compared with 64 square feet (6 square meters) for the X-MP/4 series systems.

In February, 1987, Cray Research raised the number of options from one to three. The CRAY-2/4-256, with which the model was launched, offering four processors and 256 million words of memory, was reduced somewhat in price, to $17 million. Cray Research added a two-processor option, the CRAY-2/2-128, with 128 million words of memory, at $12 million, and another four-processor option, the CRAY-2/4-128, also with 128 million words of memory, priced at $14.5 million. All CRAY-2 versions use the same software and are not field upgradable.

Cray Research claims that the CRAY-2 provides an order of magnitude increase in performance over the CRAY-1. The CRAY-2 operating system, UNICOS, is based upon AT&T's UNIX, and a set of compilers and other software tools is available. CTSS is also used. Applications programs used on the CRAY-1 and CRAY X-MP are being adapted to the CRAY-2.

Reports indicate that a new CRAY model, the Y-MP, will be announced before long, perhaps in 1987. According to this information, the Y-MP will be able to use software operating on the X-MP and will feature a larger number of processors than is available on the X-MP as well as a faster clock.

CRAY-1

Although discontinued, the CRAY-1 is still widely used and remains a factor in the resale market. (This market may, however, be affected by the recent announcement of the new lower-price CRAY X-MPse and price reductions at the lower end of other X-MP options.) A total of 63 CRAY-1 systems were installed following its introduction in 1976 as the first widely sold vector processor. X-MP systems are based upon CRAY-1 architecture.

All CRAY-1 systems have a clock time of 12.5 nanoseconds and operate on COS or CTSS. The original CRAY-1 used emitter-coupled logic (ECL) chips and was available with memory sizes of 256 thousand, 512 thousand, or one million 64-bit words. The

CRAY-1/S, introduced in 1979, substituted bipolar semiconductor technology and was offered in options with memories of 512 thousand, one million, or two million words. The CRAY-1/S, with 38 machines installed, is the most widely used version. The CRAY-1/M, using MOS memory technology, available in options of one, two, or four million words, was introduced in 1982 and discontinued in 1984.

> Cray Research, Inc.
> 608 Second Avenue South
> Minneapolis, MN 55402
> Telephone: (612) 333-5889

Sales offices at 23 locations around the United States; subsidiaries in Canada, France, the Federal Republic of Germany, Hong Kong, Italy, Japan, and the United Kingdom.

ETA Systems, Incorporated

ETA Systems, an independent company created and largely owned by Control Data Corporation, is responsible for the development and production of the new ETA-10 and supporting existing installations of Control Data's Cyber 205. The "10" in ETA-10 (expressed as a superscript in company brochures) is intended to imply an order of magnitude improvement in performance over earlier supercomputers. Early deliveries, during 1986 and the first half of 1987, are to be to Florida State University, the John von Neumann center at Princeton, and the University of Minnesota. A machine has been ordered by the Weather Service of the Federal Republic of Germany for mid-1988 delivery.

ETA-10

The ETA-10 is a multiprocessor machine, available with up to eight central processing units (CPUs). Each CPU has scalar and vector capabilities, with a local memory of four million 64-bit words. The CPUs access a shared memory, with options from 32 million to 256 million words, in increments of 32 million words. The ETA-10 is a virtual memory computer.

Like the CRAY-2, the ETA-10 emphasizes miniaturization. It utilizes complementary metallic oxide semiconductor (CMOS) chips which feature low power consumption, low heat production, and high density—on the ETA-10, 20,000 gates per chip. ETA representatives stress that the high gate density means that an entire CPU can be made with only 240 chips, permitting the CPU to be implemented on a single printed circuit board. ETA will also take another, unique step in the cooling race. According to ETA spokespersons, the use of CMOS chips and the highly compact CPU design result in a greatly decreased requirement for cooling. The machine operates without harm at room temperature. In order to achieve maximum performance from the CMOS chips, however, the ETA-10 design provides for immersion in liquid nitrogen, at a temperature about 175 degrees below zero centigrade.

ETA claims a potential performance level of ten gigaflops (ten billion floating point operations per second)—ten or more times, according to ETA, the performance of a CRAY X-MP/48. (Ten gigaflops is also the 1990 target for the Japanese high-speed scientific computer project.) Initially, the clock speed will be 10.5 nanoseconds. It will be increased later to 7 nanoseconds. The ETA-10 will run on an operating system with two user environments: VSOS, used by the Cyber 205, permitting it to run applications adapted to the 205; and an environment based on UNIX.

CYBER 205

About 40 Cyber 205's have been sold, to customers in the United States, Canada, Western Europe, and Taiwan. There are two basic options, with two or four vector pipelines. Memory sizes of one, two, eight, and 16 million 64-bit words are available. The clock speed is 20 nanoseconds. Distinctive features of the Cyber 205 include the capability to process long vectors of elements, up to 65,535, and the use of virtual memory. It operates on VSOS, developed by Control Data.

ETA Systems, Incorporated
1450 Energy Park Drive
St. Paul, MN 55108
Telephone: (612) 642-3408

Fujitsu

Fujitsu is a large Japanese integrated electrical/electronic manufacturer (although neither as large nor as diversified as a supergiant like Hitachi). It leads in market share in computer sales within Japan, followed by NEC (IBM Japan, once the leader, is now third). Fujitsu uses the name *Facom* for computers sold in Japan and many other countries. In the United States and Europe, supercomputers manufactured by Fujitsu are marketed by Amdahl. Amdahl Corporation, based in Sunnyvale, California, develops, manufactures, markets, and supports large-scale computer systems, storage products, communications systems, software programs, and educational services. Siemens, the large diversified German electrical products firm, also markets for Fujitsu in Europe. This description uses the model designations employed by Amdahl.

Amdahl 500, 1100, 1200, and 1400 Vector Processors

As the name implies, the Fujitsu-made supercomputers are vector-processing machines based upon the company's line of IBM-compatible mainframes. The Amdahl 1100 and 1200 were introduced in the United States in 1984; the 500 and 1400 in mid-1985. The scalar units are identical in scalar speed (14 nanoseconds). Vector units operate on a 7 nanosecond clock time. Differences in performance are due to successively more powerful vector units: the 1100 is roughly twice as powerful as the 500 and the 1200 four times as powerful. (The corresponding Fujitsu model numbers, used with the Facom trade-name, are VP-50, VP-100, VP-200, and VP-400.)

Options for the main memory of the 500 and 1100 range from 32 to 128 megabytes. Memory for the 1200 and 1400 is from 64 to 256 megabytes. Emitter-coupled logic chips with large-scale integration of 400 gates per chip are employed. Cooling for all models is by chilled air. The manufacturer claims peak processing speeds of 142 megaflops on the 500, 570 megaflops on the 1200, and over one gigaflop for the 1400.

In addition to stressing straightforward, reliable construction and high performance, sales literature for the Amdahl/Fujitsu machines also emphasizes compatibility with software developed for the IBM System/370 series, the established IBM architecture for mainframes up through the current 3090. The operating system used is MVS/XA, which offers easy integration into IBM installations. Fujitsu also provides a sophisticated, flexible compiler, the FORTRAN-77/VP compiler, and an Interactive Vectorizer that enables an operator to discover, diagnose, and correct sections of a program that could be improved through rewriting to increase vectorization.

Amdahl Corporation
1250 East Arques Avenue
P.O. Box 3470
Sunnyvale, CA 94088-3470
Telephone: (408) 746-6000

Hitachi, Limited

Hitachi describes its two models of supercomputers as array processing systems. The first machines of this series were shipped in October 1983. Like the Fujitsu supercomputers, Hitachi's entries are an extension of earlier mainframe machines. Peak performance of 315 megaflops is claimed for the S-810/10; 630 megaflops for the S-810/20. The Model 20 has twice as many arithmetic units, vector load and store units, and vector and scalar registers as the Model 10 and a larger maximum storage capacity.

One of the features of the Hitachi design is the inclusion of a solid-state "extended storage" that has a maximum capacity of 1000 megabytes. It is composed of 256 kilobit MOS chips. This feature functions very much like the Cray SSD, available on CRAY X-MP's. Main memory is 128 megabytes for the Model 10 and 256 for the Model 20; data can be transferred between main memory and the extended storage at 1000 megabytes per second. The machines are cooled by chilled forced air.

The high performance levels claimed by Hitachi are attributed primarily to the large number of high-speed vector processors and a consistent effort to design hardware and software tools so as to maximize vectorization. Hitachi has developed a customized compiler, the FORT77/HAP (Hitachi Array Processor), which is aimed at taking full advantage of the Hitachi design. Like Fujitsu, Hitachi also offers a tune-up tool, VECTIZER, that analyzes a program and draws attention to portions that could run more rapidly if fully vectorized. Hitachi computers are distributed in the United States by National Advanced Systems (NAS).

National Advanced System (NAS)
1705 Junction Court, No. 200
San Jose, CA 95122
Telephone: (408) 436-2400

International Business Machines Corporation

Like the Hitachi and Fujitsu machines, the IBM 3090 with vector attachments achieves supercomputer performance by adding vector processors to a basic mainframe design. The IBM philosophy is, however, somewhat different. The Japanese manufacturers achieve high theroretical performance by emphasizing very high levels of vectorization. IBM has focused upon more modest levels of vectorization, accompanied by high scalar efficiency.

The basic 3090 main frame, first shipped in 1985, is a multiprocessor machine. It is available with a single processor, two, four, or six processors. Optional vector processors can be added to one or more of these standard CPUs to achieve supercomputer performance. Multiprocessor options can run in parallel or with different tasks being divided among processors operating independently.

Cycle time for the 3090 is 18.5 nanoseconds. In the IBM tradition, each CPU has a cache storage—in this case, 64 kilobytes. Shared memory of up to 640 million bytes is available. The operating system is MVS/XA. Applications can be adapted to vector processing by using the IBM VS FORTRAN Version 2 compiler. Cooling is performed through the IBM Thermal Conduction Module system that drains heat away from circuit boards for disposal by chilled water piping.

Sales offices of IBM and its overseas subsidiaries are located throughout the United States and in most major cities abroad.

NEC Corporation

The NEC SX series of supercomputers was announced in 1983; first shipments were made in 1985; and the first installation in the United States (at the Houston Area Research Center) took place in late 1986. There are two models: the SX-1 (for which NEC claims a peak vector performance of 570 million floating point operations per second) and the SX-2 (for which 1.3 gigaflops are claimed.)

The SX-1 operates at a clock rate of 7 nanoseconds and the SX-2 at 6 nanoseconds (about in the middle between the CRAY X-MP clock speed of 8.5 nanoseconds and the CRAY-2's 4.2 nanoseconds). The additional performance of the SX-2 is primarily due to the increase in vector pipelines from eight on the SX-1 to 16. The SX-2 has four identical sets of four vector pipelines, making it possible for four vector operations to be executed in parallel.

Main memory is from 64 to 256 megabytes for the SX-1 and 128 to 256 megabytes for the SX-2. Like the Hitachi S-810, the SX series also features an extended memory unit. Composed of 256K MOS chips, it provides 128 to 2000 megabytes of solid-state memory—similar in function to the Cray SSD. A modular chilled water system based upon the same principles as IBM's is employed.

The operating program developed for the SX series is called SXCP. Like its Japanese competitors, NEC also offers a FORTRAN compiler, a vectorizer tool, and special tools called ANALYZER/ SX and OPTMIZER that make it easier for an operator to achieve high levels of vectorization and maximum efficiency.

NEC, the computer operations of the American electronic company Honeywell, and the French computer maker Groupe Bull are all technological descendants of the unsuccessful effort by General Electric to establish itself in the computer industry. Honeywell has announced that it is emulating GE, spinning off its computer business. The former Honeywell operations will be managed by a new joint operation with NEC and Groupe Bull in which the French company will take the leading role. The new corporation will presumably market supercomputers in the United States for NEC.

NEC Corporation
33-1, Shiba 5-chome
Minato-ku
Tokyo 108, Japan

Minisupercomputers

Alliant Computer Systems Corporation

The FX series of minisupercomputers was introduced by Alliant in mid-1985. The FX-8 emphasizes parallel architecture, with up to eight computational elements, or CE's. These are not conventional unary CPU's; each includes a number of individual processors. The company claims maximum vector performance of more than 90 megaflops with a full complement of eight CEs. Smaller versions of the FX/8 series can be upgraded.

The FX/1 is compatible with the FX/8 series, utilizing the same software and hardware. Peak performance in the 10-megaflop range is claimed for the FX-1. All Alliant models use an operating system based upon UNIX. FORTRAN compilers are also available. Different levels of the Alliant FX system range in price from approximately $100,000 to $1 million.

Alliant Computer Systems Corporation,
42 Nagog Park,
Acton, Massachusetts 01720
Telephone: (617) 263-9110

Convex Computer Corporation

The Convex C-1 is a 64-bit minisupercomputer with integrated vector processing, which features, as the company puts it, "Cray-like architecture." From one-half million to 16 million words of memory can be installed. The first C-1 was shipped in March, 1985, and the company states that more than 110 systems have been installed.

Using a UNIX-based operating system, the C-1 also features a compiler based upon FORTRAN '77. Prices of C-1 systems range from approximately $500,000 to $1 million, depending upon selection of memory, mass storage devices, and other options.

Convex Computer Corporation
701 Plano Road,
Richardson, Texas 75081
Telephone: (214) 952-0226

Scientific Computer Systems Corporation (SCS)

SCS offers a single model of minisupercomputer, the SCS-40, a 64-bit machine which utilizes the CRAY X-MP instruction set and operates on CTSS. UNIX will also be made available. Options include addressable memory of one, two, or four million 64-bit words. The first SCS-40 was shipped in mid-1986.

The SCS-40 operates at a clock speed of 45 nanoseconds. Company announcements emphasize that the SCS-40 can utilize over 300 widely-used engineering and scientific applications programs optimized for use on Cray supercomputers. Programs can also be vectorized with public-domain FORTRAN '77 compilers. SCS states that the SCS-40 delivers over 25% of the performance of a single-processor CRAY X-MP system. SCS prices begin at $595,000.

Scientific Computer Systems Corporation,
10180 Barnes Canyon Road,
San Diego, CA 92121
Telephone: (619) 546-1212

APPENDIX II _____

Where the Cycles Are: Supercomputer Facilities in the United States Available to Researchers and Other Users

Since the early 1980s there has been a far-reaching increase in the availability of supercomputer capacity (known to computer people as "cycles"). Access may be obtained under widely-varying conditions by academic researchers and other users, including private firms. This appendix provides basic information on equipment at selected facilities and describes the objectives, philosophy, and requirements for access of each installation. The three sections describe (1) the centers supported by the National Science Foundation (NSF), (2) other supercomputer facilities supported by the federal government which are accessible (usually on a selective basis) to outsiders, and (3) facilities at U.S. universities and major commercial service bureaus.

Section 1: Supercomputer Centers Supported by the NSF

The NSF initative provided the spark and continues to supply a substantial proportion of the gunpowder being used in the present explosive increase of supercomputer availability in the United States.

Operators of computer centers often say that their main task is to "put out [computational] cycles"—in other words, make capacity available. Not long ago, the would-be user had difficulty obtaining any cycles at all. Now, a great many more cycles are available. Finding out where they are has become a problem in itself. This appendix is a preliminary catalog.

The NSF launched its program to increase supercomputer availability in July 1984, when it began Phase 1 of a new program designed to provide U.S. researchers with access to supercomputers and encourage the growth and development of advanced scientific computing in the United States. The NSF funded several existing facilities, enabling researchers (most of whom were working on NSF-funded projects) to use supercomputer time at Purdue University, the University of Minnesota, and Boeing Computer Services. Later, three other suppliers of computer capabilities were added: Colorado State University; Digital Productions in Los Angeles, and AT&T Bell Laboratories.

Phase I was also intended to give researchers new to supercomputing an opportunity to work with various models: the CRAY-1/A and 1/S, the CRAY X-MP, the CRAY-2, and the Cyber 205, each of which was available at one or more of these facilities.

The NSF's newly formed Office of Advanced Scientific Computing allocated 22,000 hours of supercomputer time in fiscal 1985. It took a while for actual use to catch up with availability, due in part to users' frustrations over slow communications between their work sites and the computers.

Phase II of the NSF program followed briskly. It solicited proposals, reviewed them, and selected five projects that would receive NSF funding: the Center for Theory and Simulation in Science and Engineering at Cornell University (usually abbreviated Cornell Theory Center); the National Center for Supercomputing Applications (NCSA) at the University of Illinois, Champaign/Urbana; the Pittsburgh Supercomputer Center (PSC); the San Diego Supercomputer Center (SDSC), at the University of California, San Diego; and the John von Neumann Center for Scientific Computing (JVNC) at Princeton, New Jersey.

In addition to $200 million (over a five year period, beginning in fiscal 1985) from the NSF, substantial additional funding has come from other sources, especially host universities and the states in which the centers are located. Manufacturers of supercomputers, support computers, workstations, and other equipment have also supported the centers through reduced prices, technical support, outright donations of equipment and funding for development.

Increased direct involvement in supercomputing has been as significant as the increase in the number of supercomputers available for academic use. Over 60 universities and research institutions are participating directly in the program through membership in consortia or formal affiliation (see Chapter Six).

Three of the centers, those at San Diego, Princeton, and Cornell, involve consortia which span the nation. San Diego's affiliates extend from Hawaii to Maryland and include institutions in the East, Midwest, and mountain states as well as the Far West. Members of the John von Neumann consortium are located primarily in the Northeast but include the University of Arizona and University of Colorado. Affiliates of the Pittsburgh Center are concentrated in the mid-Atlantic states, Southeast, and Midwest. Cornell's consortium members are located throughout the U.S., with concentrations in the Northeast and Southeast.

In the early stages of development of the NSF-sponsored centers, two—those at San Diego and Princeton—emphasized consortia that spanned the nation. By spring, 1987, all five centers had developed systems of affiliation. Participants totalled over 100 universities and other institutions, many of which had multiple affiliations. These are reached by a wide variety of networking and dial-up arrangements. (See chart at end of Chapter Six for listing; additions continue to be made.)

The philosophies, objectives, and equipment of the NSF-supported centers reflect the diversity of the scientific community in the United States and equal diversity among those who founded and direct these centers. These differences are touched upon in the descriptions that follow.

General Information for Applicants for NSF Support

The NSF allocates 60% of total computing time available at each of the five NSF-supported centers. Decisions to award grants of computer time are based upon the scientific merit of the project and its contribution to scientific knowledge, the need for supercomputer capabilities, and the potential for successful completion of the project. Grants do not depend upon institutional affiliation. Applicants seeking computer time in the context of existing NSF grants (or grants from other federal agencies, such as the National Institutes of Health or U.S. Geological Survey) may receive priority attention. Each center has an allocation committee that allocates 30% of available time, according to criteria similar to the NSF criteria. The final 10% can be made available to private firms for non-classified research that may be proprietary. NSF applications and additional information may be obtained from Ms. Irene D. Lombardo, NSF Office of Scientific Computing, Telephone (202) 357-7558. Contact addresses and telephone numbers for each center are given following the description of the center.

Applications from academic researchers to NSF and individual centers are subject to peer review or reviewed by allocation committees. Decisions are typically made quarterly, and it is advisable to submit requests well in advance of the commencement of research. Some centers offer expedited action on small-scale requests (typically, five CPU hours or less).

The Center for Theory and Simulation in Science and Engineering

The NSF-supported center at Cornell University sought and was given an explicit mandate to focus on parallel processing in addition to providing capacity for researchers. Its director, Nobel laureate Kenneth G. Wilson, is a vigorous advocate of parallel computing and improved software methodologies. He especially emphasizes the scientific and technological "grand challenges" that more powerful supercomputers could address.

At the Cornell National Supercomputer Facility (CNSF), the main CPU is an IBM 3090-400 VF (running VM/CMS) with multiple FPS 264 scientific computers attached. The attributes of this configuration are high-speed scalar and vector processors, large virtual memory, expanded storage and potential for parallel processing. The Theory Center/CNSF sponsors a Strategic User Program to allow major portions of the resources of the 3090-400 VF to be dedicated to innovative science and engineering applications which require parallelism, extremely large memories, and/or large amounts of CPU resources.

Cornell is the principal provider of supercomputer services for NYSERNET (New York State Education and Research Network). This network is expected to reach full scale service in 1987, linking 15 major research institutions in New York State to the NSFNET backbone network. In addition to NSFNET and NYSERNET, the Center provides access to its resources via ARPANET, Bitnet, Accunet, and toll-free dialups. The Center also provides technical support for the nationwide NSFNET effort. The Cornell Center maintains an active outreach program, which includes the Smart Node program. The Center currently has 18 Smart Node institutions nationally. The Center also operates a Visitors Program to bring remote users of both the CNSF and ACF to Cornell for periods of one to three weeks to closely interact with Theory Center staff and the Cornell community.

A Research Institute has been formed to bring corporations into active participation with the Center's endeavors. Customized programs of interaction are formed to meet corporate research and supercomputing needs. Requests for time should be addressed to the NSF or to the Theory Center's Allocations Subcommittee. For more information contact:

Linda Morris:
Theory Center
265 Olin Hall
Cornell University
Ithaca, NY 14853-5201
Telephone: (607) 255-8686

The National Center for Supercomputing Applications (NCSA) at the University of Illinois, Champaign/Urbana

Inevitably, the names selected by the five NSF-supported centers shuffle similar words around in different combinations. The Illinois center, however, places "applications" in the center of its formal title. This is significant, like the choice of "theory" by Cornell. The focus at Illinois is the Interdisciplinary Research Center. The intent is to create a community of resident and visiting scholars who will explore new ways to apply the computational powers of high-performance computing systems to the widest possible range of applications in the sciences—and in the arts as well.

NATIONAL SCIENCE FOUNDATION
REQUEST FOR COMPUTING SERVICES

A. IDENTIFICATION

1. PI Name:	2. Title:	3. Address (include elec. mail & phone):

4. Education & computing experience of requesting scientist (please include co-PI's):

5. Project Title:	6. Major field of science:

7. New Applic. _____ Suppl. Req. _____	8. Other agencies/centers request submitted to:	9. Major comput. techniques:

B. RESEARCH SPONSOR (if applicable)

1. Sponsoring Agency:	2. Award No. (eg, ASC86-00000)	3. Expir. Date:

4. PI (name, instit., address, phone—if different from Section A):	5. Host Program Director/phone:

6. Endorsements (certification that computations are part of sponsored research; name, title, date)

Principal Investigator   Authorized Institutional Rep.

_____   _____

_____   _____

_____   _____

C. RESEARCH REQUIREMENTS

1. Requested center (circle one, please refer to the "Centers Information Section" for details & contacts):

Cornell   Illinois   JVNC/Princeton   Pittsburgh   San Diego

2. Service units requested:

number _____ proposed start date _____ expected completion date _____

projected use per quarter _____ _____ _____ _____

NSF 1235 (2-86)

3. Special requirements (yes or no):

extensive memory _____ extensive mass storage _____
graphics devices _____ other _____

4. How will you access the center? (eg, networks and local host)

D. PROPOSAL

(Your request will fall into one of the following categories. Please read carefully and follow instructions).

1. If your request for supercomputer time is submitted as a component of a standard NSF research proposal, send it to the appropriate NSF research program in accordance with "Grants for Scientific and Engineering Research," NSF 83-57. Sufficient information should be provided to allow peer review of both the science and numerics. A breakdown of computer usage must be included.

2. If this is a request for additional time to complete work in progress at the center, please send the following to the center:

    a) a summary of progress to date,
    b) a justification for additional supercomputer resources, and
    c) plans to complete the project.

3. If this is a request for supercomputer time in conjunction with a currently sponsored research project, please attach a copy of the grant proposal, complete items a, b, and c in number 4 below, with respect to the supercomputer request, provide a rationale for the amount of time requested, and send either to the appropriate NSF research programs or to the center.

4. If this is a request solely for supercomputer resources, please submit the following information to the center:

    a) Abstract (<200 words).
    b) Significance of the research project and its contribution to scientific knowledge (<500 words).
    c) Objectives of this project (<500 words).
    d) Methodology (<500 words).
    e) Description of previous studies or preliminary results that have bearing on this project and its potential for success (<500 words).
    f) Available resources (<1,000 words). Please include: (i) qualifications of PI(s) [attach vita(e), list of relevant publications], (ii) institutional support and or other sources of funding, and (iii) a description of local computing environment relevant to the project.
    g) Please provide the name, address and phone number of three people who are familiar with the research for which the computing resources are requested.

MAILING ADDRESSES FOR THE CENTERS APPEAR IN THE "CENTERS INFORMATION SECTION" OF THE ACCESS DOCUMENT. THIS REQUEST FORM MAY BE SUBMITTED TO EITHER NSF OR THE CENTER DIRECTLY.

Larry Smarr, the center's director, talks enthusiastically about "coupling supercomputers into the human eye-brain system." He also seeks a "fusion of art and science." The NCSA emphasizes the complete system, not just the capacity of the supercomputer itself. Attention will be concentrated upon improving imaging and upon improving algorithms and software tools so that scientists who are not programmers can take full advantage of these capabilities. The center is acquiring a large number of workstations and personal computers—including Suns, IBM PC/ATs, and Apple Macintoshes— for use by resident and visiting users.

The equipment at NCSA is not experimental. Operations began with a two-processor CRAY X-MP/24 that was later upgraded to a four-processor X-MP/48 with a 128-megaword solid-state storage device. The operating system is CTSS; two VAX 785s running VMS serve as a front end. Operational experience has been good, and attention is now being focused on improvements in communications protocols and other facilities in order to improve remote users' productivity.

Professor Smarr has pointed out that NCSA offers corporate users a chance to participate in the intellectual atmosphere of the research center and be able to know what is going forward in supercomputer technology and applications. The goal is ten corporate participants, each of whom would contribute $1 million a year. At the end of May, 1986 Smarr announced that Eastman Kodak was the first corporation to join.

Contact: Applications may be made to NSF or direct to the NCSA, emphasizing detailed justification for computer time and a clear statement of priorities. Applicants seeking small start-up authorizations (up to five hours) in order to optimize their codes or prepare proposals are encouraged. For visits, contact the Visitor's Program Coordinator at (217) 244-0074.

National Center for Supercomputing Applications
Center for Supercomputing Research and Development
University of Illinois at Champaign/Urbana
154 Water Resources Building
605 East Springfield Avenue
Champaign, IL 61820
General number: (217) 244-0074

The Pittsburgh Supercomputer Center (PSC)

In June 1986, the Pittsburgh Supercomputer Center dedicated a CRAY X-MP/48 with a 128-megaword SSD—which had in fact been operational since April. The center is a joint undertaking of Carnegie-Mellon University and the University of Pittsburgh. The supercomputer itself is managed by the Westinghouse Corporation, which has operated supercomputers in Pittsburgh for a number of years.

Its objectives are similar to the other NSF centers: to advance basic research, provide quality supercomputer capability to the scientific and engineering communities, offer training opportunities, and educate users about the capabilities of supercomputers. To assure a high level of participation in the activities of the center, the PSC has formed a group called Academic Affiliates, chosen primarily from top research universities. This group forms an advisory committee for the PSC.

The operating system is COS, the standard system developed by Cray Research, modified by Westinghouse. The central unit has four processors, 64 megabytes of memory, and 19.2 gigabytes of very fast disk storage. The front ends are two VAX 8650s running VMS with their own tape and disk storage capabilities. Permanent data storage is managed by an automatic file system, transparent to the user, which moves rarely used files from disk to tape.

PSC is on several major networks. It will be a major node for NSFNET, the network linking the NSF-supported national centers and NCAR. It will also have high-speed connectivity to SURANET (linking universities in the Southeast). It will be a national ARPANET node for NSFNET.

Like other NSF-supported centers, the PSC is permitted to allocate 10% of total time for proprietary research. It encourages the participation of industrial affiliates that would like to become more familiar with supercomputing and use supercomputer time for their proprietary work.

Contact: For consultation and training, contact Robert Stock; for industrial affiliates, contact Beverly Clayton, Executive Director. Applicants for time should contact the NSF or apply direct.

Pittsburgh Supercomputing Center
4400 Fifth Avenue
409C Mellon Institute
Pittsburgh, PA 15213
General telephone: (412) 268-4960
Executive Director: (412) 268-4860

The San Diego Supercomputer Center (SDSC)

The SDSC is located on the campus of the University of California, San Diego, in La Jolla, on the coast north of the main part of the San Diego municipality. It is operated by GA Technologies, Inc., and is linked with a 25-member consortium over a 56-kilobit per second network (SDSCNET) consisting of ground and satellite circuits.

SDSC's primary mission is "to foster near-term scientific achievements and advances by providing a broad national community of researchers with state-of-the-art hardware, software, and user services." Like the other NSF-supported centers, it welcomes participation by industrial affiliates. Affiliate relationships with SDSC have been established by Aerojet General, AMOCO, Battelle Memorial Institute, International Telephone and Telegraph (ITT), MACOM Linkabit, Omnibus, Science Applications International (SAIC), and the Rohr Corporation.

Basic resources include a CRAY X-MP/48 supercomputer with eight million 64-bit words of memory and an SCS-40 minisupercomputer with four million 64-bit words of memory. Both CPU's run the CTSS operating system. (The SDSC is described in greater detail in Chapter Two.)

Contact: Applicants should contact NSF or directly to the SDSC Allocation Committee, c/o Dan Bender, SDSC Program Manager, (619) 534-5030. Inquiries about industrial participation should be directed to Robert Randall, Resource Development Manager, (619) 534-5060.

San Diego Supercomputer Center
GA Technologies, Inc.
P.O. Box 85608
San Diego, CA 92138

The John von Neumann Center for Scientific Computing (JVNC)

The JVNC center is located in Princeton, New Jersey, in a technology park on traffic-clogged Highway 1, a few miles from the university. It is operated by the Consortium for Scientific Computing, a grouping of universities and other institutions, mainly in the northeastern and mid-Atlantic states, but also including the University of Arizona and the University of Colorado.

Named after one of the most creative pioneers of computing, the JVNC seeks to be a pioneer in pressing the boundaries of computation forward. During the first half of 1987, it will install one of the first production models of the ETA-10 (shortly after another ETA-10 is delivered to Florida State University). In the interim, its main resource is a Cyber 205, running on the VSOS operating sysem. The 205 is a two-pipeline machine with a memory of four million 64-bit words. A VAX 8600 cluster acts as front end.

The stated objective of the JVNC center is to "provide state-of-the-art computing and communications to university, government, and industrial researchers." In addition to NSF support, the project received a $12 million construction grant from the State of New Jersey. Much attention has been given to development of the network serving consortium members. The University of Arizona and the University of Colorado are served through 56 kilobit/second satellite links, and the University of Rochester is served by a land line of the same capacity. Closer consortium sites are served by T1 links. Other customers are served via dial-up links.

Contacts: Applications should be submitted to NSF or to Brenda McNamara, (609) 520-2000. For general information: Ben Bryan, (609) 520-2000. Industrial relations: S. Orszag, (609) 452-6206.

The John von Neumann Center
Consortium for Scientific Computing
P.O.Box 3717
665 College Road East
Princeton, NJ 08543

Section 2: Federal Supercomputing Facilities Available to Outside Researchers

Federal agencies in the United States operate a number of super-computer centers and networks that are available to academic researchers in certain fields and, in some cases, to private companies as well (on a reimbursable basis if research is proprietary). These resources are growing in number, capacity, and accessibility. For many disciplines, especially fluid dynamics, energy research, atmospheric and oceanographic research, and medical research, these federal facilities constitute a large part of total available super-computing resources.

Specialized government users like the Department of Energy's national laboratories and NASA played crucial roles in stimulating the development of supercomputers and creating the software, networks, and support technology needed to make supercomputers work. The National Center for Atmospheric Research (NCAR), operated by a nonprofit consortium of universities and supported primarily by the National Science Foundation, was also able to stay at the forefront of supercomputing.

By emphasizing their special needs and demonstrable requirements for high-speed computing, these federally-supported activities were able to display remarkable ability at dodging the budget cycle. In addition to contributing to the development of hardware, operating systems, and applications software, these agencies made services available to outside researchers and demonstrated that supercomputing is an essential tool of science. Individual academic researchers and whole scientific disciplines complained at being excluded, but these specialized uses helped to prepare for the rapid expansion in general-purpose supercomputer facilities that is now taking place.

In recent years, federal agencies have continued to provide much of the impetus to improvements in the availability and accessibility of supercomputers and in the diversity of supercomputer applications. NASA and the DOE laboratories are increasing their capacity and broadening access. New supercomputer facilities established by other federal agencies, including the National Cancer Institute and the National Bureau of Standards, are also accessible to scientists participating in cooperative programs and other outside users.

Other federal departments—including the military services—are starting new supercomputer programs or adding to present resources. Many of these facilities are accessible to defense contractors and to other researchers outside the Department of Defense. Most of these uses are specialized, and special procedures (including classification) may be involved. For these reasons, DOD resources are not catalogued here.

The equipment, fields of specialization, and procedures for access of federal facilities vary widely. Federal supercomputing programs most likely to meet the needs of broad categories of academic researchers and potential industrial users are described in this section. To the student of the sociology and politics of supercomputing, these supercomputer centers present a fascinating contrast in philosophy, aspirations, and approach.

The National Center for Atmospheric Research (NCAR)

Ever since its foundation in 1960, the National Center for Atmospheric Research in Boulder, Colorado has made every effort to obtain access to the most powerful computers available. As an NCAR bulletin points out, it is "dedicated to furthering our understanding of atmospheric, oceanographic, and related sciences through the use of modern research applications, including the use of large-scale computing services." Computations are prominent because "Most broad and innovative research in the atmospheric and oceanographic sciences depends upon large-scale computing, primarily in the analysis of very large data sets and various types of simulation modeling." (See Chapter Eight for a brief review of supercomputing applications in atmospheric and oceanographic research from the scientists' point of view.)

In its first few years, NCAR had access to computers located nearby on the campus of the University of Colorado and at the Boulder branch of the National Bureau of Standards: an IBM 1620, a Control Data 1604, an IBM 7090 and an IBM 709. In 1964, NCAR purchased its first computer, a CDC 3600, a 48-bit machine with 32K of memory. A CDC 6600 (designed by Seymour Cray) was bought in 1965, replacing the CDC 3600, and A CDC 7600 was obtained in 1971. In 1977, NCAR installed a CRAY-1/A, whose computational capacity was roughly 50 times that of the CDC 3600.

NCAR's current inventory includes a CRAY X-MP/48 with a 256-million word SSD and eight million words of bipolar memory shared among the four processors. It also operates a CRAY-1/A, with over one million words of central memory. Both machines run Cray's COS batch-mode operating system. An IBM 4381, which runs IBM's VM/CMS operating system, provides front-end services, including remote job entry access to the supercomputers for users who prepare jobs on computers at their own distant sites. On-line storage is provided by an IBM 3380 disk system that can contain 960 billion bits; long-term data storage is carried out by an IBM 3480 magnetic cassette system. Special equipment includes two laser printers and two Dicomed graphics processors which can produce high-quality graphic output, including microfiche and three sizes of film for still images and movies.

These facilities, operated by NCAR's Scientific Computing Division, can be reached over a remote user network (UNINET) from more than 150 terminals at almost 100 universities and research organizations in the United States and Canada. Users can reach the UNINET packet switching network via local telephone calls to the nearest UNINET access location. NCAR is a major node on the NSFNET coast-to-coast trunk line that is now being established. In addition, NCAR has office space and support facilities for scientists who come to Boulder to conduct their research.

NCAR's allocation guidelines reserve about 42% of available resources for researchers on the NCAR staff; 42% goes to scientists outside NCAR. The remainder is used for joint projects. NCAR policy emphasizes large projects beyond the scope of university computing facilities or requiring special capabilities. The services are intended to extend rather than duplicate computing resources available at an applicant's home institution.

Applications for small amounts of NCAR supercomputer services are reviewed by the director of the Scientific Computing Division, guided by a peer review process. Requests for larger projects are also reviewed by an advisory panel. Research should fall within NCAR's definition of atmospheric or oceanographic science, which includes relevant areas of earth science, solar physics, and astrophysics. Other criteria include estimated scientific contribution, originality, justification of the resources requested, and efficient use of computing resources. Applicants requesting National Science

Foundation grants that include NCAR computational resources should submit applications simultaneously to NCAR. User fees are charged to investigators not supported by the NSF. As with other applications processes employing peer review, applications should be submitted well in advance.

Contact: Application forms may be obtained from:

JoAn Knudson
Scientific Computing Division
National Center for Atmospheric Research
P.O. Box 3000
Boulder, CO 80307
Telephone: (303) 497-1207

Completed applications should be submitted to the Director, Scientific Computing Division, at the same address. Requests for general information about NCAR should be sent to the Information Office at the same address.

The National Bureau of Standards (NBS)

The supercomputing system at the National Bureau of Standards Gaithersburg laboratories, based upon a Cyber 205 that went on-line in spring 1985, is a child of compromise. The NBS is a unit of the Department of Commerce, a mansion with many chambers. The Consolidated Scientific Computing System has established close cooperation among some of those chambers.

NBS had a long history of using high-performance computers, and it yearned for its own supercomputer. In a decision at the departmental level, Commerce concluded that such a computing facility should provide services to other units, notably the five sites of the Environmental Research Laboratories (ERLs) of the National Oceanic and Atmospheric Administration (NOAA) and the Institute for Telecommunications Sciences (ITS) of the National Telecommunications and Information Administration (NTIA).

The ERL sites are in Boulder, Colorado (where ITS is located and the NBS also has a branch); Seattle, Washington; Ann Arbor, Michigan, Norman, Oklahoma; and Miami, Florida. Each specializes in topics appropriate to its location: localized severe storms at Norman; the Pacific and phenomena of large bodies of water (such as the El Niño cycle of weather and oceanic temperature) at Seattle, oceanographic and meteorological studies at Miami, and the Great Lakes at Ann Arbor.

The NBS has established a network of leased lines. The overall plan is to integrate local capabilities, including VAXs at all sites and a Cyber 180/846 at Boulder, with those of the central system. It was assumed that the requirements of the ERLs would be modest—for example, an estimated 150 hours of CPU time on the Cyber 205 per year for Seattle. Once the system was established, however, Seattle began to use time at an annual rate of 350 hours—and rising. By the summer of 1986, ERL use had reached 25% of the total; long-range plans call for a split of 60% for the NBS and about 40% for the rest of the system.

At the NBS itself, major users of the system have included investigators in thermal physics, fire modeling, and the specialized field known as characterizing surfaces (their degree of smoothness and roughness). According to Glenn Ingram, NBS's associate director for computing at the Center for Applied Mathematics, problems of characterization are an ideal vector application, well suited to the Cyber 205. He said that access to the new facility had enabled researchers in this field at the NBS to advance to the forefront of research in their speciality.

The NBS Center for Building Technology has applied the supercomputer to problems of structural collapse, the effects of high wind forces upon glass-sided buildings, and snow-load capacity of wooden beams. The solidification of alloys and other problems in materials science are major consumers of supercomputer time at the NBS.

As it turned out, the Department of Commerce decision has worked out to everyone's benefit. The system is saturated already, and thought is being given to future augmentations.

Cooperative and collaborative projects with scientists and engineers from universities and industry have a long tradition at the NBS and the ERL. The laboratories can now accommodate investigators whose projects require high-performance computing. Researchers engaged in collaboration with NBS or ERL scientists may be able, with the approval of their NBS or ERL collaborators, to obtain access to time on the Cyber 205.

The National Cancer Institute (NCI)

Since April 1986, the National Cancer Institute has been operating the first supercomputer facility in the United States to be dedicated entirely to biomedical research. An NCI announcement states that "The philosophy of operation is to provide a strong research environment through collaboration, training, and independent research. The scope of operation is to apply current technology computational capability and special emphasis on analysis of rapidly expanding molecular biology data using the methods of advanced computation and mathematical biology." It is intended to provide support for the scientific community associated with the Department of Health and Human Services, HHS grantees, and other biomedical researchers.

The NCI's Advanced Scientific Computing Laboratory is at the Frederick Cancer Research Facility located at Fort Detrick in Frederick, Maryland, 40 miles north of Washington, D.C. Its central resource is a CRAY X-MP 2/2U, using the COS operating system. This is now a single-processor machine; it is planned to add to memory and place another processor in service. The facility is being linked over a T1 circuit to the main laboratories of the National Institutes of Health in Bethesda, 30 miles to the south. Specialists at Frederick manage and develop hardware and software resources and develop programs and systems for applications in the center's fields of concentration.

Applications from researchers will be reviewed by a board including representatives from the NCI, the Laboratory of Mathematical Biology, and outside scientists. Criteria are scientific merit, potential for successful completion, appropriateness of computing resources for the research, availability of time, and support services required.

Contact: Dr. Jacob Maizel, Chief
Laboratory of Mathematical Biology
P.O. Box B
Frederick, MD 21701
Telephone: (301) 698-5532

The National Magnetic Fusion Energy Computer Center (NMFECC)

The NMFECC is located at Livermore, Calfornia and operated for the Department of Energy by the Lawrence Livermore National Laboratory. Its exceptional concentration of supercomputer capability includes a CRAY-1, a CRAY-1/S, a two-processor CRAY X-MP/22, and the first CRAY-2 to go into regular service. The network serviced by the NMFECC, called MFENET, also has access to the resources of the San Diego Supercomputer Center and to a Cyber 205 at Florida State University, which also installed in late 1986, on an experimental basis, the first ETA-10 to be delivered. Since mid-1985, the NMFECC has also operated a link with the Institute of Plasma Physics in Nagoya, Japan. It is the oldest supercomputer network (started in 1974) and is still the largest. The NMFECC is used only for unclassified research and is separate from the Livermore Computer Center (LCC), which is used primarily for the laboratory's classified research on programs in support of national security requirements.

These resources are provided to users over a network composed of a mixture of satellite and terrestrial links, most of which operate at 56 kilobits per second. The NMFECC rents transponders on two satellites, providing a dual capability—one link can take over if the other fails. A NMFECC history notes that "By retaining control of the entire network (rather than purchasing access to someone else's network) NMFECC has been able to provide services that are integrated with our supercomputers."

As one of the pioneers in supercomputer operation as well as networking, the NMFECC has developed software and inaugurated procedures and practices which are now used widely within the supercomputer community—especially time-sharing systems. (As noted in Chapter Two, the Livermore-developed time-sharing operating system, CTSS, is also used by the NSF-supported centers at San Diego and Illinois.) The NMFECC has also developed a multilevel file storage system, a distributed personal computer workstation software system, and other tools.

Initially, NMFECC served a single set of customers: researchers in the field of magnetic fusion energy. In 1983, the DOE's Office of Energy Research, responsible for a much wider spectrum of energy-related disciplines, asked the center to expand its services. Research programs now supported include high energy physics, nuclear physics, materials sciences, chemical sciences, carbon dioxide research, engineering and geosciences, heavy ion fusion, applied plasma physics, and health and environmental research. By 1985, the total number of NFMECC users had approximately doubled, to 3500, and by the summer of 1986 the total had come close to doubling once again.

> *Contact:* National Magnetic Fusion Energy Computer Center
> Lawrence Livermore National Laboratory
> Post Office Box 808
> Livermore, CA 94550
> Telephone: (415) 422-1544

NASA Supercomputing Facilities—
The Numerical Aerodynamic Simulation (NAS) Project

NASA is no stranger to high-performance scientific computing. On the contrary, it has in fact been among the earlier and most intensive federal users of supercomputing. Supercomputers have been in operation for some years at the three NASA installations designated research centers: Ames, at Moffett Field (near Mountain View), California (a Cyber 205 and CRAY X-MP); Langley, at Newport News, Virginia (Cyber 205); and Lewis, at Cleveland, Ohio (CRAY X-MP). The Marshall Space Flight Center in Huntsville, Alabama is in the process of acquiring a supercomputer. Principal applications at the research centers include computational aerodynamics, computational fluid mechanics, and analysis of the thermal and structural performance of components of aerospace propulsion systems.

Beginning in 1975, participants in the computational fluid dynamics program at the Ames Research Center set several ambitious goals. As an Ames paper described it, they "proposed the development of a special-purpose Navier-Stokes processing facility which would have several orders of magnitude more speed than the ILLIAC IV computer [an experimental multiprocessor machine then in use at Ames] for solving the equations of fluid physics." (For an introductory discussion of the use of supercomputers in fluid dynamics, including the significance of the Navier-Stokes equations, see Chapter Seven.)

The ILLIAC IV was a sensitive, stubborn creature, difficult
to program and hard to use. Additional goals were set. The proposed
new machine "had to be user-oriented, easy to program, and capable
of detecting systematic errors when they occurred." During the
succeeding years, the goals of the program were revised to adjust
to new capabilities; discussions with users raised additional issues.
In the early 1980s, it was decided that system architecture and
advanced system networks were as important as the supercomputers
themselves. In order to reduce dependence on specific machines
or manufacturers, the center would need to develop its own technical
capability to achieve maximum overall performance capability.

In later stages of planning, three principal programmatic goals
were defined: "(1) Provide a national computation capability, available to NASA, DOD, other government agencies, industry, and
universities, as a necessary element in insuring continuing leadership
in computational fluid dynamics and related disciplines; (2) act as
a pathfinder in advanced, large-scale computer system capability
through systematic incorporation of state-of-the-art improvements
in computer hardware and software technologies; and (3) provide
a strong research tool for NASA's Office of Aeronautics and Space
Technology."

The fruit of this long preparation is in reach. The NAS Production
System went into initial production in July, 1986, with about 100
users in 20 locations throughout the U.S. It moved to a new facility
in early 1987. (NAS is a national facility, separate from the supercomputers at the Ames central computational facility, that primarily serve researchers on the site.)

A number of supercomputing projects, including the NSF-
supported centers at Cornell and Illinois, have made declarations
that they intend to remain in the forefront of supercomputer performance, using phrases like "second to none." The NAS program
at Ames has adopted a formal policy toward this end, endorsed
by NASA. At any given time, NAS hopes to have two main high-
speed processors. One is to be the most powerful machine available
at the time of purchase, domesticated so that it can serve as the
principal day-to-day source of computational horsepower. The other
is to be an even more advanced machine, still snorting and inclined
to buck. It will in due time be subjected to the discipline of saddle
and snaffle and become a steady performer. At that time, NAS

will phase out the older machine while it identifies another skittish but promising new colt to bring into the stable.

This means that NAS has to have some pretty skillful horse trainers. This task is to be made less overwhelming by the development of an operating system and basic software that are, in NAS jargon, "vendor-independent." NAS was one of the first facilities to install a CRAY-2. Ames specialists worked with experts from Cray and NMFECC to explore capabilities of the first production CRAY-2 at Livermore. One of their most important objectives was to obtain maximum performance from UNICOS, a new Cray-developed operating system based on UNIX.

The CRAY-2 is supported by two Amdahl 5840s, managing mass storage and input/output duties, and a bank of four VAX 11/780 minicomputers. The central role of fluid dynamics at NAS—and the importance of high-performance workstations in displaying supercomputer output about fluid dynamics in graphic form—led NAS to purchase 25 IRIS workstations made by Silicon Graphics, Inc. Already, the system developed at Ames has demonstrated a kind of stop-time interactive capability. An operator using the system to display flow-patterns around an object—which are, of necessity, a simplified depiction of the complete flow—can use the mouse on the workstation to select a particular point. The supercomputer and the rest of the system will then display the flow-line from that point. NAS is also establishing a network, linking it via satellite and terrestrial channels to a total of 13 sites around the United States.

Time on the NAS is to be allocated as follows: NASA: 55%; Department of Defense: 20%; other federal agencies: 5%; aerospace industries: 15%; university researchers: 5% (to be allocated by the NSF). The primary focus of NAS is aerodynamics, but other disciplines of interest to NASA, such as astrophysics and other space sciences and atmospheric sciences can also qualify. During the first months of use of the facility, leading uses were aerodynamics (35%), studies of propulsion and aerodynamics for the proposed hypersonic National Aerospace Plane project (30%), studies of turbulence (17%), computational structural mechanics (8%), astrophysics and atmospheric sciences (2%) and computational chemistry (2%). Miscellaneous uses accounted for the other 6%.

Projects submitted by commercial firms and other government

agencies are submitted to a peer review process. Policies also aim at ensuring that equal access will prevent any commercial organization from acquiring a competitive advantage through research using NAS facilities.

> *Contact:* Ms. Leslie J. Chow
> NAS User Interface Manager
> NASA Ames Research Center
> Mail Stop 233-1
> Moffett Field, CA 94035
> Telephone: (415) 694-6535

NASA Supercomputing Facilities—
NASA Space and Earth Sciences Computing Center (NSESCC)

The NSESCC, located at the Goddard Space Flight Center in Greenbelt, Maryland, is operated by NASA's Office of Space Sciences and Applications to support scientific research at Goddard and elsewhere. The percentage of time used by remote users, now 15%, is expected to be raised to 25% in 1987.

NSESCC's central resource is a two-pipeline Cyber 205, with a memory of four million 64-bit words. It operates on the standard Cyber 205 VSOS operating system. It interfaces with outside users through an IBM 3081 running VM/CMS and MVS/TSO.

Since May 1983, the NSESCC has also been operating the Massively Parallel Processor (MPP), made by the Goodyear Aerospace Corporation. This machine was designed to carry out very high-speed processing on the ground of images obtained by satellites. It consists of an array unit that has a 128-by-128 array of 16,384 bit-serial processing elements, each of which has 1024 bits of local memory. These are controlled in turn by an array control unit. A staging memory transforms conventional data into the special format required by the array unit. The MPP is thus one of the finest-grained parallel processors in actual service. Access is through two minicomputers, a PDP-11/34A and a VAX 11/780, which also manage operation of the computer, acting as control interfaces that load applications programs.

Goodyear sources state that the MPP has demonstrated very efficient performance at its designated principal function, image processing. An initial test showed that the MPP could do image processing at a rate 2000 times faster than a VAX 11-780. Tests with a weather forecasting program showed substantial, but less dramatic, improvements in performance.

Contact: Requests for allocation of time should be directed to the NSESCC, which will forward applications to NASA headquarters.

NASA Space and Earth Sciences Computing Center
Code 630.1
Goddard Space Flight Center
Greenbelt, MD 20771
Telephone: (301) 286-8541

Section 3: Supercomputer Facilities at U.S. Universities and Service Bureaus

The NSF initiative did not introduce current-generation supercomputers to American universities. Several operated their own supercomputers before the NSF decided upon large-scale federal support for supercomputing. The state of Minnesota and its university work hard to make sure that Minnesota is an important—and visible—center of high technology. The university decided that this required that it operate a major computer center; the state legislature endorsed this view with money. Colorado State University bought a Cyber 205 in the early 1980s, hoping to meet some of its costs by selling time to oil companies. Purdue University and Florida State University also acquired supercomputers before the NSF-supported centers were established.

Other universities are currently setting up their own supercomputing programs outside the framework of the five NSF-supported centers. The University of Georgia and the University of California at Berkeley have established their own supercomputer facilities, and two installations (one at Austin and another in Houston) are serving universities in Texas. UCLA is now operating an IBM 3090 with vector processors, as is the University of Michigan.

Through local and regional networks, these facilities are accessible to researchers on other campuses and, in many cases, to private industry as well. Some provide services on a national scale; this is likely to become more significant as new national networks are established and others are upgraded. This section describes the facilities at these supercomputing centers and procedures for arranging access, including sources to contact for more complete information. It also provides information on Boeing Computer Services, the largest commercial supercomputing service bureau.

The brief descriptions that follow are limited to fully-functional centers using conventional commercial supercomputers to service users on their campuses and at remote sites. Many experimental projects, most of them emphasizing multiprocessors or massively parallel machines, are in operation at universities in the United States. Some of them are used by local and distant customers, but, as a general rule, they are not in the business of providing a wide range of standardized services. These are not discussed here. This omission does not imply a lack of interest in this evolving dimension of high-speed computing. It is, rather, an admission of the difficulty of keeping track of these numerous facilities and fitting adequate descriptions of them into an already crowded book.

University of California, Berkeley

Stanford University and Berkeley are cooperating in a project funded by the NSF calling for the establishment of a Bay Area Regional Research Network (BARRNet) that will link these two universities, the University of California at San Francisco, and NASA's Ames Research Center. The University of California campuses at Davis and Santa Cruz and perhaps other nearby institutions will be added to the network before long. This network will provide access to supercomputers at SDSC and Ames as well as other facilities.

One of the supercomputers that will be serviced by this network is a CRAY X-MP/14, a single-processor machine with four million words of memory, which was installed on the Berkeley campus in summer 1986. The facility also operates an IBM 3090-200, with two vector processors, providing another source of high-speed computing. The X-MP was obtained from Ames, where it was running the UNIX-based UNICOS operating system on a test basis before the transfer.

Like Apple Computer (see Chapter Three), Berkeley is running its X-MP on UNICOS. Computer scientists at Berkeley have played a major role in the development of UNIX: the "Berkeley utilities" are prominent in the software library of many UNIX users. On the Berkeley campus, the supercomputing facility serves a local network and a number of workstations using UNIX. Principal applications expected at Berkeley include chemistry, biological sciences, physics, mathematics, earth sciences and geophysics, computer science, and civil, mechanical, and electrical engineering.

> *Contact:* Raymond K. Neff
> Assistant Vice Chancellor
> Information Systems and Technology
> 209 Evans Hall
> Berkeley, CA 94720
> Telephone: (415) 642-4095

Colorado State University

A Cyber 205 operating on VSOS is the supercomputing resource at Colorado State University's University Computer Center. It is linked with two mainframes, a Cyber 830 and a Cyber 840, which meet basic computing requirements on the campus. The Cyber 205 is a two-pipeline machine with a memory of two million 64-bit words. The center welcomes applications from researchers and others from outside the campus, including applicants who secure NSF support.

> *Contact:* John Cooley
> University Computer Center
> University Services Center
> Colorado State University
> Fort Collins, CO 80523
> Telephone: (303) 491-6017 (applications) or
> (303) 491-6900 (general inquiries)

Florida State University

A number of universities have chosen to divide supercomputing activities into two parts: a production facility and a research center. The production facility, the Florida State University Supercomputing Center, has been operating a Cyber 205 since April 1985. The 205 operates on VSOS, has two pipelines, and has a memory of four million 64-bit words. It is supported by funding from the U.S. Department of Energy, the university, the state of Florida, and

Control Data Corporation. In connection with the DOE's support for the center, recipients of DOE research grants have first access to 65% of its resources. The balance is allocated by the university for research and instructional use. The Florida State facility can be reached by remote users in the United States, Europe, and Japan who are regular participants in the DOE MFENET. MFENET access is by satellite to Oak Ridge National Laboratory and thence by a 9600 baud land line to the center. It is also connected with BITNET and the Florida Information Resources Network (FIRN).

The Florida State center relies upon Control Data Corporation hardware; all its ancillary computers are CDC machines, except for a DEC VAX 11/780 which serves as a front end for access to MFENET. At the end of 1986, Florida State took a leap into the unknown. It is the research test site for the first ETA-10, made by a subsidiary of Control Data (see Appendix I). The ETA-10 project also has DOE support.

The Supercomputer Computations Research Institute (SCRI), located at Florida State, describes itself as a "university-based industrial/governmental partnership in basic research and training in supercomputer computational science and technology." It emphasizes university-based, nonclassified, energy-related research, concentrating upon the properties of elementary particles. The SCRI encourages users in the fields of accelerator design, lattice gauge theory, event simulation, and quantum chromodynamics,

Meteorologists and oceanographers based at Florida State are taking part in an international effort to apply mathematical models to large-scale natural systems such as the El Niño phenomenon. The SCRI is conducting or planning investigations relying upon supercomputers in geophysical fluid dynamics, astrophysics, polymer chemistry, molecular dynamics, materials design, cancer research, beach erosion, and pollution by hazardous wastes.

> *Contact:* Joseph E. Lannutti, Director
> The Supercomputer Computations Research Institute
> Florida State University
> Tallahassee, FL 32306
>
> For applications: Client Relations
> Florida State University Computing Center
> Tallahassee, FL 32306-3042
> Telephone: (904) 644-2764

University of Georgia

The Advanced Computational Methods Center (ACMC) is located at the University of Georgia in Athens. Since spring 1986, it has been operating a Cyber 205 purchased by the state of Georgia. Operating on the VSOS operating system, the Cyber 205 is a two-pipeline machine with two million 64-bit words of memory. It is linked with 33 institutions throughout the state. Most channels are 9.6 kilobit per second circuits. Georgia Tech, in Atlanta, is the other main node in the system; when SURANET (for Southeastern Universities Regional Network) is fully operational, the Georgia Tech node will be used for access.

In addition to research and educational functions, the ACMC is charged with stimulating cooperative efforts between academic and industrial sectors to promote business ventures requiring large-scale computer simulations. It is also to serve as a state and regional facility supporting educational, governmental, and industrial applied research. The center aims to explore possibilities of parallel processing for high-speed computing and has installed a Cyber Plus parallel system. Allocations are made by ACMC.

> *Contact:* Advanced Computational Methods Center
> University of Georgia
> Computer Services Annex Building
> Athens, GA 30602
> Telephone: (404) 542-5110

Houston Area Research Center (HARC)

Four Texas institutions, Rice University, Texas A&M University, the University of Houston University Park, and the University of Texas at Austin are included in the Houston Area Research Center, a non-profit consortium.

HARC is the first university-related facility in the United States to install a Japanese-made supercomputer. It became operational in late 1986. The NEC SX-2 is a distinctive machine—even in Japan, only a few are in operation. It is a very fast computer (claiming peak performance of 1.3 gigaflops).

The consortium is actively soliciting participation by industrial associates. In addition to assisting HARC in meeting its costs, the associates program is aimed at meeting one of HARC's goals: "to transform scientific and technological advances into practical commercial applications."

    Contact: Computer Systems Applications and Research Center
               Houston Area Research Center
               2202 Timberloch Place, Suite 200
               The Woodlands, Texas 77380
               Telephone (713) 367-1348

University of Minnesota

The Minneapolis campus of the University of Minnesota possesses more supercomputing capability than any other university campus. The Minnesota Supercomputer Institute is, in fact, one of the largest concentrations of supercomputers in the world, surpassed in size only by a few federal installations and the DOE-owned Los Alamos, Sandia, and Livermore national laboratories.

Minnesota also pioneered operation of current-generation supercomputers. It was the first U.S. university to acquire a CRAY-1, a one megaword CRAY-1/A installed in September 1981. A Control Data Cyber 205 was added in early 1985. In addition, Minnesota was one of the first CRAY-2 installations and remains the only university in the United States that operates a CRAY-2. Its first, a single-processor system with 16 megawords of directly accessible memory, was delivered in October 1985. Another CRAY-2, in the four-processor mode, with 256 megawords of directly accessible memory, was acquired at the end of 1986. The extensive support facilities include advanced graphics workstations.

The Supercomputer Institute plans to replace its Cyber 205 with an ETA-10, tentatively a four-processor machine. One of the institute's objectives is to "provide the user community with access to the highest performance supercomputing technology available." This is interpreted as providing access to a diversity of architectures as well as sheer capacity. With this in mind, the Minnesota institute also expects to replace its CRAY-2 with one of the next generation of Cray Research machines, presumably a CRAY-3.

In 1984, the Minnesota state legislature established the Supercomputer Institute and gave it a muscular charter. Its objectives include familiar academic goals: to make its capabilities available to educational institutions in the United States and abroad, and to carry out education and training. In addition, it is charged to "promote the supercomputer industry and research in the state of Minnesota," to promote development of supercomputer-related industries and services in Minnesota, and "to work with manufacturers of supercomputers, pursuant to contractual relationships, in the development of supercomputer and related equipment, systems and applications software, services, and processes." Supercomputer services can also be made available to private companies in other states and abroad as well as in Minnesota on a full cost-recovery basis.

The legislature did more than grant a charter. It appropriated $6 million per year for the institute's operation and a large part of the cost of a new $11.5 million supercomputer center, with 120,000 square feet of office and computer space, 100,000 square feet of which are assigned to supercomputer-related activities. The new center is one of major links in a technology corridor being developed by the city of Minneapolis, the state, and the university.

Minnesota aims at becoming a national center for education and training about supercomputers as well as a source of services for research using supercomputers. It was selected as one of the early participants in the NSF's Phase I program for providing capabilities at existing supercomputer facilities to academic researchers. In 1985 and again in 1986, the Minnesota institute operated one of the summer institutes supported by the NSF. Minnesota has also the Institute of Mathematics and Its Applications, supported by the NSF. The 1986-1987 program emphasis of the mathematics institute is on scientific computing and will involve extensive interaction with the supercomputer institute.

Recent research and educational projects at the Minnesota Supercomputer Institute include physics and astronomy (40%), chemistry (11%), biochemistry (6%), engineering (all specialities, 35%) and all other (3%)—all figures are rounded.

Contact: Minnesota Supercomputer Institute
1200 Washington Avenue South
Minneapolis, MN 55415
Telephone: (612) 376-8323

For applications other than NSF:
Research Equipment, Incorporated
2520 Broadway Drive
Lauderdale, MN 55113
Telephone: (612) 373-7878

Purdue University

The Purdue University Computing Center operates a Cyber 205, a two-pipeline machine with a memory of two million 64-bit words. Front-end services are provided by a VAX 11/780, a CDC 6600, and a CDC 6500. The center can be accessed through ARPANET, GTE Telenet, and the Indiana University Network which links it with other academic institutions in the state.

Contact: Saul Rosen
Mathematical Sciences Building
Purdue University Computing Center
West Lafayette, IN 47907
Telephone: (317) 494-1787

University of Texas System

A two-processor CRAY X/MP-24 is operated at Austin, Texas by the University of Texas System Center for High-Performance Computing. It is not administered by the Austin campus but was established to serve the seven academic campuses and six health institutions of the university system. It is separate from HARC, although the Austin campus also participates in the HARC consortium. The new system was funded entirely from university resources and serves as an instrument for research programs at the university system's installations throughout Texas.

Inaugurated in May 1986, the new X-MP uses COS; UNICOS is used in a test mode. The center plans to switch to UNICOS operation when this can be done without undue disruption to the needs of current users.

Contact: The Director
University of Texas System Center for High-Performance Computing
Balcones Research Center
10100 Burnet Road
Austin, TX 78738
Telephone: (512) 471-2472

Boeing Computer Services (BCS)

Several aerospace companies, including Boeing and McDonnell Douglas, have diversified by developing substantial computer-services subsidiaries. These activities, starting out as efforts to achieve fuller utilization of facilities also used for the companies' own needs, developed into profit-centers in their own right. Boeing is the only aerospace company to offer supercomputing services. It is one of the principal providers of straightforward cash-on-the-line supercomputer time. Such services are also offered by Control Data. The Control Data service bureau subsidiary has recently undergone reorganization. Several academic centers, including Minnesota, offer services for cash and are sometimes referred to as service bureaus. Boeing has recently acquired several SCS-40 minisupercomputers.

The central supercomputing resource at BCS is a CRAY X-MP/24 with two processors, a four million word memory, and a 128 million word solid state storage device, operating on COS. Two IBM 3031 computers act as front end. Support computers include two Cyber 760s, a Cyber 875, a Cyber 730, and a Cyber 825. Services include a very broad library of diverse applications software.

Access is possible over the Boeing network, one of the largest proprietary computing networks, with local dial-up access available in 160 U.S. cities. Requests for purchasing computer time may be made to BCS sales offices in major regional centers around the United States.

Contact: BCS Data Center
2600 160th Avenue, S.E.
Boeing Computer Services
Bellevue, WA 98008

Sources and References

Note: Numbers in parenthesis indicate the page number of occurrence in text.

The best way to learn more about supercomputing is to communicate directly with people who are doing it. Most of the information in this book was obtained through interviews and visits, and we have emphasized listings of sources for additional information so that readers know where to turn in their own pursuit of up-to-date information.

Perodicals and Journals

Until recently, the only publications specializing in supercomputing have been issued by the manufacturers. *Cray Channels* has evolved from a conventional house organ into an informative source of articles about supercomputer applications, written by researchers as well as by Cray publicists. Other sources of information about supercomputer applications have been spread over a very broad spectrum of academic and professional journals. Researchers prefer to report to their own professional colleagues; if results were obtained in part through supercomputing, that fact is often buried in the article.

Beginning in 1986, the flow of publications about supercomputing has widened and deepened. The five NSF-supported supercomputing centers all publish newsletters. The primary audiences are users of each center's services, and much space is given to technical notes of interest to those readers. The newsletters are also an up-to-date source of information about supercomputing in general and about research being done at those centers. Distribution of some of these newsletters rose from a few hundred to five thousand or more between January 1986 and spring 1987. Most other supercomputing facilities listed in Appendix II publish newsletters, occasional bulletins, and other material valuable to the potential user and often of broader interest.

The first scholarly journals devoted to supercomputing are beginning to appear in 1987.

The International Journal of Supercomputer Applications, quarterly, Vol. 1, no. 1 appearing spring 1987. Subscriptions: MIT Press, 55 Hayward Street, Cambridge, MA 02142. Editorial communications: Joanne L. Martin, Editor, IBM T.J. Watson Research Center, H2-A17, P.O. Box 218, Yorktown Heights, NY 10598.

The Journal of Supercomputing, quarterly, Vol. 1, no. 1 appearing about June 1987. Subscriptions: Kluwer Academic Publishers, 101 Philip Dr., Norwell, MA 02061. Editors: Harlow Freitag and John Riganati, c/o Mary Ann Grandjean, Supercomputing Research Center, 4380 Forbes Blvd., Lanham, MD 20706.

SuperComputing Magazine, first issue appeared winter 1987. Editorial correspondence and subscriptions: 570 South Mathilda, Suite 4419, Sunnyvale, CA 94086. Editor: Christopher Willard.

Books

Supercomputer books have not been numerous and have tended to emphasize technical descriptions. The numbers are now beginning to increase rapidly. Most books devoted to supercomputing have been compilations of papers presented at conferences. All age quickly.

Access to Supercomputers, National Science Foundation, Office of Advanced Scientific Computing. Overview booklet, available from NSF.

Fernbach, Sidney, ed. *Supercomputers: Class VI Systems, Hardware and Software*. Amsterdam and New York: Elsevier/North Holland, 1986.

Matsen, F.A., and T. Tajima, eds. *Supercomputers: Algorithms, Architectures, and Scientific Computation*. Austin: University of Texas Press, 1986.

Metropolis, Nicholas, ed. *Frontiers of Supercomputing*. Berkeley: University of California Press, 1986.

Schneck, Paul B. *Supercomputing Architecture* (tentative title). Norwell: Kluwer Academic Publishers, 1987 (expected summer 1987).

Speed and Power (Time-Life Books, Alexandria, 1987) one of a series called *Understanding Computing*, is aimed at general readers. It emphasizes the history of supercomputing but includes well-illustrated discussions of parallel processing and other technical matters. Volumes on scientific computing and computers in government, planned for this series, should provide additional information on applications.

Supercomputers: Government Plans and Policies. Washington: Office of Technology Assessment, 1986.

Torrero, Edward A., ed. *Next-generation Computers*. New York: Insitute of Electrical & Electronics Engineers, 1985.

Chapter 1. Numbers (4): An estimate of 244 supercomputers installed as of December 1986 was made by Piper, Jeffrey, and Hopwood, Inc., a brokerage house in Minneapolis (*Computerworld*, March 16, 1987, p. 89). This figure does not count IBM 3090s with vector boards. As a matter of policy, IBM does not release figures about numbers of machines installed. An informed guess places IBM vector-processing machines at about two dozen, suggesting a total of at least 275 supercomputers. Sales of $1 billion per year is a conservative estimate; Cray alone had sales of almost $700 million in 1986. The total value estimate of $5 billion is based on an estimated cost of $20 million per installed facility, including buildings and peripheral equipment. Entry-level prices are dropping, but a substantial proportion of buyers is opting for the most powerful machines with high memory options—often exceeding $15 million before peripherals are added.

Projections (4): The higher forecast (60%) refers to site intallations, not total sales, and is from a research paper dated November 1985 prepared by the brokers Sanford C. Bernstein & Co., Inc. User projections are the authors' estimates. Performance comparisons (7): authors' estimates, intended to be indicative rather than literal.

Chapter 2. Programs (24): The classical (and highly readable) discussion of the hardware/software illusion is Brooks, Frederick P., Jr. *The Mythical Man-month: Essays on Software Engineering*. Reading: Addison-Wesley, 1975 and 1982. Additional information on the SDSC is available from its newsletter, *Gather/Scatter*, and other materials that can be obtained from the center. (Address: Appendix II.)

Fifth Generation (43): Bramer, Max, and Bramer, Dawn. *The Fifth Generation: An Annotated Bibliography*. Reading: Addison-Wesley, 1984, provides a concise, informative summary of this topic as well as a well-selected bibliography. Feigenbaum, Edward A., and Pamela McCorduck. *The Fifth Generation: Artificial Intelligence and Japan's Computational Challenge to the World*. Reading: Addison-Wesley, 1983. Mostly computational polemics, now out of date, but still quoted.

Chapter 3. Based upon interviews at AT&T Bell Laboratories in June 1986, and at with Tony Rappe at Colorado State University, September 1986, supplemented by correspondence. *Cray Channels*, Vol. 5, no. 3 (1983, no other date), pp. 2–10, provides additional information on chip design. Information about Apple and Aerojet- General applications is based upon personal and telephone interviews in May and September 1986 respectively. Presentations

by Van-Catledge, Bridenbaugh, and Dodd at a seminar co-sponsored by In-
dustrial Research Institute and Lawrence Livermore National Laboratory at
Pleasanton, California, June 1986, provided initial material for the items on
Dupont, Alcoa, and General Motors, supplemented by later correspondence.
Glenn Ingram quote (59) from interview at Gaithersburg, Maryland, June 1986.
Caldwell McCoy of the NASA space directorate also provided valuable insights
on saturation. Fell quote (60) from telephone interview.

Chapter 4.   Drawn primarily from interviews with Bash, De Young, Kuti,
Bruce Smith, Kollman, and Olson in San Francisco, Mountain View, and San
Diego between April and August 1986, supplemented with correspondence.
Centrella quote (81) reprinted from *Supercomputers and the Direction of
American Science*, an account of a roundtable at the University of Maryland,
College Park, October 30, 1985, reprinted by the Media Outreach Program,
American Association for the Advancement of Science, n.d., pp. 10–11, con-
firmed by telephone interview. Zwanzig was interviewed by telephone in June
1986. Information on National Radio Astronomy Observatory is from brochures
and other documents supplied by NRAO.

Chapter 5.   Based upon technical manuals and brochures supplied by manufacturers. Early IBM supercomputers (90) from Fishman, Katharine Davis.
The Computer Establishment. New York: McGraw-Hill, 1982, pp. 117–124.
Additional detail on initial IBM efforts is available in *Speed and Power*, cited
above, pp. 16–18. Sidney Fernbach's 1986 book, cited above, and "Supercomputers Hit Their Stride," with contributions by Tom Manuel, Jerry Lynman,
and Alexander Wolfe, in *Electronics*, March 10, 1986, pp. 44–52, provide
useful additional technical and general information.

Chapter 6.   This chapter is based primarily upon conversations with NSF
officials and staff of the NSF-supported and other supercomputing centers,
supplemented by correspondence and publications provided by the centers.
The listings of consortium members (110–113) are drawn from documents
obtained from the centers supplemented by correspondence and telephone
contacts.

Chapter 7.   Interviews at NASA's Ames Research Center, Mountain View,
California, May and June 1986, provided most of the material for this chapter.
Terry Holst and Ron Bailey were especially informative; assistance by Vic
Peterson and Tony Gross was also very helpful. Quote (119) and comment
(124) about problems with aircraft designs from Ballhaus, W.F., "Computational
Simulation and Supercomputers," undated paper issued by NASA Ames Re-
search Center, p. 4. More detail available in series of articles on computational

fluid dynamics (including turbines) in *Cray Channels*, Vol. 8, no. 2, (summer 1986), pp. 2–17. Survey of current state of ultra high bypass (ducted and unducted fan) technology in *Aviation Week and Space Technology*, April 13, 1986, pp. 52–93.

Chapter 8. Visits to NCAR (September 1986) and the Scripps Institution (July and August 1986) provided most of the material for this chapter. In addition to those mentioned by name, Paul Swarztrauber, Paul Rotar, and JoAn Knudson were very helpful. Washington, Warren M., and Parkinson, Claire L. *An Introduction to Three Dimensional Climate Modeling.* Mill Valley: University Science Books (also distributed by Oxford University Press), 1987, describes climatic computations in greater depth. The Barron/Washington study is in "The Role of Geographic Variables in Explaining Paleoclimates: Results from Cretaceous Climate Model Sensitivity Studies," Journal of Geophysical Research, Vol. 89, No. D1, pp. 1267–1279, Feb. 20, 1984.

Nuclear winter (136): TTAPS findings in: Richard Turco, O. Brian Toon, Thomas Ackerman, James Pollack, and Carl Sagan, "Nuclear Winter: Global Consequences of Multiple Nuclear Explosions," *Science*, Dec. 23, 1983, pp. 1283–1292). Starley L. Thompson and Stephen H. Schneider, "Nuclear Winter Reappraised," *Foreign Affairs*, Vol. 64, no. 5 (Summer 1986) examines the TTAPS findings. Mike Waller and Ken Kelly of AMOCO Production Company and Tom Wyman of Chevron assisted with the material on seismic exploration and fossil fuels (142–146).

Chapter 9. Computer animation (149–157): interviews with Kleiser and Rudd in Hollywood, September 1986; presentation by Gary Demos at seminar organized by Ames Research Center, June 1986; information on animation in Japan from *Cray Channels*, Vol. 5, no. 2, (1983, no further date) pp. 19–20. *America's* Cup (157–161): Articles by Mike Ross in Lawrence Livermore National Laboratory *Weekly Bulletin*, July 2, 1986, p. 3, and December 17, 1986, p. 7; "Supercomputers, the *America's* Cup and Winning," *Cray Channels*, Vol. 8, no. 2 (Summer 1986), pp. 20–23. Computer chess (161–166): article by Cynthia Ivanetich in LLNL *Weekly Bulletin*, June 25, 1986, p. 1, and Dewdney, A.K."Computer Recreations," *Scientific American*, Vol. 254, no. 2 (February 1986), pp. 13–21.

Chapter 10. Presentations at a conference on the supercomputer environment at Ames Research Center in June 1987 were helpful in drawing together this material. Nelson quote (171) from June 1986, interview at Bell Labs. Dennis M. Jennings, Lawrence H. Landweber, Ira A. Fuchs, David J. Farber, and W. Richards Adrion, "Computer Networking for Scientists," *Science*, Vol. 231, pp. 943–950 (February 28, 1986) is a useful reference on networking and an important source for this section (175–179). An interview with Dennis Jennings at Princeton, New Jersey, in June 1986 was also very informative. Information on "Walnut"(181) primarily from Perrin F. Smith, who as an IBM engineer worked on the project.

Chapter 11. Ewald comment (187) from presentation at IRI/LLNL conference in Pleasanton, June 1986. Information on Floating Point Systems projects from manufacturer's promotional material. BBN information (188–190) from *Computerworld*, July 7, 1986, p. 4, and August 25, 1986, p. 14. *Science*, Vol. 232, pp. 1090–1091, has article on the Connection Machine (187). Gilmore, Paul A., "The Massively Parallel Processor," in Fernbach, cited above, pp. 183–217, describes this machine (192) in detail. Wilson quote (192) from June 1986 interview in Ithaca, N.Y., supplemented by corrrespondence.

Chapter 12. A number of people were exceptionally helpful in making this chapter possible. They were: Dr. Ing. Karl-G. Reinsch, Director of the Regional Computer Center, University of Stuttgart (Europe generally, especially Germany); Lloyd Parker of Toronto University and Jack Miller of the Toronto *Star* (Canada); Seymour Goodman and R.A. Stapleton and of the University of Arizona (USSR and China); Michael A. Harrison of the University of California at Berkeley (Japan), George Lindamood of the National Bureau of Standards and Hood College (Japan) and Hiroshi Mizuta of the Japan National Space Agency (Japan). Information was obtained through a mixture of interviews, telephone contacts, and draft articles and other documents generously made available by these sources. Special appreciation is due to Mr. Stapleton, who took the time to prepare draft reports on the USSR and PRC containing information that otherwise would have been impossible to develop, especially on a tight schedule.

Eureka project (200): Summary of current projects (including one on gallium arsenide) in *Aviation Week and Space Technology*, September 1, 1986, pp. 134–135. See also *New York Times*, July 1, 1986, p. 33. Controls on supercomputer use in U.K. (209): See *Science*, Vol. 233, p. 279 (July 18, 1986) and "US and Britain Tangle Over Supercomputers," *New Scientist*, May 29, 1986, p. 18. Issue of IBM 3090 in Finland (208) from *Computerworld*, September 1, 1986, p. 15. Report on Gorbachev offer to India (209): New Delhi dispatch by Salamat Ali, *Far Eastern Economic Review* (Hong Kong), December 11, 1986, pp. 18–19. Information on Japanese high-speed project (212–214) primarily from Kashiwagi, Hiroshi: "The Japanese Super-speed Computer Project," in *Future Generations Computer Systems*, Vol. 1, no. 3 (Feb. 1985), pp. 153–160. An estimate in *Computerworld*, (March 16, 1987, p. 89) reports that Japanese supercomputer sales worldwide have totaled 57 (42 by Fujitsu, 8 by Hitachi, and 7 from NEC). This suggests that the number in the text for total supercomputer installations in Japan (210) is conservative. Charles Smith, Tokyo dispatch, "The Yen Strikes Home," *Far Eastern Economic Review*, December 25, 1986, pp. 61–68, reviews effects of "hollowing-out." *The Asian Wall Street Journal Weekly* and *The Japan Economic Journal* (English-language weekly published by Nihon Keizai Shimbun) provided information on running story of trade disputes between the U.S. and Japan.

Chapter 13. Descriptions of the two training sessions (219–223) based on attendance by authors. Other material based upon personal interviews (Henry, Brikowski, Berry, Golden, and Maizel) and telephone interviews (McQueen, Wetherill, Melosh, and Becker), supplemented in most cases with correspondence. Peskin and McQueen quote (222) from McQueen, David M. and Charles S. Peskin, "Computer-Assisted Design of Butterfly Bileaflet Valves for the Mitral Position," *Scandinavian Journal of Thoracic and Cardiovascular Surgery*, 19:139–148, 1985. Articles in *Issues in Science and Technology*, Vol. 3, no. 1 (Spring 1987), pp. 25–56, "Sequencing the Human Genome," provide a balanced discussion, with contributions by Walter Gilbert, Leroy Hood and Lloyd Smith, David Baltimore, and Fracisco J. Ayala. See also *Science*, Vol. 232, pp. 1598–1600 (27 June, 1986) and Vol. 233, pp. 620–621 (August 8, 1986). Moon origin studies at Los Alamos (240): see *Scientific American*, Vol. 254, no. 6 (June 1986), pp. 67–68. See also Gleick, James "Moon's Creation Now Attributed to Giant Crash," *New York Times*, June 3, 1986, p. C1. Wetherill. George W.: "Occurrence of Giant Impacts During the Growth of the Terrestrial Planets," *Science*, Vol. 228, pp. 877–879 (May 17, 1985) summarizes planetesimal research.

Appendix I. All information is derived from presentations, brochures, press releases, and manuals provided by the manufacturers. Claims about performance are those of the manufacturers. Every effort has been made, including follow-up correspondence and telephone contacts, to assure that information is accurate and current as of early 1987. Models, specifications, and prices change rapidly; however, manufacturers or their sales offices should be contacted directly for up-to-date information.

Appendix II. Direct contact with staff of the facilities described—by visits, correspondence, and telephone—has been the basis for this appendix. Newsletters, brochures, and promotional material have also been valuable. Every effort has been made to verify accuracy through subsequent follow-up. More detailed technical specifications on many of these facilities may be found in *Earth and Environmental Science in the 1980's: Part I. Environmental Data Systems, Supercomputer Facilities, and Networks*, NASA Contractor Report 4029, October 1986, prepared by Science Applications International Corporation.

Obtainable from National Technical Information Service, Springield, VA 22161. Our thanks to Carroll Hood of SAI for sharing information on centers and providing an early copy of this study.

Many of these facilities are still in their formative stages; hardware, software, and networks at all of them are evolving rapidly. Once again, direct inquiry is the best way to obtain up-to-date information.

Glossary

Note: Acronyms used in the text are identified in the index.

Algorithm A procedure for solving a problem, analogous to a recipe; not dependent upon a specific program language or architecture.

Analog The representation of numbers approximately by assigning them locations on a continuum. Grandfather clocks, slide rules, and old-fashioned mercury thermometers are analog devices. (The usual dictionary spelling "analogue" is not used in this case.)

Applications program (or software) Programs which instruct a computer to produce a specific result such as the solution to an equation, or to rearrange the text in a document, or to draw a picture on a plotter. Applications programs sometimes need to be adapted to operating systems and specific architecture, at least for optimum performance.

Architecture The basic design of a computer system, governing how it does calculations, handles memory, and carries out programs. A single architecture can be used by various sizes of computer. An analogy to building architecture would be a type, e.g. Cape Cod or ranch house.

Binary notation Numbers are represented by combinations of two states, conventionally represented as 0 and 1, as opposed to a decimal (0 through 9) notation. Some early computers were decimal, but binary notation (which can be represented by the presence or absence of electrical charges) became universal when digital electronic processors became standard.

Benchmark A standardized program used to determine the performance, especially the speed, of a computer in comparison with other computers.

Bit (contraction of "binary digit") The fundamental unit of digital information,

297

corresponding to a 0 or 1. A *byte* is the conventionally meaningful unit; it usually consists of eight bits and can represent a character, decimal digit, or other symbol. A *Word* in computing is the unit a computer uses to manipulate information such as floating point numbers. It ranges in size from eight bits for microcomputers to 64 bits in high-performance computers, including supercomputers. A larger word size can increase accuracy in handling numbers as well as speed up manipulation of data.

Bus   A trolley track is a better analogy. A bus is a communications channel that transmits information among parts of a computer system.

Byte   See Bit.

Central Processing Unit (CPU)   The central unit of a computer, accepting and acting upon instructions, carrying out calculations, and overseeing the transfer of data in and out. Often used casually to apply to the entire principal machinery of a computer, including the main memory.

Clock time or clock cycle   The interval in which the smallest cycles of synchronized events take place in a computer. Architecture determines how much work is done in each cycle. Supercomputers typically have very fast clock times and can accomplish multiple operations in a single cycle.

Computer   In U.S. military nomenclature through World War II, it referred to a *person* who did calculations, usually for artillery trajectories, often with the use of mechanical calculators or matrixes of numbers called firing tables. The need for accurate firing tables was one of the most urgent tasks spurring the earliest development of the modern electronic computer. The term migrated to *machines* by the 1950s. It became firmly attached to electronic devices that manipulate digital data according to standardized systems in order to perform calculations and other tasks.

Data   The usual term for information (not limited to numbers) manipulated, produced, and stored by a computer. Originally plural (as in "data about mating habits in the Paleolithic are sparse"), but being singularized inexorably through habitual use by computer people. The scholarly singular "datum" is a seriously endangered species, approaching extinction.

Digital   The expression of numbers in discrete form, as in handwritten arithmetic and binary notation. Digital computation has become the universal standard, although lonely advocates occasionally point out that analog computations are suitable for some uses.

Floating-point Arithmetic   Also called scientific notation, it permits large numbers (as well as very small numbers with numerous decimal places) to be represented compactly and accurately. For example, the price of a supercomputer in dollars can be represented as $.05 \times 10$ to the eighth power as well as by 5 million; the decimal point moves, or floats. Special hardware is required to perform floating-point operations efficiently.

FLOPS Floating-point operations per second. The usual measure of performance in high-speed computers.

Gallium arsenide A compound of two metals that has semiconductor properties (somewhat like silicon) but can operate faster, requires less power and generates less heat. The technology, especially appropriate for supercomputers, is under intensive development in Japan as well as the U.S. and Europe.

High-electron-mobility transistor (HEMT) An experimental form of high-speed semiconductor switch, being explored by the Japanese high-speed computer project and in other laboratories.

Gigaflops or GFLOPS Billion floating-point operations per second.

Input-Output (I/O) The process by which data is transferred from the world into a computer and removed for storage, transmission or reference. Used adjectivally for devices which do this. Extremely high I/O capacity is one of the prerequisites of a true supercomputer.

Image processing A specialized, computer-intensive task involving the transformation of digital signals (received, for example, from a scientific satellite) into recognizable images. The programs used may enhance images—for example, by adding artificial colors. Like other signal processing (such as the analysis of data obtained by devices which use acoustical means to hunt for submarines) image processing is relatively well-adapted to parallel processing.

Integrated circuit A single electric circuit, consisting of a collection of transistors and other electrical components, concentrated upon a single very small semiconductor chip. The distinction VSLI, for very large scale integrated circuit, implies collections consisting of thousands or even tens of thousands of individual elements on a chip.

Josephson junction A high-speed switching device, a potential replacement for current chip technology, which functions only at superconducting temperatures. IBM and Japanese researchers have explored this experimentally, but practical use seemed out of reach. Recent developments in superconductivity might change this outlook.

Kernel A part of a larger program, performing a small but often essential task, usually relatively simple but repetitive. Manufacturers speak of kernels that remain the same within operating systems which offer differing options.

Mainframe computer Often simply "mainframe;" refers to large computers that typically service a number of users, operating through peripherals with substantial capacity. Traditionally, mainframes have peformed a large majority of total computational business, especially in large organizations. This is still true, but other categories of computer are increasing their shares rapidly. Supercomputers typically have different architectures, faster clock speeds, larger memories, and greater I/O capacity.

Megaflops or MFLOPS   Millions of floating point operations per second. The usual unit in which performance of supercomputers is measured, although Gigaflop will soon prevail.

Memory   Data stored within a computer for accessing and manipulation during the computational process; also applied to the devices (now usually semi-conductor chips) on which the data is stored. Individual processors in a multi-processor machine may possess individual memory, share a central (or global) memory, or combine both.

Microcomputer   A personal computer, usually of desktop size, (although some IBM models include a component under the desk). Some microcomputers weigh only a few pounds and can be used on the lap.

Minicomputer   A middle-sized general-purpose computer with relatively moderate cost and substantial performance.

Minisupercomputer   A high-performance general-purpose computer, optimized for scientific purposes and in some cases emulating supercomputer architecture. The aim is to offer, at relatively moderate cost and compact format, performance corresponding to a fairly substantial fraction of typical supercomputer performance.

MIPS   Millions of instructions per second. The most common unit of performance for mainframes and for scalar processing generally, although an often inadequate and misleading measure.

Mouse   A device which translates analog instructions (created by moving a vaguely rodent-like object over a surface) into digital input. "Pointing devices" is appearing as a generic term, including roller balls, joysticks, and other means for achieving the same end. Mice usually also have one or more clicker switches for digital input.

Multiprocessor   Machines with more than one processor; several tasks can be done at once, or all processors can be used simultaneously in order to process a single task.

MWords   Millions of words of memory.

Nanosecond   One billionth of a second.

Operating System   Also operating program. The program which manages the work of the computer. Must be adjusted to the architecture of the particular machine, but more than one operating system can be run on most computers. Some operating systems (including UNIX) have been adapted for use with many different computers.

Parallel processing   The execution of several instructions or several parts of a single instruction at the same time. Increasingly, the term implies multi-processing and is often applied to systems that have moderate or very large numbers of processors.

Peripheral Storage devices, front-end computers, printers, and other equipment separate from the CPU which enables an entire computer system to function.

Scalar processing Calculations in which each number is processed one at a time, as in familiar primary-school arithmetic.

Storage Devices that retain data in digital form for relatively short periods or indefinitely ("archival storage"). Magnetic media, notably disks and tapes, are now the usual storage media. Optical disks may become the next generation.

Supercomputer The fastest, most powerful (usually general-purpose) computers available at any given time; typically significantly more powerful than other computers. (See *Mainframe* for some differences.)

Superconductor A compound which offers little or no resistance to electricity under certain conditions. Until very recently, the only known conditions for superconductivity were at temperatures very close to absolute zero. In early 1987, scientists all over the world have developed compounds capable of superconductivity at higher (though still low) temperatures.

Superminicomputer Still somewhere between an advertising slogan and a recognized category; refers to minicomputers with exceptionally high performance. At least in manufacturers' claims, the distinction between superminis and minisupers is tending to blur. The distinction between superminis and mainframes has been blurred for several years.

Vector processing Calculations in which a single instruction is executed simultaneously on an entire list, or vector, of numbers. Vectorizing or vectorization is the reorganizing of a program so that the maximum proportion of operations can be executed through vector processing.

Word See Bit.

Workstation (also used: Engineering Workstation, High-performance Workstation) Increasingly, the term implies a class of computer midway in performance between microcomputers and minicomputers, typically possessing strong graphics capabilities, usually used for engineering, design, and scientific applications, often networked with a minicomputer or larger system, and increasingly networked with supercomputers.

Index